ABOUT THE AUTHOR

GILBERT RIST has for many years been a leading Swiss scholar of development. Before joining the staff of the Graduate Institute of Development Studies (IUED) in Geneva, where he has been a professor since 1986, he first taught in Tunisia and then spent several years as Director of the Centre Europe–Tiers Monde. One of his principal intellectual interests has been to construct an anthropology of modernity in which he sees Western society as being every bit as traditional and indeed exotic as any other.

Professor Rist is the author of a number of intellectually pathbreaking books highly critical of conventional thinking in the field. These include:

Il était une fois le développement (with Fabrizio Sabelli et al.);

Le Nord perdu: Répères pour l'après-développement (with Majid Rahnema and Gustavo Esteva);

La Mythologie programmée: L'économie des croyances dans la société moderne (with Marie-Dominique Perrot and Fabrizio Sabelli);

La Culture: Otage du développement? (editor).

The present book is his first to be published in English.

THE HISTORY OF

DEVELOPMENT

From Western Origins to Global Faith

GILBERT RIST

Translated by Patrick Camiller

ZED BOOKS
London & New York

The History of Development was first published in English in 1997 by
Zed Books Ltd, 7 Cynthia Street, London N1 9JF, UK, and
Room 400, 175 Fifth Avenue, New York, NY 10010, USA

Distributed in the USA exclusively by St Martin's Press Inc.,
175 Fifth Avenue, New York, NY 10010, USA

Copyright © Presses de la Fondation Nationale des Sciences Politiques, 1996
English edition © Zed Books, 1997

The translation of this book into English was made possible thanks to the
generous contributions of the Fondation Antoine Duchemin and the Fondation
Charles Léopold Mayer pour le Progrès de l'Homme.

The moral rights of the author of this work have been asserted by him
in accordance with the Copyright, Designs and Patents Act, 1988

Typeset in Monotype Bembo by Lucy Morton, London SE12

Printed and bound in the United Kingdom by Redwood Books Ltd,
Kennet House, Kennet Way, Trowbridge, Wilts BA14 8RN

A catalogue record for this book is available from the British Library

Library of Congress Cataloging-in-Publication Data
Rist, Gilbert, 1938–
   [Le Developpement. English]
   The History of Development : from western origins to global faith
/ Gilbert Rist : translated by Patrick Camiller.
   p. cm.
   Includes bibliographical references and index.
   ISBN 1–85649–491–8. — ISBN 1–85649–492–6 (pbk.)
   1. Economic development—History. 2. Economic assistance—
History. 3. Sustainable development—History. I. Title.
HD78.R5713 1997
338.9′009—dc21
                                97–7618
                                  CIP

ISBN 1 85649 491 8 (Hb)
ISBN 1 85649 492 6 (Pb)

CONTENTS

v

INTRODUCTION

The strength of 'development' discourse comes of its power to seduce, in every sense of the term: to charm, to please, to fascinate, to set dreaming, but also to abuse, to turn away from the truth, to deceive. How could one possibly resist the idea that there is a way of eliminating the poverty by which one is so troubled? How dare one think, at the same time, that the cure might worsen the ill which one wishes to combat? Already Ulysses, to avoid giving in to the Sirens' song, had to plug his companions' ears and tie himself to the mast of his ship. Such is the opening price to be paid, if one is to emerge victorious from the test of lucidly examining the history of 'development'.

How could it have been thought necessary and urgent to do everything to speed up the process of 'development', ostensibly favouring the prosperity of countries in both North and South? After all, for centuries no one – or virtually no one – took it into their head to relieve the misery of others by structural measures, especially when they lived in different continents. What is the origin of this collective task which, though constantly criticized for its lack of success, appears to be justified beyond all dispute? What sense can we make of the numerous debates which, for nearly fifty years, have offered a solution to the problems that majority destitution poses in the face of minority opulence? How are we to explain this whole phenomenon, which mobilizes not only the hopes of millions but also sizeable financial resources, while appearing to recede like the horizon just as you think you are approaching it?

These are some of the questions that this work will seek to answer. Its aim is not to add one more theory to all the others formulated so far but, rather, to scrutinize the aura of self-evidence surrounding a concept which is supposed to command universal acceptance but which – as many have doubtless forgotten – was constructed within a particular history and culture. Our perspective will therefore be historical or genetic – for we must locate in the long-range movement of history the sequences whereby the 'international community' has given 'development' the central place it occupies today. Hence the necessity of going back to the distant origins of a concept which (on the grounds that its practical implications first appeared in the middle of the twentieth century) is too often taken to be modern. Hence, too, the importance we shall attach to the continuity of discourse, beyond the controversies which led some to believe that each new approach corresponded to an original, innovative conception different from all that had gone before.

Every perspective involves a particular point of view, which should be defined so as to dispel the illusion of objectivity or exhaustiveness. As far as the latter is concerned, there was never any question of discussing one after another the numerous theories that have fuelled the debate on 'development' since the Second World War.[1] Rather, the aim has been to identify, and to draw out the logic of, the 'great texts' which have claimed in each period to offer an original solution. As for objectivity, it is known to be a vain pursuit so long as we refuse to accept that the object is always constructed by the one who observes it. In this respect, the case of 'development' has exemplary value. The images associated with it, and the practices it entails, vary from one extreme to the other depending on whether we adopt the viewpoint of the 'developer' – committed to bringing about the happiness he wishes for others – or the viewpoint of the 'developed' – who is forced to modify his social relations and his relationship to nature in order to enter the promised new world. And that leaves out two further viewpoints: that of the technocrat with a brief to display the originality of the institution for which he works; and that of the researcher determined to prove that his chosen parameters are the only ones capable of accounting for the phenomenon under study.

---

1. The reader may refer to a number of works on this question, including: Christian Comeliau, *Les relations Nord–Sud*, Paris: La Découverte, 1991; Elsa Assidon, *Les théories économiques du développement*, Paris: La Découverte, 1992; André Guichaoua and Yves Goussault, *Sciences sociales et développement*, Paris: Armand Colin, 1993; *États des savoirs sur le développement: Trois décennies de sciences sociales en langue française* (under the direction of Catherine Choquet, Olivier Dollfus, Etienne Le Roy and Michel Vernières), Paris: Karthala, 1993; Louis Baeck, *Post-War Development Theories and Practice*, Paris: UNESCO and the International Social Science Council, 1993.

To locate this work straight away within a critical perspective is thus the least of the explanations we owe to the reader. (We should merely add that the term 'critique' is understood in its Kantian sense of free and public examination rather than its ordinary sense of unfavourable judgement – there being, of course, a considerable difference between the two.) What really matters here is that we do not yield to ready-made appraisals deriving from the presuppositions of conventional think-ing, which would make us take it for granted that 'development' exists, that it has a positive value, that it is desirable or even necessary.[2] None of this is actually established in advance. For the definition given of the 'development' phenomenon changes according to the implicit *a priori* that serves as the starting point for reflection. The same may be said of the (probably less common) procedure that starts from the opposite hypothesis and saddles 'development' with every evil. More than ever, then, epistemological distrust is in order. An effort will be required to free ourselves from the connotations of the term, to keep at arm's length the value judgements we are supposed to make, especially when the sight of extreme poverty, and the legitimate desire to put an end to it, make 'development' look like a panacea.

These methodological precautions should not, however, lead us into tame neutrality or mechanical indifference – quite the contrary. The rule never to judge anything before examining it means that we remain free to take sides afterwards. The danger lies in unavowed assumptions, not in appraisals made after we have shown how the mechanism func-tions. It is moralism as a starting point – not to discourage people of good will, or to keep the most desperate from losing all hope – which activates self-censorship and obscures what is really at issue. On the other hand, nothing seems more legitimate than to spotlight what a discourse has been trying to hide, or to take a position on the conse-quences flowing from it.

The fact remains that this work, too, rests upon a series of choices: choice of distance from the object of study, but also choice of how this object is to be dissected. The very first point is that 'development', far from being confined to the countries of the South, concerns the whole of the world, including the industrial heartlands. How could we forget that it was there that the phenomenon first appeared? Or that it was in

2. This point has been brought out especially well by Marie-Dominique Perrot in 'Passager clandestin et indispensable du discours: le présupposé', in Gilbert Rist and Fabrizio Sabelli, eds, *Il était une fois le développement*, Lausanne: Éditions d'En Bas, 1986, pp. 71–91.

the North that it acquired its fullest extent (as the South is still 'under-developed')? What would one say of an anthropologist who, in order to study Bambara society, conducted his investigations in the suburbs of Paris without ever setting foot in Mali – on the grounds that Malians, even when they are in Paris, do not lose their Bambara quality? Or what would one say of a political scientist who, in order to describe parliamentary democracy, based himself only on the way in which it is practised in Zaïre – on the grounds that even if Zaïrean institutions have seized up, the fiction of their existence is not in doubt? We shall therefore have to consider 'development' as a global phenomenon; for although some countries declare themselves to be 'developed', they are far from lacking interest in their own 'development'. The proof is that whenever a proposal is made for measures to improve the lot of the poorest countries, there is a rush to explain that their success is inti-mately bound up with the prosperity of the richest. On the road to growth, no one can stop and wait for the slow-movers. However much one pretends to believe that the 'development' problematic began with decolonization and mainly concerns the South (because it is there that the most unbearable poverty prevails), it is actually the opposite which is the case – not only historically, but also because the great themes of contemporary debate (the environment, debt repayment, liberalization of international trade) directly stem from the preoccupations of the industrialized countries.

Next, there has been a choice of what seemed to us the most signifi-cant 'episodes' in the history of 'development'. No doubt this has in-volved a degree of arbitrariness, but the main emphasis has anyway fallen upon the second half of the twentieth century. Although it seemed essential to go back to Antiquity, we have passed over the transformations that took place in the Middle Ages and especially the Renaissance, when conquest and colonization – legitimated through the duty of evangeli-zation – combined with the appearance in Europe of new attitudes to work and capital. These were important changes, of course, but their consequences (in terms of inequalities between nations) fully manifested themselves only after the Industrial Revolution. Similarly, the chapter on late-nineteenth-century colonialism mainly refers to the French case: not because other European powers (especially Britain) played an insig-nificant role in this attempt to dominate the world, but because the example of France seemed sufficient to bring out the similarities and the differences between this period and the 'age of development'.

Finally, the 'great texts' used here for the contemporary period are obviously not an exhaustive set,[3] and quite a few problems have been

posed in selecting them. For example, President Truman's Point Four,
which went almost unnoticed at the time, has exerted a much greater
influence than the New International Economic Order about which so
many streams of ink have flowed. Yet these various documents do have
a guiding thread, which strikes us all the more forcefully in that it
seems to fly in the face of the evidence; that is, each theory or
declaration makes a claim to be original (or novel), to pass itself off as
the solution at last discovered to the 'problems of development'. When
we look more closely, however, we see that the apparent innovations
are merely variations on a single theme which allow the various actors
to assert their legitimacy within the field of 'development'. In addition
to the banal obligation of adapting to changes in the international
environment, they each feel a pressing need to distinguish themselves
from rival theories or declarations on the 'development market', so as
to boost the fortunes of their intellectual lineage or their particular
institution. Indeed, one might say that each text sees itself as part of
the 'development mosaic', the variety of forms and shades serving to
bring out the overall 'design' (in both senses of the word). Thus, if
certain fragments have been left out, this by no means prevents us from
perceiving the general pattern.

It is this general pattern which is the most useful to us today, precisely in an age when the picture seems to be growing blurred. With
regard to 'development', the successive novelties to which we grew
accustomed over five decades have become a rarity. The moment is
therefore right to take a fresh look at the history of the ideas – to go
back to the drawing board, as it were, so that the elements which have
in turn claimed to occupy the whole space will appear as so many
parts of a broader fresco. To use a historical approach for a synchronic
view of 'development' – that would not be the least paradoxical aspect
of this work!

We shall begin, then, by defining what is to be understood by the
word 'development'. Even if everyone thinks they know what is involved, the favourable consensus surrounding the term is at the heart
of a misunderstanding that paralyses debate. To grasp its origins, we
shall concern ourselves with Ancient Greece, and then with the
Christian reinterpretation and the Enlightenment transformation, which
discloses something radically new beneath the appearance of sameness.

3. See Gilbert Rist, *Towards a 'New' United Nations Development Strategy? Some Major United Nations Resolutions in Perspective*, Nyon: International Foundation for Development Alternatives (IFDA), 1977, mimeo.

Then we shall move on to the colonial period, to show that the practices which are today claimed as new have a long history behind them, and that control over the lands of the South has long dressed itself up as high-minded internationalism. The question will then present itself of how President Truman – as much by accident as by inspiration – came up with the concept of 'underdevelopment' which helped to change the course of history. Following the work of Rostow, it was imagined that every country would be able to share in the promise of abundance; but then the dependency school tempered such hopes by stressing the responsibility of the industrial heartlands for the acute poverty of the South. With the proclamation of the New International Economic Order, it was thought that a way had at last been found to reduce the inequalities between nations; the satisfaction of 'basic needs' would put an end to the devastating plight of those living in countries with the least resources. But then the debt problem and the environmental crisis thrust themselves to the centre of attention, all the more insistently because they affected the finance and supply systems of the countries of the North. Not being able to solve them, everyone joined in hoping that 'development' would be both durable and humane. Such was the justification, in both North and South, for the humanitarian operations perpetuating a system which maintains and reinforces exclusion while claiming to eliminate it. In a concluding chapter, it will be shown why 'development' has gradually been drained of content, so that it is now a mere residue used to justify the process of globalization.

This résumé will have given some idea of the present work. Its main thesis is based upon a series of texts which marked their particular epochs; each was considered in its time to furnish an original solution, but in fact unwittingly followed an ancient problematic that must now be abandoned if we are to understand the nature of 'post-development'. What is at issue is so important that it warrants detailed demonstration. This accounts for the inevitable apparatus of notes, which may be passed over if they are thought excessive but which serve as a control on the argument and render it more precise.

The text was composed during sabbatical leave granted me by the Graduate Institute of Development Studies in Geneva. It has benefited from the comments, all the more critical for being friendly, which were submitted by my colleagues Marie-Dominique Perrot, Christian Comeliau, Philippe Durand, Serge Latouche, Fabrizio Sabelli and Rolf Steppacher. I would like to thank them all most sincerely – even if, of course, the contents of the book commit no one except its author.

Finally, I am immensely grateful to Patrick Camiller, who not only translated what I believe to be a difficult text, full of French turns, into brilliant English, but who also took pains to check every single reference and drew my attention to a series of blunders which had so far escaped my vigilance. Thanks to his exceptional shrewdness and professional conscience, the present version has been considerably improved. What a pleasure to transform a mere collaboration into real teamwork!

CHAPTER I

DEFINITIONS OF
DEVELOPMENT

CONVENTIONAL THINKING

When psychologists speak of the development of intelligence, mathematicians of the development of an equation or photographers of the development of a film, the sense they give to the word 'development' is clear enough. Its definition is shared by everyone working within the same area. The situation is quite different, however, when it comes to the use of the word in ordinary language to denote either a state or a process associated with such concepts as material well-being, progress, social justice, economic growth, personal blossoming, or even ecological equilibrium. Let us take just three examples.

1. Under the general heading '*développement*', the *Petit Robert* dictionary (1987) contains the following entry (among the meanings close to growth, blossoming, progress, extension, expansion): '*Developing country or region*, whose economy has not yet reached the level of North America, Western Europe, etc. Euphemism created to replace *underdeveloped*.'
2. The Report of the South Commission, produced under the chairmanship of the former Tanzanian president Julius Nyerere, was supposed to sum up the aspirations and policies of 'developing' countries. It defined development as 'a process which enables human beings to realize their potential, build self-confidence, and lead lives of dignity and fulfilment. It is a process which frees people from the fear of want and exploitation. It is a movement away from political, economic, or social oppression. Through development, political inde-

pendence acquires its true significance. And it is a process of growth, a movement essentially springing from within the society that is developing.'[1]

3. The *Human Development Report* of 1991, published by the United Nations Development Programme, stated: 'the basic objective of human development is to enlarge the range of people's choices to make development more democratic and participatory. These choices should include access to income and employment opportunities, education and health, and a clean and safe physical environment. Each individual should also have the opportunity to participate fully in community decisions and to enjoy human, economic and political freedoms.'[2]

We might comment at length on these definitions and demonstrate their various presuppositions: social evolutionism (catching up with the industrialized countries), individualism (developing the personality of human beings), economism (achieving growth and access to greater income). We might also show how the definitions themselves are either normative (what should happen) or instrumental (what is the purpose), and register the abundant use of intensifiers (e.g. 'more democratic and more participatory') which actually point to things presently 'lacking' or deficient. The most important question, however, is whether these really are *definitions*.

A METHODOLOGICAL WORD OF CAUTION

We cannot go over here the conditions necessary for something to be defined.[3] Let us simply note that for a definition to be operational – that is, for it to allow us to identify an object without the possibility of error – it must first of all eliminate all 'preconceptions', 'the fallacious ideas that dominate the mind of the layman',[4] and then base itself upon

---

1. *The Challenge to the South: The Report of the South Commission*, Oxford: Oxford University Press, 1990, p. 10.

2. UNDP, *Human Development Report 1991*, Oxford: Oxford University Press, 1991, p. 1.

3. See Emile Durkheim, *The Rules of Sociological Method* [1895, 1937], New York: The Free Press, 1964.

4. Ibid., p. 32. For example, 'to lead lives of dignity and fulfilment' or 'to participate fully in community decisions' means completely different things according to the context.

certain 'external characteristics' common to all phenomena within the group in question.[5] Or – to put it more bluntly – we must define 'development' in such a way that a Martian could not only understand what is being talked about, but also identify the places where 'development' does or does not exist. It is thus understandable why talk of 'realizing people's potential' or 'expanding the range of individual choice' does not help us to reach a definition – for it refers to individual (context-bound) experience that can never be apprehended by means of 'external characteristics'. At most, a normative injunction might be regarded as a kind of compass allowing us to hold a certain course. But to continue the journey, we may need to know where the North is without having any intention of proceeding there.

The principal defect of most pseudo-definitions of 'development' is that they are based upon the way in which one person (or set of persons) pictures the ideal conditions of social existence.[6] Of course, these imagined worlds – laid out according to the personal predilections of those who produce them – are often inviting and desirable, and it would be bad form to attack those who dream of a more just world where people are happy, live better and longer, and remain free of disease, poverty, exploitation and violence. This way of proceeding has the huge advantage of assembling a broad consensus at little cost and on the basis of unchallengeable values.[7] But if 'development' is only a useful word for the sum of virtuous human aspirations, *we can conclude at once that it exists nowhere and probably never will!*

Yet 'development' does exist, in a way, through the actions that it legitimates, through the institutions it keeps alive and the signs testifying to its presence. How could it be denied that there are developed and developing countries, development projects, development co-operation

5. Ibid., p. 35. Durkheim states very clearly: 'This rule, as obvious and important as it is, is seldom observed in sociology. Precisely because it treats everyday things ... we are so accustomed to use these terms, and they recur so constantly in our conversation, that it seems unnecessary to render their meaning precise' (ibid., p. 37).

6. The definition of these pictures is totally dependent on the subjectivity of the speaker: a believer will define God as 'the supreme Being', whereas an agnostic will speak of mystification or, even more radically, of a term lacking any referent.

7. A good example of such consensual – and tautological – usage of the term 'development' may be found in the first paragraph of the Declaration on the Right to Development (Resolution 41/128 of the General Assembly of the United Nations, 4 December 1986): 'The right to development is an inalienable human right by virtue of which every human person and all peoples are entitled to participate in, contribute to, and enjoy economic, social, cultural and political development, in which all human rights and fundamental freedoms can be fully realized.'

ministers, a United Nations Development Programme, an International
Bank for Reconstruction and Development (better known as the World
Bank), institutes for development studies, NGOs responsible for furthering development, and many other institutions and activities with the
same stated aim. In the name of this fetishistic term – which is also a
portmanteau or 'plastic' word[8] – schools and clinics are built, exports
encouraged, wells dug, roads laid, children vaccinated, funds collected,
plans established, national budgets revised, reports drafted, experts hired,
strategies concocted, the international community mobilized, dams
constructed, forests exploited, deserts reafforested, high-yield plants
invented, trade liberalized, technology imported, factories opened,
wage-jobs multiplied, spy satellites launched. When all is said and done,
every modern human activity can be undertaken in the name of
'development'.

For conventional thinking, the quest for a definition therefore
oscillates between two equally irrepressible extremes: (a) the expression
of a (doubtless general) wish to live a better life, which seems
deliberately to ignore the fact that the concrete ways of achieving it
would run up against conflicting political choices; and (b) the great
mass of actions (also often conflicting with one another) which are
supposed eventually to bring greater happiness to the greatest possible
number. The weakness of these two perspectives is that they do not
allow us to identify 'development': it appears in the one case as a
subjective feeling of fulfilment varying from individual to individual,
and in the other as a series of operations for which there is no *a priori*
proof that they really contribute to the stated objective.[9]

To escape from this dead end, we must return to Durkheim's twofold requirement of a definition: that it should cover all the phenomena

---

8. See Uwe Poerksen, *Plastic Words: The Tyranny of a Modular Language* [1989],
University Park, PA: Pennsylvania University Press, 1995. For Poerksen, the hallmark
of a plastic word is that it first had a clear and precise meaning as part of ordinary
language (in our case, the 'development' of an equation), was then used in scientific
discourse (Darwin's development of the species), and has now been so widely adopted
in technocratic parlance that it no longer means anything – except what the individual speaker wishes it to mean.

9. Not only is there nothing to suggest, for example, that the building of a dam
or the encouragement of exports for a particular product will actually increase the
well-being of the people supposed to benefit from it. We also see that, according to
context, the same operation is considered either as 'development' or as normal commercial activity: the purchase of an American company by a Japanese corporation is
not viewed in the same way as the setting up of an enterprise in Burkina Faso by
Japanese capital.

in question, and that it should include only their external character-istics.[10] In other words, it is necessary to identify sociologically, by reference to practices that anyone may observe, what allows us to say that certain countries are 'developed', while others are 'developing'. The point is not to contrast two different sets of countries by showing that one has more of this (schools, roads, currency reserves, average calorie consumption, cars, democracy or telephones) but less of that (illiteracy, cultural traditions, children per family, 'absolute poor', time, skilled labour, etc.), while the other set has the reverse.[11] Rather, the process at the root of this contrast needs to be brought into the light of day – a process whose rhythm differs in the two sets of countries and which transforms them, both quantitatively and qualitatively, in ways that cannot be reversed. For 'development' does not concern only the countries of the 'South', nor only operations conducted under the auspices of 'development co-operation'. It is a global, historically dis-tinctive phenomenon, whose functioning first needs to be explained before it can be detected as either present or absent.

ELEMENTS OF A DEFINITION

To satisfy the methodological requirements outlined above, and to embrace all the phenomena entering the field in question, our defini-tion will have to describe the ubiquitous mechanisms of the contem-porary world that determine social change in accordance with a special structure-creating logic. It is not enough to say that in the end 'develop-ment' boils down to social change, for social change has been a constant feature of life in every society since the dawn of humanity. What has to

---

10. Of course, the definition of these 'external characteristics' itself presupposes weighing and choosing activity; no method will ever allow us to embrace the whole of 'reality'. For Durkheim, then, a definition is like a map: it provides enough detail for us to recognize the geographical area, but does not pretend to describe all the life unfolding there.

11. Such a way of defining 'development' is quite widespread. (See, for example, the *Encyclopédie universelle Tempo*, vol. 7, 1967, under the entry '*sous-développement*'.) It enables the dominant group itself to define the characteristics of 'development', and then to identify a series of 'lacks' that are supposed to be filled within an evolutionary perspective. In reality, the so-called 'underdeveloped' countries are 'those which have more or less directly undergone Western domination, … which do not manage to find the answers required for their reproduction, [and which are characterized not by a lagging behind the industrial countries but by] the impossibility of following the same path.' Alain Lipietz, *Mirages et miracles. Problèmes de l'industrialisation dans le tiers monde*, Paris: La Découverte, 1985, p. 19.

be shown is the characteristic of 'developmental' change *which distinguishes modern societies from those which have gone before.*

Our starting point will be the following definition: *'Development' consists of a set of practices, sometimes appearing to conflict with one another, which require — for the reproduction of society — the general transformation and destruction of the natural environment and of social relations. Its aim is to increase the production of commodities (goods and services) geared, by way of exchange, to effective demand.* Let us look in turn at each element of this definition.

The *'practices'* in question (economic, social, political and cultural) correspond to the 'external characteristics' that Durkheim invoked to exclude from a definition any normative aspect stressing what is hoped as against what actually occurs. The facts, then, should not be considered on the basis of one or another currently available theory of 'development', for we know that what is envisaged in a theory does not necessarily happen in practice, and that similar practices can lay claim to opposing theories. This is why, as we have already noted, these practices are innumerable and appear at first sight to contradict one another. At the level of economics, for instance, some practices are geared to profit (direct investment, technology 'transfers', trade, etc.), while others involve a degree of generosity (loans on favourable terms, all kinds of NGO assistance, etc.); some foster international trade (raw material exports, cash crops, industrial relocation, etc.), while others hold it back (import restrictions as part of a restructuring drive, import substitution, customs duties, etc.); some aim to enhance the role of the State (creation of nationalized corporations, subsidization of basic commodities), others to limit it (deregulation, privatization, etc.); some have the effect of increasing external debt (new loans or rescheduling of old ones), while others seek to reduce it (cancellation, agreements playing the environment off against external financing).

'The reproduction of society.' To put it simply, these practices enable the world system to reproduce itself by expanding the area within its grasp, so that it assures the existence of societies (or social classes) included within the system, and washes its hands of those excluded from it.

'The general transformation and destruction of the natural environment...' The economic process which, for example, transforms ore into steel, oil into exhaust gas, or forest into 'resources', necessarily entails destruction. A previously available resource is thus converted into an object or a product whose recycling is either problematic (requiring new energy costs) or impossible — with the result that the destruction of the natural environment becomes worse still (pollution). This entropic

phenomenon is by no means new – indeed, it accompanies every physical process on the planet[12] – but its effects have grown considerably
since the Industrial Revolution. Simplifying a great deal, we could say
that industry has been producing energy by replacing watermills or
windmills (which use naturally renewable sources) with 'fire machines'
(steam engines, internal combustion engines) which, besides mainly
using non-renewable resources, irrevocably disperse a large part of the
resulting energy in the form of heat.[13] Whereas 'normal' economic
science[14] considers the industrial process only in terms of production, it
must be stressed that every phenomenon of production always involves
destruction, and that for roughly two centuries this has been increasing
in importance (though it went unnoticed for a long time). It is also the
case that the transformation of nature takes other forms bound up with
the transformation of institutions and techniques: the simplest such
example was the original appropriation of the land,[15] or the creation of
dams which allowed control and, consequently, market exploitation of
hydroelectric resources; the most complex has to do with genetic
engineering, which makes it possible not only to control but also to
manipulate nature or living organisms, and then to patent the results.
Space itself does not escape this process, as access to geostationary orbits
becomes a matter of dispute.[16] Of course, these are mere illustrations of
a worldwide process spreading to the whole of the natural environment; the economic–financial power of transnational corporations is

---

12. See Nicholas Georgescu-Roegen, *The Entropy Law and the Economic Process*,
Cambridge, MA: Harvard University Press, 1971.

13. See Jacques Grinevald, 'Science et développement. Esquisse d'une approche
socio-épistémologique', in *La pluralité des mondes*, Geneva: Théories et pratiques du
développement, Cahiers de l'IED, 1975, pp. 31–98. This massive growth in entropic
phenomena is linked to the difference in temporality between 'living' phenomena
(including wind-power and water-flow within the biosphere) and the exploitation of
minerals. Living reproduction has a slow rhythm that determines modes of use, whereas
the extraction of minerals depends only upon the technical means available, so that
improvements make for faster cumulative growth. (This point was made to me by
Rolf Steppacher.)

14. According to Thomas S. Kuhn (*The Structure of Scientific Revolutions*, Chicago:
University of Chicago Press, 1962/1970), 'normal science' is based on a series of past
results that are deemed sufficient to define the orientation of new research. It is
inserted within a paradigm which defines the problems and the ways of solving them.

15. See Karl Polanyi, *Primitive, Archaic and Modern Economies*, ed. George Dalton,
New York: Anchor Books, 1968.

16. The 'Space Commerce – Space for Your Business' conference, held in
Montreux in March 1992, said as much in its unvarnished publicity: '*Space is a common heritage, make it work for you!*'

also part of this generalization, which is today synonymous with globalization of markets.

'...and of social relations.' Social relations are not free from the rule of
the commodity and exploitation – that is, from exchange-value determined by supply and demand.[17] In this respect, the most important
change took place with the appearance – and gradual generalization –
of wage-labour in modern societies.[18] It was a major revolution whose
effects continue to make themselves felt, in at least two ways. First, in
economic theory, the new American thinking influenced by the recent
Nobel Prizewinner Gary Becker does not hesitate to extend the
'economic approach' to family relationships, including marriage,
domestic production, fertility, and even altruism.[19] Whereas Marx wrote
indignantly that the bourgeoisie had 'torn away from the family its
sentimental veil, and reduced the family relation to a mere money
relation',[20] the 'new economics' actually exults that 'no other nexus
between man and man than naked self-interest' remains.[21] This revolution in the way of approaching social relations is expressed in many
different ways. It can be seen, for example, in the massive expansion of
the leisure market or in the new possibilities offered by medical science.
Things that used to be personal and intimate, supposedly outside the

---

17. 'Quite irrespective, therefore, of their natural form of existence, and without
regard to the specific character of the needs they satisfy as use-values, commodities
in definite quantities are congruent, they take one another's place in the exchange
process, are regarded as equivalents, and despite their motley appearance have a common denominator.... The exchange-value of commodities is, consequently, determined not by the labour-time contained in them, but by the relation of demand and
supply.' Karl Marx, *A Contribution to the Critique of Political Economy*, London: Lawrence & Wishart, 1971, pp. 28, 62.

18. See Karl Polanyi, *The Great Transformation: The Political and Economic Origins of
Our Time* [1944], Boston, MA: Beacon Press, 1957. Polanyi (pp. 86–102) traces the
creation of a labour market back to the repeal of the Speenhamland Law, which until
1834 had given the poor a 'right to live' in the form of a guaranteed minimum
income independent of their earnings.

19. The 'economic approach' maintains that *everything is scarce*: not only natural
resources, energy or money, but also – and above all – time. Nothing is free, then,
and everyone must weigh the opportunity cost of everything they do. Is it worth not
taking a job in order to study? What price do I attach to leisure if I am offered
overtime? What is the cost of the sacrifices that would have to be accepted to keep
a family? See Gary Becker, *The Economic Approach to Human Behavior*, Chicago: University of Chicago Press, 1976. See also Henri Lepage, *Demain le libéralisme*, Paris: Le
Livre de Poche, 1980, pp. 25 ff.

20. 'Manifesto of the Communist Party' [1848], in Karl Marx, *The Revolutions of
1848*, London: New Left Review/Penguin, 1973, p. 70.

21. Ibid.

realm of the market, can today be the object of a contract for paid services. The practice of womb-leasing or drawing on sperm banks clearly shows that the commodity form is continuing its march into every area of social relations.

'*To increase the production of commodities (goods and services).*' The process is geared to increased production, on the assumption that 'more' necessarily means 'better'.[22] Many instances do, it is true, tend to confirm this postulate, but it should be borne in mind that all production necessarily involves destruction. This is largely covered up by the dominant trend in economics, which most often abandons any reckoning of the 'external costs' of production, or passes them off as an extra gain.[23] The most serious aspect, however, is that the process cannot be interrupted without endangering the social reproduction of those who benefit from it. It is therefore entirely focused upon production of the maximum rather than the optimum − for it can exist only by spreading extensively (geographically) or intensively (into new natural or social domains).[24] In other words, *growth is not a choice but a necessity*, as is amply demonstrated by the numerous strategies to 'reflate' the economy and (ideally) create more jobs.[25]

In most societies other than modern society, the circulation of goods is organized according to relations of kinship or hierarchy, and this confers on things a special role in which they are subordinate to social ties. Certain goods (e.g. those set aside for a dowry) can be exchanged only between certain persons (the eldest of the family), and only in precise

---

22.   This assumption is decidedly modern. Although the classical economists celebrated the 'progress of opulence' (Adam Smith), they nevertheless expected that a 'stationary position' would one day be reached.

23.   The recent current of 'environmental economics' has been trying to combat this blindness, particularly by including in the selling price of certain products their implicit costs of recycling or destruction. These operations, however, make it possible to sustain a new energy-destroying form of industry, and therefore do no more than postpone the problem. The 'polluter pays' principle may, in some cases, reduce the level of pollution (through the incorporation of 'externalities'), but it will not put an end to it. Even if pollution becomes a luxury, there will always be economic actors willing to 'afford it' (or to will it on others).

24.   In addition, growth has the ideological function of making people believe that inequalities are decreasing, given that the cake is said to be growing bigger all the time (and so its fairer distribution is not an issue).

25.   For example, *Le Monde* of 4 October 1994 carried the headline: 'G-7 Members Back Growth as a Remedy for Unemployment'. And Bill Clinton's solution to the crisis − when he was running for president − was quite simply to double the GNP of the United States within a generation. See Michel Beaud, 'Face à la croissance mortifère, quel développement durable?', *Revue Tiers Monde*, XXXV (137), January–March 1994, p. 136.

circumstances (restricted exchange);[26] in other cases, the social bond is expressed through the exchange of identical goods; or the 'big men', in order to maintain their prestige, have an obligation to redistribute goods obtained through the fruits of their labour, and so on. These numerous and diverse practices are not unrelated to *bargaining*, where the (not yet defined) rate of exchange corresponds to the 'value' that the two parties attach to each other. Quite different, however, is the system that appears together with the commodity. Now people are considered free in relation to one another, and their isolated mutual dealings are mediated through objects whose autonomy is established by a market price insensitive to any individual intervention.[27] In market exchange, individuals encounter one another not directly but 'around' an object sold by the one and bought by the other – after which each is all square with the other and resumes his initial freedom. This autonomization of the object legitimizes the autonomization of economics, which now strives to keep itself free from political, ethical and personal 'interference'.[28] Once again, this is a major feature of modern society.

'*Geared to effective demand.*' People produce in order to sell, and they sell so that they can buy something else.

> Give me that which I want, and you shall have this which you want … ; it is in this manner that we obtain from one another the far greater part of those good offices which we stand in need of. It is not from the benevolence of the butcher, the brewer, or the baker, that we expect our dinner, but from their regard to their own interest. We address ourselves, not to their humanity but to their self-love.[29]

This axiomatics of self-interest, explicitly excluding any reliance on the kindness of others, stands in radical contrast to the practices of generosity and gift-exchange that characterize most societies – including certain aspects of modern society made invisible by the ruling

26. We have already noted, following Polanyi, that the conversion of labour and land into commodities took place quite recently in Europe. As to so-called 'primitive' or 'traditional' societies, the anthropological literature abounds in examples of objects made to conform to the position held by their holder within the social system.

27. The Paribas Group sums this up nicely in its advertising slogan for the 'first telephone bank': 'No need to see each other to get on well.'

28. It should be noted, however, that this form of 'market economy' exists nowhere in a pure state, and that especially in OECD countries, numerous laws and regulations limit 'unfair competition'. Paradoxically, it is the formerly state-managed economies which now come closest to the 'ideal type', with all the consequences this entails.

29. Adam Smith, *The Wealth of Nations* [1776], London: Methuen, 1961, vol. 1, p. 18.

economism.[30] According to Smith, it is the exchange of commodities, resting upon individual interest, which is the best guarantee of the social bond; for 'man has almost constant occasion for the help of his brethren, and it is vain for him to expect it from their benevolence only'.[31] *But this modern anthropology, based upon the supposed equality and liberty of individuals who are no more than utility-seeking traders, leads to consequences that totally contradict its premises.* For 'gentle commerce',[32] which is supposed to assure social cohesion, assumes that everyone is able to exercise their talents and receive due remuneration for their labour, so that they have the wherewithal to obtain what they need. In other words, solvency of the exchange-partners is the basic precondition of the whole system. But in reality it is far from being guaranteed, as the conversion of commodities into money permits accumulation and therefore inevitable inequalities, both within a country and at an international level. In the end, if solvency is the only criterion for the management of resources, it becomes impossible to take account of intertemporality; the demand of future generations, which is real enough, is theoretically anticipated but not to a sufficient extent, because it cannot manifest itself on a market. What price will a Japanese natural history museum pay in the middle of the next century for the last barrel of oil produced by Saudi Arabia?

For roughly two centuries, then, as we have seen in broad outline, a distinctive process has led one part of the world along the path of 'development', and for the last fifty years it has been striving to maintain its momentum by drawing in the rest of humanity. The definition we have used above has the advantage that it describes a historical phenomenon, synthesizes what is common to a mass of diverse practices, and shows how difficult it is for other forms of social organization to survive on the margins of the dominant system.

---

30. On the persistence of gift-exchange in modern societies, see MAUSS [Mouvement anti-utilitariste dans les sciences sociales], *Ce que donner veut dire. Don et intérêt*, Paris: La Découverte, 1993.

31. *The Wealth of Nations*, p. 18.

32. The expression '*doux commerce*' keeps cropping up in the eighteenth century, to indicate that market exchange is a guarantee of peace because it ties people to one another. Only Rousseau rejects the optimism of the Encyclopaedists: 'Everything that facilitates communication among the various nations carries to some, not the virtues of the others but their crimes, and among all of them alters the morals that are proper to their climate and the constitution of their government.' Preface to *Narcissus, or The Lover of Himself* [1782], in *The Collected Writings of Rousseau*, vol. 2, Hanover, NH: University Press of New England, 1992, p. 190.

A SCANDALOUS DEFINITION?

It may be objected that the essence of 'development' is not worldwide expansion of the market system. Is it not different from mere economic growth?[33] Does it not set itself 'human goals' that conflict with the cynicism of the process presented above? Is it not the generous expression of a real concern for others? Indeed, is it not a moral imperative? Despite inevitable mistakes and reprehensible perversions of original intentions, does it not aim to put an end to the extreme poverty that is the scourge of most of the world?

These are understandable questions. They betoken a collective hope of improving the conditions of life of the majority of mankind. They express a will not to be discouraged by past setbacks. They reveal a (mostly sincere) commitment to the most deprived, and a real desire to help them by taking action. All this can only excite our approval and admiration.[34] So how are we to explain the discrepancy between such high-minded goals and practices hindering their achievement?

A comparison may help to clarify this point. Suppose that a group of Christians (belonging to different Churches) are asked to define Christianity.[35] They might well state that it is essentially a religion based upon love of one's neighbour which seeks to establish peace and justice among men. Even if such a definition is criticized for a lack of theological profundity, it might still command widespread allegiance among the believers concerned. Does this mean that a sociologist of religion can be satisfied with it? Or, in other words, is it sufficient for an agnostic to identify where Christianity exists and where it does not exist? The answer is obviously negative, because the definition in question fails to base itself upon the distinctive practices of Christianity, and mentions only unverifiable (and indubitable) feelings that come under the heading of spiritual experience.

---

33. It is often said that 'development' is not the same as economic growth, but this is by no means certain. As the *Human Development Report 1991* puts it: 'Just as economic growth is necessary for human development, human development is critical to economic growth' (p. 2). Or, in the 1992 edition: 'The issue is not only how much economic growth, but *what kind* of economic growth' (p. 2). It is easy to see that in practice, economic growth is what is pursued, in the name of 'development'.

34. Beyond any moral judgement of this way of presenting 'development', it should be noted that everyone chooses the definition that suits them best in the light of their practical interests, allowing them to retain the position they occupy within the particular field.

35. The choice of Christianity for this comparison does not imply any value judgement. The same conclusions would be reached by asking members of the Communist Party to define classless society.

Once again we may profitably turn to Durkheim, who defined religion in general as 'an eminently social thing' and 'religious representations' as 'collective representations that express collective realities'.[36] He thus excluded from his definition that which seems most important on a common-sense view – namely, the idea of the supernatural, of mystery or divinity. For 'religions can be defined as they are now or as they have been, not as they may be tending more or less vaguely to become'.[37] What remain are the beliefs and rituals, the separation between the sacred and the profane, the notion of the 'Church' or the community of believers. *To put it in another way: religion is the belief of a given social group in certain indisputable truths, which determine obligatory behaviour in such a way as to strengthen social cohesion.* It is 'the way in which the special being that is society thinks about the things of its own experience';[38] it reflects and expresses the experience of society.

This detour via the phenomenon of religion shows that the definition which seems best to someone located within a belief system is of no use to a sociologist seeking to understand it from the outside. However real and profound the believer's religious experience may be, 'it by no means follows that the reality which grounds it should conform objectively with the idea the believers have of it. The very fact that the way in which this reality has been conceived has varied infinitely in different times is enough to prove that none of these conceptions expresses it adequately.'[39] On the other hand, if it is accepted that religion is the product of social causes and a reality needed to assure 'agreement of minds', then it must be interpreted on the basis of social practices, however remote these appear from the ideals proposed by the belief itself.[40] It is not up to the sociologist to pass a value judgement on the content of the belief, or even to take a position 'for' or 'against' development. Such questions have no meaning for him as a sociologist; he is content to point out that the act of belief entails a number of practices on the part of believers, and that they cannot evade them without

---

36. Emile Durkheim, *The Elementary Forms of Religious Life* [1912], New York: The Free Press, 1995, p. 9.

37. Ibid., p. 44.

38. Ibid., p. 436.

39. Ibid., p. 420.

40. It is well known that the religion based upon love of one's neighbour has also served to justify, among other things, slavery, the Inquisition, witch-hunting, wars of religion, and colonization – not because the belief content has varied, but because society could not but lay claim to it (by reinterpreting it) in order to assure its own cohesion.

endangering the cohesion of the group whose belief they share. This explains the diversity, or even the conflicting nature, of the viewpoints, and hence the definitions. Seen from a distance, a social phenomenon inevitably appears in a different light from that in which it is experienced by a participant: a fish is the worst-placed creature to discover the existence of water.

'DEVELOPMENT' AS AN ELEMENT IN THE RELIGION OF MODERNITY

Our detour via religion raises a new question. What if 'development' is part of our modern religion? Without repeating the argument developed elsewhere,[41] let us make a couple of points that will allow us to put forward such a view.

(a) To consider modern society as different from others, on the pretext that it is secular and rational, is actually a result of Western arrogance. As there is no society which is not based upon traditions and beliefs, nothing indicates that Western society is lacking them either – even if they are different from those of other societies. *It is necessary to reject the 'great divide' between 'tradition' and 'modernity'*,[42] *for modernity itself lies within a certain tradition.*

(b) The modern belief to which we are referring needs to be qualified. It should not be confused with the message proclaimed by Christianity – for although that is unquestionably part of the Western heritage, progressive secularization has taken away from the Churches their monopoly of defining the beliefs shared by society as a whole. Nevertheless, from a sociological point of view, this marginalization of ecclesiastical institutions does not mean that religiosity has disappeared. Rather, it has 'migrated elsewhere' – above all, to where one does not expect to find it, in what generally passes as secular. Moreover, since beliefs are positioned beyond dispute, they should not be confused with ideology.[43] An ideology is open to debate: one may, for example, be a liberal, a social democrat or a communist, and accept the pluralism of

---

41. See Marie-Dominique Perrot, Gilbert Rist and Fabrizio Sabelli, *La Mythologie programmée. L'économie des croyances dans la société moderne*, Paris: PUF, 1992.

42. See Bruno Latour, *We Have Never Been Modern* [1991], New York: Harvester Wheatsheaf, 1993.

43. The ruling ideology – to quote Marx – is produced by the ruling class. But as it happens, the ruling class is itself mystified by its belief in 'development'.

sociopolitical perspectives. But social beliefs (human rights or 'develop-ment', for example) are a kind of collective certainty; their concrete forms may be debatable, and they may even be doubted in private, but it would be improper to question their validity in public. Such beliefs correspond in a way (homeomorphically) to the myths of non-Western societies – except that myths can be recounted, whereas modern society has no real founding narrative. Still, the shared beliefs of modern society can be linked to ancient myths or fragments of myths peculiar to West-ern society. Beliefs, in fact, are not dogmatic truths to which everyone subscribes by personal conviction; they are expressed in the form of simple propositions widely held to be true, which people believe – unable to do otherwise – because they hear everyone else saying them, and think that everyone believes them. For example: 'economic recovery will solve the problem of employment'; 'technological progress will allow today's problems to be solved'; or 'most citizens support the govern-ment'. They are 'floating propositions', then, which rely upon obscure authorities (opinion polls, the experts) and are legitimized by fragments of ancient beliefs. As 'reserves of meaning', these beliefs play the same role that bank gold did when it used to guarantee paper money with-out ever being checked by anyone. Still today, it is enough if everyone plays the game by trusting in the banknotes they are offered (that is, by agreeing to grant credit).

(c) These beliefs are effective. They compel those who share them to act in a particular manner. Even if everyone personally questions the validity of such and such a proposition, it is impossible to escape the collective obligation that it involves. However many doubts one may express in private about whether economic growth can create jobs for everyone who is out of work, it is necessary to act as if that were, if not true, then at least plausible, on pain of being treated as a bad citizen. *The act of belief is performative, and if people must be made to believe, it is so that they can be made to act in a certain way.* Indeed, the action determined by the belief is obligatory, and does not rest upon any choice.

(d) Finally, in so far as these beliefs are religious, life is constantly imparted to them through signs and rituals. For example, shows, fairs and exhibitions of every kind (especially 'world fairs') sustain the idea that 'progress is under way', and the opening of a school or a dam in a distant country means that people can be made to believe that a better life is just around the corner. Just as the Azande had their sorcer-ers and the Romans their haruspices, so does modern society consult economic experts whose job it is to keep an eye on the conjuncture, to scrutinize the 'broad indicators', and to prophesy the future being stored up in 'pregnant trends'. Predictions are piously considered at the grand rituals of political 'summits', G-7 meetings, trade negotiation 'rounds', and various sessions of the UN General Assembly. Mistakes happen to each and every one, but this does not diminish the respect in which their ministry is held. Their authority depends not upon results but on the care they take in discharging their duties.

If 'development' is regarded as an element of modern religion, this explains not only the discrepancy between the sociologist's definition and the believer's vision, but also why it does not threaten the existence of the belief in any way.

It may well appear surprising that, fifty years after the international community officially set its sights on extending 'development' to the South, this has still not come to pass. If a politician makes too many demagogic promises, he ends up a failure in the eyes of his electorate. And if a researcher persists too long with experiments that show no result, he is eventually dismissed by his employer. But nothing of the kind happens in the field of 'development': *promises are tirelessly repeated and experiments constantly reproduced. So why is it that each failure leads to another reprieve?*

Just as Christians know all about the numerous crimes committed in the name of their faith, yet continue to uphold it, so do the 'development' experts increasingly recognize the mistakes without questioning their reasons for soldiering on. Belief is so made that it can easily tolerate contradictions[44] – especially as, unlike scientific theories, it cannot be refuted. This is why science changes faster than belief, which has immunity against anything that might place it in question. The Truth cannot lie, so lies – or mistakes – are always attributed to faulty interpretation, human failings, or lack of information. The Zande sorcerer did not proceed otherwise. Never ceasing to believe in the truth of the oracle, he could turn its decisions around by repeating his operations or changing his methods until the result suited him ... or the person who had come to consult him. As for the latter, if he thought the advice wrong, or deceitful, he would cast doubt not on sorcery in general but only on the skills of this particular sorcerer; he was always

---

44. Thus, it is often said in one and the same breath that 'development' co-operation is motivated both by disinterestedness (solidarity) and by self-interest.

free to turn to a more competent one.[45] Nor is it necessary to go a
long way to find examples of beliefs which persist despite being contradicted by the practices they justify. In different times and places, did
not Christianity condemn then rehabilitate Galileo, despise then honour the Jews, tolerate slavery and then preach the equal dignity of all
human beings, support colonialism then salute independence, blacklist
democracy then exalt human rights?

For Edgar Morin, 'the ultimate defence of a belief lies in the feeling
of abandonment that wells up when one contemplates abandoning it....
In this way, the hard core is defended through fear of emptiness.'[46]
How could one not tremble to think that hopes cherished, struggles
fought, actions engaged in, have suddenly lost all value because the
belief underpinning them has been declared vain and empty? That
which is irrational in the act of belief is not the least worthy of respect.
This becomes apparent when one listens to those who, also for fifty
years, sincerely believed in the radiant future promised by the people's
democracies of Eastern Europe. For belief, let us repeat, does not arise
directly out of personal illumination but takes shape collectively in the
course of a history. Belief clings to age-old indisputable truths, seals
membership in a group and defines what is legitimate discourse; it
makes acceptable measures which, one knows, conflict with the hoped-
for goal, on the pretext that they are in the 'order of things'.

'Development' thus appears to be a belief and a series of practices which
form a single whole in spite of contradictions between them. The belief is no
less real than the practices, because they are indissolubly linked to each
other. Together, they reflect the logic of a society undergoing globalization which – in order to accomplish the programme it has set itself
(whose consequences are not equally heartening for all) – has to draw
its legitimacy from a number of widely shared, indisputable truths that
have the character of myth. The next chapter will consider the gradual
construction of this Western myth, while recognizing that 'history has
not reached a stagnant end, nor is it triumphantly marching towards
the radiant future. It is being catapulted into an unknown adventure.'[47]

---

45. 'Scepticism, far from being smothered, is recognized, even inculcated. But it
is only about certain medicines and certain magicians. By contrast, it tends to support
other medicines and magicians.... The experience of an individual counts for little
against accepted opinion. If it contradicts a belief, this does not show that the belief
is unfounded, but that the experience is peculiar or inadequate.' Edward Evans-
Pritchard, Witchcraft, Oracles, and Magic among the Azande [1937], Oxford: Clarendon
Press, 1976, p. 202.
46. Edgar Morin, Pour sortir du vingtième siècle, Paris: Fernand Nathan, 1981, p. 102.
47. Edgar Morin, 'La terre, astre errant', Le Monde, 14 February 1990.

CHAPTER 2

METAMORPHOSES OF
A WESTERN MYTH

There might well have been hesitation about the right generic term for the many different practices designed to increase human well-being, as well as for the new meaning given to history. 'Civilization' in the transitive sense of a process – widely used until the end of the First World War – could have been brought back into currency; 'Western-ization' could have been employed to highlight the origins of the implicit model; the seemingly neutral concept of 'modernization' also had its supporters; and in a militant perspective, 'liberation' could have been favoured in reference to the life of society as a whole. In the end, however, it was 'development' that carried the day – no doubt because concepts do not fall from heaven and the choice was not as open as we have just suggested. The word 'development' had many advantages: it already enjoyed a certain respectability within scientific discourse; it allowed the conditions under which the desired process could unfold to be postulated; and it linked up with a tradition of thought (going back into mythology) which underwrote its legitimacy.[1]

WHAT THE METAPHOR IMPLIES

To describe social change is a difficult, even impossible, undertaking. For its object is not only economic production, material infrastructure and the political system, but also attitudes, relationships with other

---

1. The various elements in this chapter rely heavily on Robert A. Nisbet's *Social Change and History: Aspects of the Western Theory of Development*, New York: Oxford University Press, 1969.

people, and perceptions of nature. Moreover, these multiple changes
are themselves imperceptible, and it would be hard to identify them as
and when they appear. Hence the usefulness of metaphor or comparison, which 'borrows from something foreign a palpable and natural
image of the truth',[2] and makes it possible to express a complex idea
by means of an image. How many explanations would be needed to
account for what is meant by referring to France as the *le coq gaulois*?
It is a common procedure, which allows us to pass from the familiar to
the unfamiliar by applying to one domain reasoning or concepts valid
in another. Thus, we understand electrical phenomena better if we
compare them to a hydraulic system, with its flows, its strength and its
pressure. Analogy – which allows us to pass from one object to another
by drawing on similarities established by the imagination – is therefore
a useful aid to reflection, *on condition that image is not confused with
reality, analogy with real meaning.*

The fact that 'development' already has a range of meanings associated with unfurling and growth makes it especially suited to describe
change in society that stems from the economic process. Whereas it is
difficult to give a precise account of the many social transformations
due to the influence of modernity, everyone knows what is meant by
the development of a child or a plant. It is an imperceptible process,
impossible to grasp at any one moment of time yet clear enough when
followed over a period; and despite the appearance of immobility, the
way in which it unfolds is both spontaneous and predictable. By means
of this analogy, a social phenomenon is related to a natural phenomenon, as if what is true of the one must necessarily be true of the
other. It is this metaphor, then, this transfer from the natural to the
social, which we have to examine first.

A number of things are implied by talk of the development of a
plant or an organism, of natural or living beings.[3] First of all, there is
the negative idea that change is not a matter either of chance or of
external aspects grafted on to the process itself. Of course, the context
should not be hostile, and in some cases it can be made more favourable. For a plant to grow, it must avoid frost and be able to count on
the sun; it is also advisable to pull up undesirable vegetation nearby
and, perhaps, to mix in some fertilizer. The fact remains, however, that

---

2. Boileau, *Sat. IX*, quoted in *Littré*, vol. 5, Paris: Gallimard–Hachette, 1957,
col. 177, article '*métaphore*'.
3. The following remarks relate to knowledge derived from common sense. A
biologist would not necessarily speak the same language.

the plant will develop spontaneously in accordance with well-established 'laws'. To put it more positively, we could say that the 'development' of a living organism involves four basic features.

1. *Directionality*. Growth has a direction and a purpose. It follows a number of clearly identified stages. Even when the transformations are considerable, the final stage is already given at the beginning; one can know the shape of the tree in advance by looking at the seed. 'Development' in general may be considered synonymous with 'growth', but here there is also the idea of perfecting or completing which characterizes a 'fully developed' organism. 'Development' is thus seen as necessarily positive.

2. *Continuity*. Nature makes no leaps. Even when the bud bursts open or the chrysalis turns into a butterfly, it is still the same organism which gradually changes its appearance, not its 'nature'. This permanence through change is indeed one of the conditions of life, and comes to an end only in death.

3. *Cumulativeness*. Each new stage depends upon the preceding one, in accordance with a methodical progression. Blossom precedes the fruit; a heifer must calve before giving any milk; and in children, symbolic thinking is prior to the mastery of logical operations. In each case, there is a passage from a lower to a higher stage, a maturing which leads to a state of completion. In other words, the variations that make themselves felt as time goes by are always interpreted as a positive (quantitative or qualitative) addition.

4. *Irreversibility*. When a stage is passed or a new level reached, it is not possible to go back: the adult does not become a child again, nor does the fruit blossom a second time or the leaf turn back into its seed.

These various remarks are a matter of common wisdom. But they do show what is presupposed in likening society to a live organism, where social change or 'development' is thought of in terms of the growth characteristic of biological systems.[4] The convenience of the analogy no doubt makes it seem more plausible, but the price is that sociohistorical specificities tend to be overlooked. *Far from making it easier to understand the phenomenon, the metaphor obscures it by naturalizing history.* For there is no proof that each little village is 'destined' to become a big town.

---

4. See Pierre Achard, Antoinette Chauvenet, Elisabeth Lage, Françoise Lentin, Patricia Nève and Georges Vignaux, *Discours biologique et ordre social*, Paris: Le Seuil, 1977.

External factors operating on a society (migration, political alliances, wars) often radically change the 'course' of history. Even the greatest empires collapse (the former Soviet Union, for example), and societies marginalized today look back fondly on their past prosperity.

The process of social change that is qualified as 'development' is by no means the only historical phenomenon caught in the clutches of naturalist ideology. Economics, 'behavioural science' and political sociology – which ought, after all, to give greater importance to specificities and contingencies – frequently resort to biological models in support of their demonstrations.

> The key instrument in this permanent project is discourse, a sufficient guarantee of social power. For it is words that are given the responsibility not only to classify, but actually to ground the existence of a representation meant to be generally applied. Words too are asked to justify practices and powers. Biology becomes the unchallengeable reference that ceases to appear sociopolitical because it is a 'natural' guarantee.[5]

Nevertheless, 'development' occupies a quite special place within naturalist ideology, for it evokes a tradition stretching throughout the long history of the West.

LANDMARKS IN THE WESTERN VIEW OF HISTORY

Aristotle and Antiquity

Antiquity relied upon two sources of knowledge, one relating to myth and the other to the theories put forward by philosophers. Among the themes attracting special attention, a major priority was change – that is, how the permanence of the same should be reconciled with the appearance of newness. According to the mythological tradition, the transformations of the world were to be explained by a succession of 'ages' [αἰῶνες] metaphorically designated by the metals symbolizing their relative perfection (gold, silver, bronze, iron), each of which unfolded in the mode of a cycle of growth, apogee and decline.[6] This way of conceiving evolution could also draw upon everyday experience of the common trajectory followed by humans and plants – which helped to reinforce the veracity of the myth. Thus, in a matter as important as

---

5. Ibid., p. 10.
6. See, for example, Ovid's *Metamorphoses*, I: 90 ff.

the cultivation of wheat, myth had it that the earth goddess Demeter – displeased at the abduction of her daughter Persephone by Hades, the god of the Underworld – decided to blight the growth of the plants in her care. As long as her daughter was held by her lover in the nether regions, nothing more would grow. It was an impossible situation for human beings, who found themselves without food. Zeus, moved by their complaint, came to their rescue by negotiating a compromise between Demeter and Hades, so that Persephone would spend only part of the year with her lover and then come back to the world of human habitation. This was an ingenious way of explaining the *reason* for what everyone could observe: namely, that the seed has to lie in the ground before it can grow, and that after developing to the full it has to return to the soil to assure the perpetuation of the cycle.

Against this background, Aristotle (384–322 BC) sought to ground scientific knowledge by distinguishing as clearly as possible between what can be known for certain and what depends upon unforeseeable circumstances. There was thus a radical break between science and history: the one tried to grasp the sequence of causes determined by necessity, while the other (viewed as an art) dealt only with the contingent or accidental.

For Aristotle, the field of science was coextensive with nature, although the latter was given rather a different meaning from the one it has today. The Greek word for 'nature', *physis* or φύσις, comes from the verb *phuo* [φύω], which means 'to grow' or 'to develop'. So whereas we usually think of 'nature' as that which does not change ('it's in his nature!'), for Aristotle 'nature' [φύσις or 'development'] means (1) 'the genesis of growing things [literally: which participate in the phenomenon of growth]'; and (2) 'that immanent part of a growing thing from which its growth first proceeds.... Nature in the primary and strict sense is the essence of things which have in themselves, as such, a source of movement ... and processes of becoming and growing are called nature because they are movements proceeding from this.'[7] This being so, science may be defined as the theory of the 'nature' – that is,

---

7. *Metaphysica*, 1014^b and 1015^a, in *The Works of Aristotle*, ed. W.D. Ross, vol. 8, Oxford: Oxford University Press, 1966. The problem of translation is especially acute here, as the text constantly plays with terms that should be simultaneously rendered as 'nature', 'growth' and 'development'. See ibid., 982^b: 'The science which knows to what end each thing must be done is the most authoritative of the sciences ...; and this end is the good of that thing, and in general the supreme good in the whole of nature.'

the 'development' – of things,[8] and to examine things scientifically is to consider them 'according to their nature' – that is, in conformity with their 'development'.[9] Thus – to stay within the field of botany – a scientist is one who seeks to understand plants on the basis of their 'normal' (or, pleonastically, their 'natural') growth from seed to fruit, without going into their 'history', into what may happen if there is too much sun or frost, if a bird digs up the seed, or if a child plucks the blossom. 'Nature is therefore that which exists independently of human activity; but nor is it to be confused with "matter". Matter is chance – a mode of existence not only independent of human production but also indifferent to any principle and any law. As soon as an order manifests itself … it is held to be natural.'[10]

For Aristotle, however, 'nature' is not limited to the frontiers within which modern thought confines it. In his eyes, every being has a *physis* of its own – that is, its own principle of 'development'. Thus 'the State is by nature [that is, seen in terms of development] clearly prior to the family and to the individual, since the whole is of necessity prior to the part; … he who is unable to live in society, or who has no need because he is sufficient for himself, must be either a beast or a god: he is no part of a State.'[11] This quotation shows that things should be understood in accordance with their end, and in so far as man is a 'political animal' [ζῷον πολιτικόν] his ultimate goal is given by the polis or the State, which is 'prior' to the individual, just as the tree is 'already' contained in the seed. For Aristotelian science, the 'historical character of the State' does not concern the political convulsions or power games that occur within it, but only its 'natural reality'[12] – that is, the course of things which is necessary to make it what it should be. Whereas the historian is interested in accounts of 'accidents' taking place within a given period, and will try, for example, to set a date on them, the scientist offers a

---

8. 'He who thus considers things in their first growth and origin, whether a state or anything else, will obtain the clearest view of them.' *Politica*, 1252ᵃ, in *Works*, vol. 10.

9. 'We also speak of a thing's nature as being exhibited in the process of growth by which its nature is attained.… What grows *qua* growing grows from something into something. Into what then does it grow? Not into that from which it arose but into that to which it tends.' *Physica*, 193ᵇ, in *Works*, vol. 2.

10. Clément Rosset, *L'Anti-nature. Eléments pour une philosophie tragique* [1973], Paris: PUF, 1986, p. 11.

11. *Politica*, 1253ᵃ. Cf. 'And therefore, if the earlier forms of society are natural, so is the state, for it is the end of them, and the nature of a thing is its end. For what each thing is when fully developed we call its nature, whether we are speaking of a man, a horse, or a family.' Ibid., 1252ᵇ.

12. Ibid., 1252ᵇ.

'natural history' of institutions and things (that is, a description of their silent, invisible and necessary development).

'Nature', to be sure, assigns to each being a 'final' state, which corresponds to its perfect form.[13] But this does not at all mean that growth can continue to an unlimited extent. For Aristotle, that which has no term or limit [το ἄπειρον] is by definition incomplete and imperfect, and 'coming-to-be and passing-away must occur within the field of "that which can be-and-not-be"'.[14] Aristotle therefore remains faithful to the theory of cycles: that which is born and grows up will also fade and die, in a perpetual series of new beginnings. This is his solution to the basic question concerning persistence in change and the ceaseless return of the same.

Saint Augustine and the Theology of History

The authority of Aristotle's views spread to the whole of the ancient world. When Lucretius (98–55 BC) wrote his *De Rerum Natura*, he thought of 'nature' as the principle of growth, the word itself deriving from the verb *nasci*, 'to be born'. And if the world is still in its youth, he argued, that does not mean it will not one day have to face its decay. For

the things you see growing merrily in stature and climbing step by step the stairs of maturity – these are gaining more atoms than they lose ... until they have touched the topmost peak of growth. Thereafter the strength and vigour of maturity is gradually broken, and age slides down the path of decay.[15]

The convulsions of the Roman Empire in the first few centuries AD lent credence to the idea that the world was at the end of a cycle, and that it was 'natural' for imperial power to be drawing to a close.[16] It was in this politically unstable context of an ageing world that Augustine of Hippo (354–430) attempted to reconcile the philosophy of history of his time with Christian theology. But the Aristotelian view posed a problem for Christian theology on at least three points.

---

13. 'Final' in the sense of Aristotelian logic: that is, 'which corresponds to the end' or 'which is determined by the final cause' (principle of entelechy). 'For in all things, as we affirm, Nature [= development] always strives after "the better".' *De Generatio et Corruptione*, 336^b, in *Works*, vol. 9.

14. Ibid., 335^b.

15. *De Rerum Natura* II: 1122 ff. Lucretius, *On the Nature of the Universe*, Harmondsworth: Penguin, 1951, p. 93.

16. It is true that during his brief reign as emperor, Philip the Arabian celebrated the thousandth anniversary of Rome on 21 April 248, and launched a huge propaganda effort to make people believe in the coming of a new age. (Evidence of this

The first concerned God's intervention in history. Whereas Aristotle refused to concern himself with the 'accidents' of history and concentrated on the silent force at the origins of 'development', Christianity set store by the divine pedagogy which conferred a new meaning upon the particular events of history. The Old Testament testified to the presence of Revelation within a series of historic moments (Noah and the Flood, Moses and the dispensation of the Law, David and messianic royalty, etc.). And of course, the New Testament presented the incarnation of God in the human person of Jesus as the decisive moment of Revelation. Thus, whereas Aristotelianism excluded chance and accident from its 'science' of 'natural' necessity, Christianity transformed them into signs of divine providence.

The second area of disagreement has to do with the spontaneity of 'natural' phenomena. Christianity both added a 'supernature' to 'nature' and replaced the impersonal principle of growth with divine omnipotence. God could act in a supernatural manner, but he was also the creator of a world that he unceasingly continued to sustain and direct.

The third contradiction stems from the fact that Aristotle allowed both for change and for the return of the same. Christianity could not conceive of the 'eternal return' – for history unfolded according to a plan that had a beginning and an end. Besides, history embraced all nations and was dominated by the incarnation of Jesus Christ, the one and only saviour, whose intervention took place 'once and for all'. Hence the struggle against the pagans, who keep 'walking in circles'.[17]

---

are the coins struck for the anniversary, which bear the inscriptions *saeculum novum* or *miliarum saeculum*.) Nevertheless, the feeling of the end was very strong, intensified in the case of the Christians by their expectation of the end of the world. Thus in 252 Saint Cyprien (*Ad Demetrianum*, ch. 3) noted everyone's observation that the sun's rays were less brilliant, trees bore less fruit, and wells were drying up – for 'such is the law of the world and the will of God'. [*Haec sententia mundo data est, haec Dei lex est: ut omnia orta occidant, et aucta senescant et infirmentur fortia et magna minuantur.*] Such descriptions were common at the time and harked back to Lucretius's assertion: 'Already [the earth] is far past its prime [and] has scarcely strength to generate animalcules.... The same earth in her prime spontaneously generated for mortals smiling crops and lusty vines, sweet fruits and gladsome pastures, which now can scarcely be made to grow by our toil' (*De Rerum Natura*, II: 1145 ff.; *The Nature of the Universe*, p. 94).

17. *Qui in circuitu ambulant.* Augustine mocks 'the absurd futility of this circular route', and concludes: '...there is no reason to believe in those strange cycles which prevent the appearance of anything new, since everything has already existed in the past and will exist in the future and at certain periods of time' [*Nunc enim contra opinionem disputamus, qua illi circuitus asseruntur, quibus semper eadem per intervalla temporum necesse est repeti existimantur*]. *Civitas Dei*, XII: 18, 21; *The City of God*, Harmondsworth: Penguin, 1984, pp. 495, 500.

Augustine's solution is to preserve the constituents of the cyclical theory by applying them to world history as a whole. In other words, he integrates the totality of 'natural' phenomena and sociohistorical events by considering them as an expression of God's plan for humanity. But he also reduces the multitude of successive cycles to a single one – corresponding to the history of salvation – which has the same features as the objects of Aristotelian science: birth, apogee and decline.[18] Starting with the creation of the world and of Adam, the father of humanity, world history 'develops' according to a necessity that has been present from all eternity;[19] it progresses throughout the ancient alliance and culminates in the appearance and sacrifice of Jesus Christ, so that the history of the world cannot but tend towards its own end, summed up in eschatological doctrine and the 'Last Judgement'. In the difficult times of the late fourth and early fifth centuries, this would merely have confirmed the dominant feeling of the end, if not of *the* world, then at least of *a* world. Augustine, then, took over, and applied to the whole of humanity, the metaphor frequently employed by pagan writers which compared the Empire to a man passing from youth to maturity and then ineluctably entering old age.[20]

With regard to the subject of this book, Augustine's originality bore on three aspects that would considerably influence the history of 'development'.

1. His philosophy of history – in the form of a history of salvation – concerns the whole of humankind. Unlike earlier authors, who were concerned with local, national or imperial history, Augustine stressed the universality of his schema, insisting that all nations on earth are subject to divine providence.

---

18. Beyond history, there is also a kind of 'return' to the paradisiacal time of the beginning. See the final paragraph of the *City of God* (Book XXII, chapter 30), where Augustine compares the history of the world to the succession of days of the week, and looks forward to 'an eighth day, as it were, which is to last for ever.... Behold what will be, in the end, without end! For what is our end but to reach that kingdom which has no end?' (ibid., p. 1091). We can see how wrong it is to see as 'Judaeo-Christian' the linear conception of time as tending towards 'progress'.

19. This notion of necessity was no doubt inherited from Aristotle, but it was also fundamental for Augustine and his ardent defence of predestination.

20. *Sicut autem unius hominis ita humani generis ... recta eruditio per quosdam articulos temporarum tamquam aetatum profecit accessibus* (*Civitas Dei*, X: 14). 'The experience of mankind in general ... is comparable to the experience of the individual man. There is a process of education ... as through the successive stages of a man's life' (*City of God*, p. 392). Or, in more scholarly language, ontogenesis (individual development) recapitulates phylogenesis (development of the species).

2. Particular historical events have no importance for Augustine except in so far as they are part of God's plan. Concrete history is not ignored or referred to others, as was the case with Aristotle, but reinterpreted within the framework of the conflict between the city of man and the city of God. In other words, history does occupy an important place, but this is secondary to the philosophy of history.

3. Despite its tortuous appearances, history does obey necessity. The historical progression from the creation to the end of time cannot be deflected either by chance or by human artifice.[21] God's design, decreed from all eternity, must inevitably come to pass.

Thus, Augustine's doctrine preserves from Aristotle the constituent parts of the cycle (growth/decay) and the notion of necessity, but it differs by constructing a philosophy of world history that excludes the return of the same. In a way, these two perspectives are not antagonistic to each other, for the main function of the cyclical idea was to assure the repetition or reproduction of 'natural' beings. We might represent the difference by saying that the historical succession of cycles in Aristotle is replaced in Augustine by a history constructed as a single cycle. But this 'adjustment' was not exactly unimportant, given that it opened the way to a linear view of history.[22]

---

21. For Augustine, the events that people put down to chance are the ones they do not understand.

22. We should stress the importance of Christian theology in this reinterpretation of Aristotle which led to the linear view of history. A contrasting case is that of Ibn Khaldun (1332–1406), often regarded as one of the originators of sociology, who was also a close reader of Aristotle, and based his theory upon the notion of the cycle. Significantly, he gave the concept of 'nature' [tabi'a] the same meaning as Aristotle's. 'The world of the elements,' he wrote, 'and all it contains comes into being and decays. This applies to both its essences and its conditions. Minerals, plants, and all the animals, including man, and the other created things come into being and decay, as one can see with one's own eyes.' Ibn Khaldun, The Muqaddimah: An Introduction to History, trans. Franz Rosenthal, London: Routledge & Kegan Paul, 1958, vol. 1, p. 278 [I (2), §14]. Moreover, after asserting that man is 'political by nature' (and deriving madani from medina, just as Aristotle had derived πολιτικόν from πόλις), he adds: 'If, then, senility is something natural in [the life of] the dynasty, it must come about in the same way natural things come about, exactly as senility affects the temper of living beings. Senility is a chronic disease that cannot be cured or made to disappear because it is something natural, and natural things do not change' (ibid., vol. 2, p. 117 [II (3), §44]). What is rendered here as 'senility of a dynasty' appears in W.M. de Slane's French translation (Algiers, 1852–56) as 'dépérissement d'un empire', while Nassif Nassar (La pensée réaliste d'Ibn Khaldun, Paris: PUF, 1967, p. 208) suggests 'décrépitude de l'Etat'. These remarks clearly indicate the scale of the changes that the Christian (and then the Western) tradition inflicted upon Aristotelian thought.

The Enlightenment and Infinite Progress

The Augustinian heritage was devoutly gathered and utilized down the ages, especially in the medieval period. Theology was the most concerned with the ceaseless invocation of Augustine's authority, but his influence was also felt in more earthly domains – especially in the awareness of depending in most areas upon the supposedly superior wisdom of the Ancients. Whether in philosophy, grammar, rhetoric or astronomy, it was impossible to put anything forward that was not somehow associated with the views of the most celebrated predecessors. This attitude was itself related to the Aristotelian–Augustinian notion, widely shared at the time, according to which the irreversible decline of the world made it necessary to refer back to the model of the Ancients, who had lived in happier times.

The famous aphorism attributed to Bernard of Chartres – 'We are dwarfs perched on the shoulders of giants' – does imply that the progress of knowledge is cumulative, but only by giving more than their due to the recognized authorities, and suggesting that it would be difficult to go beyond them. In a way, the Renaissance takes the same approach: the rediscovery of Antiquity is mainly a question of copying unsurpassable models such as Homer, Aeschylus or Virgil.[23]

The possibility of advances in knowledge began to be debated in the mid-seventeenth century. Descartes, for instance, criticized the superiority attributed to the Ancients: 'It is we ... who should be called Ancient. The world is older now than before and we have greater experience of things.' And Pascal, in his *Traité du vide*, argued the same point of view. The way was thus paved for the famous quarrel between Ancients and Moderns which raged between 1687 and 1694,[24] died down for a while, and then flared up again between 1713 and 1715 before concluding with the victory of the Moderns. Beyond the excellence or perfectibility of literary models, what was at issue was the

---

23. It should be remembered that although the poets of the sixteenth-century *Pléiade* posed as defenders of the French language, and insisted that it was as capable as Greek or Latin of producing beautiful works, they remained heavily dependent upon the models of Antiquity. Ronsard, for example, began by writing odes (Pindaric, Horatian and Anacreontic) and all but ended his work with the *Franciade*, following the example of Virgil's *Aeneid*.

24. Racine, La Bruyère, and especially Boileau were in the camp of the 'Ancients', against Fontenelle and Perrault, who founded *Le Mercure galant* to defend their views.

new role of reason (now said to act in an autonomous and cumulative manner).[25]

It was in this context that Fontenelle, an ardent champion of the Moderns, brought out his *Digression sur les anciens poètes et modernes* in 1688. In a celebrated passage, he completely alters the ancient way of comparing the history of mankind to individual human existence:

> The comparison we have just drawn between men of all centuries and a single man may be extended to our whole question of the Ancients and the Moderns. A fine cultivated mind is, so to speak, composed of all the minds from preceding centuries; there is one and the same mind which has been cultivated all that time. Thus, the man who has lived since the beginning of the world until the present day has had his infancy (when he busied himself only with the most pressing needs of life), and his youth (when he was quite successful in the things of the imagination, such as poetry or eloquence, and when he even began to reason, albeit with more fire than substance). Now he is in the age of virility, when he reasons with more force and greater knowledge than before, but he would be much more advanced if the passion for war had not occupied him for so long and made him contemptuous of the sciences, to which he has at last returned.
>
> It is vexing that such a smoothly flowing comparison cannot be carried to the end, but I have to admit that that man will not have an old age. He will always be equally capable of the things to which his youth was appropriate, and ever more capable of those befitting his manhood: that is, to leave the allegory, men will never degenerate, and the healthy views of all the fine minds to come will always be added to one another.[26]

This basic text implements a major turnaround. For to say that the knowledge of people living today will be added to that of their predecessors, and that a decline of science can be excluded, is to come out in opposition both to the Greeks (for whom infinity had a negative connotation) and to the Augustinian tradition (which saw the end of the world as inescapable). What remains, and is still considered necessary, is the principle of growth.[27] For both Fontenelle and Perrault, the only

---

25. Reference should be made here not only to the works of René Descartes but also to those of Francis Bacon, who published in 1620 his *Novum Organum*, and above all, in 1623, the significantly titled *De dignitate et augmentis scientiarum* (On the Dignity and Advancement of the Sciences).

26. Bernard Le Bovier de Fontenelle, *Poésies pastorales avec un Traité sur la nature de l'églogue et une Digression sur les Anciens Poètes & Modernes*, The Hague: Louis van Dole and Estienne Foulque, 1688, pp. 227–8.

27. It is significant that in the same period another 'Modern', Charles Perrault, expressed himself in a similar way in *Parallèles des Anciens et des Modernes*. To the Knight who based his argument on the metaphor of man's inevitable ageing, the Abbé (representing the author's position) objects: 'That idea is quite correct, but

things which can hinder the advancement of learning – and explain why the Middle Ages were a kind of parenthesis in the process – are superstition, despotism and war. When a historical period is too much taken up with the conduct of hostilities, or with assuring the survival of the population, the arts and sciences vanish like a river that suddenly enters an underground course. Yet Perrault makes it clear that they are later seen re-emerging with the same abundance, to the great satisfaction of monarchs who, 'by restoring calm and peace in their States, make all the fine branches of knowledge to flourish again'.[28]

Thus, from the end of the seventeenth century, *what had previously been unthinkable became quite reasonable*: the intellectual landscape suddenly shifted, and the ideology of progress acquired a dominant position. Even if 'development' – and growth – have never ceased to be regarded as 'natural' and positive within the Western tradition, they were for long kept in check by the awareness of a limit, of a kind of optimum level after which the curve necessarily moved downward to comply with the laws of 'nature' and God's plan. This was the barrier which then collapsed, allowing Leibniz (1646–1716) to place infinite progress on a rational footing.

> It may be objected that this advance does not come into view, and that there even seems to be much disorder driving it back, so to speak. But this is so only in appearance.... Thus, not only is there order in everything, but even our minds must be more and more aware of this as they progress further.[29]

Of course, it would be an exaggeration to say that this was a unanimous view in the eighteenth century – indeed, there were often quite major disagreements. Rousseau (1712–78), for example, in answering

---

custom has dictated otherwise. As regards the almost universal prejudice that what are called the Ancients are cleverer than their successors, it comes from the fact that children – usually seeing that their fathers and grandfathers have more knowledge than themselves, and imagining that their great-grandparents had much more still – have unwittingly attached to age an idea of sufficiency and aptitude all the greater as it recedes more into distant times. But if it is true that the advantage of fathers over children, and of all old people over the young, lies solely in experience, it cannot be denied that the experience of men coming last into the world is greater and more consonant than that of the men who arrived before them, since the last to come have, as it were, collected the legacy of their predecessors and added to it a great number of new acquisitions which they have made through their labour and their study.' (*Parallèles des Anciens et des Modernes* [1688], Geneva: Slatkine Reprints, 1971, vol. 1, pp. 50–51).

28. Ibid., p. 53.

29. G.W. Leibniz, *La naissance du calcul différentiel*, introduction and notes by M. Parmentier, Paris: Vrin, 1959, p. 51, note 139.

the question of the Academy of Dijon 'concerning the origin of inequality and whether it is authorized by natural laws', made himself
known for the scandalous notion that 'progress' is the result of our
vices and our idle curiosity:

> What is even crueller is that, as all the progress of the human Species continually
> moves it further away from its primitive state, the more new knowledge we
> accumulate, the more we deprive ourselves of the means of acquiring the
> most important knowledge of all; so that it is, in a sense, by dint of studying
> man that we have made ourselves incapable of knowing him.[30]

Rousseau's scepticism was shared by the Scottish philosophers David
Hume (1711–76) and Adam Ferguson (1723–1816), the latter devoting
a chapter in his *Essay on the History of Civil Society* (1766) to 'the decline
of nations'. On the Continent, however, the philosophy of progress
largely carried the day. Two writers were particularly representative of
the new current: Buffon and Condorcet.

Buffon (1707–88), in sharp opposition to Rousseauian pessimism,
composed a vast panorama on the origins of the earth and mankind,
with the significant title *Histoire naturelle*. His first assertion, directed
against Voltaire and the polygeneticists, was that there is a single 'human
species' overarching all the different 'varieties': 'There is in nature a
general prototype in each species upon which each individual is
modelled, but which seems to become debased or perfected [according
to climate or customs] as it takes concrete form.'[31] It is in the temperate
latitudes, however, that man becomes most perfect, especially as white
is 'nature's primal colour':

> It is through the European that civilization arrives. Buffon thus gives the
> force of law to a historical reality – to the difference in potential which
> reaches a maximum between the civilized and the uncivilized world, and to
> the expansionist thrust that results from it.... Precisely because of their supe-
> riority, the civilized peoples are responsible for an evolving world.[32]

---

30. Jean-Jacques Rousseau, 'Discourse on the Origin and Foundations of Inequality among Men' [1755], in *Collected Works*, vol. 3, ed. Roger D. Masters and
Christopher Kelly, Hanover, NH: University Press of New England, 1992, p. 12.
Man's 'goodness' in the state of nature is, for Rousseau, the precondition of a critique
of society.

31. Chapter on 'Animaux domestiques', *Histoire naturelle*, vol. X [1749], p. 225,
quoted in Georges Louis Leclerc, comte de Buffon, *De l'homme*, Paris: Maspero,
1971, p. 21. In Buffon, man belongs to the animal realm (and may be studied as
such), yet radically distinguishes himself from it – especially through language.

32. Michèle Duchet, *Anthropologie et histoire au siècle des Lumières* [1972], Paris:
Flammarion, 1977, p. 35.

Condorcet, the last of the Encyclopaedists,[33] summed up all the great ideas of the eighteenth century when he finished his *Esquisse d'un tableau historique des progrès de l'esprit humain*, before dying in prison on 29 March 1794.[34] He divides history into ten periods or stages, the last of which should permit 'the abolition of inequality between nations, the progress of equality within each nation, and the true perfection of mankind'.[35] A critic, like Buffon, of slavery and the exactions of the colonizers, he foresaw that Europe would eventually come to respect the independence of its colonies, and help to spread there 'the truths that will promote their happiness'. For 'these vast lands ... need only assistance from us to become civilized [and] wait only to find brothers amongst the European nations to become their friends and pupils'.[36] 'Development co-operation' thus comes in a straight line from the ideology of the Enlightenment.

At the heart of Western thought, then, lies the idea of a natural history of humanity: namely, that the *'development' of societies, knowledge and wealth corresponds to a 'natural' principle with its own source of dynamism, which grounds the possibility of a grand narrative*.[37] It is on the basis of this idea – sometimes temporarily hidden beneath practices or events such as wars – that a totalizing discourse can be constructed which reveals the continuity of a single process, from the origins down to our own times.[38] This is why the founding text of economics is called *An Inquiry into the Nature and Causes of the Wealth of Nations*, where the 'progress of

---

33. See Elisabeth and Robert Badinter, *Condorcet (1743–1794): Un intellectuel en politique*, Paris: Fayard, 1988.

34. The work was first published posthumously by Agasse in Paris, in Year III of the Republic.

35. Antoine-Nicolas de Condorcet, *Sketch for a Historical Picture of the Progress of the Human Mind*, London: Weidenfeld & Nicolson, 1955, p. 173.

36. Ibid., p. 177. Here Condorcet completes the work of his friend Turgot, who had argued: 'Thus the human race, considered over the period since its origin, appears to the eye of a philosopher as a vast whole, which itself, like each individual, has its infancy and its advancement.... [Imperceptibly] manners are softened, the human mind becomes more enlightened, and separate nations are brought closer to one another. Finally commercial and political ties unite all parts of the globe, and the whole human race, through alternate periods of rest and unrest, of weal and woe, goes on advancing, although at a slow pace, towards greater perfection.' 'A Philosophical Review of the Successive Advances of the Human Mind' [1750], in *Turgot on Progress, Sociology and Economics*, trans. and ed. Ronald J. Meek, Cambridge: Cambridge University Press, 1973, p. 41.

37. On the hypothesis that an autonomous dynamism is characteristic of capitalism, see Serge Latouche, *Faut-il refuser le développement?*, Paris: PUF, 1986.

38. Even when he sets his course against 'progress', Rousseau argues in accordance with the same model. The well-known formula of the *Second Discourse* – 'Let us

opulence' is presented as an 'order of things which *necessity* imposes in general', and which 'is promoted by the *natural* inclinations of man'.[39] In this view, the 'order of things' – that is, progress – cannot be stopped: 'development' is not a choice but the finality – and fatality – of history.

The Triumph of Social Evolutionism

The new paradigm was given the finishing touches in the nineteenth century, when the doctrine of social evolutionism firmly rooted in the popular imagination the supposed superiority of the West over other societies. There were differences on how to define the 'stages' through which every society had to pass, but there was general agreement on the three essential points: that progress has the same substance (or nature) as history; that all nations travel the same road; and that all do not advance at the same speed as Western society, which therefore has an indisputable 'lead' because of the greater size of its production, the dominant role that reason plays within it, and the scale of its scientific and technological discoveries. Largely sharing these postulates, the various authors of the time related the history of the world according to their specific field of cognitive interest.[40] For Jean-Baptiste Say (1767–1832), humanity started out with savage hordes ignorant of property rights and capable only of satisfying limited needs; it then passed through inferior civilizations such as those of India or Egypt, and eventually

---

begin by setting all the facts aside...' (p. 19) – clearly means that in order to understand the fundamental tendency, we must avoid being distracted by appearances and construct the original nature of man, even if it is a state 'which no longer exists, which perhaps never existed, which probably never will exist, and about which it is nevertheless necessary to have precise notions in order to judge our present state correctly'. Ibid., p. 13.

39. *The Wealth of Nations*, vol. 1, p. 402. Emphasis added. Similar formulations may be found in the Physiocrats (precisely!), and it is no accident that Pierre-François Lemercier de la Rivière called his work *L'ordre naturel et essentiel des sociétés politiques*, London: Jean Nourse/Paris: Desaint, 1767.

40. Social evolutionism always proceeds in the same way, by constructing a fictitious 'genealogy' (always the biological metaphor!) upon the basis of one particular aspect of things. For example, if speed is the aspect given special importance, a succession of stages is said to lead from walking on foot to the supersonic aeroplane, via the invention of the wheel, the internal combustion engine, and so on – as if each of these modes necessarily 'begat' the next. In 'Race et histoire' (published in *Le racisme devant la science*, Paris: UNESCO, 1952 – the classic critique of social evolutionism), Claude Lévi-Strauss already pointed out that one axe does not beget another axe, and Thomas Kuhn (*The Structure of Scientific Revolutions*) showed well that science proceeds not in a linear-cumulative fashion but through the replacement of paradigms.

reached the higher civilization characterized by industrial production
that allows a great variety of needs to be met. As to societies on the
margins of this process: 'either they will become civilized or they will
be destroyed. Nothing can hold out against civilization and the powers
of industry. The only animal species to survive will be those that industry multiplies.'[41] Auguste Comte (1798–1857) tried to show that all
nations have passed through a theological and then a metaphysical stage,
before reaching the 'positive state' where science triumphs on the basis
of facts verified by experience.[42] Karl Marx (1818–83) reread history
and found in it laws 'winning their way through and working themselves out with iron necessity';[43] the sequence from feudalism to bourgeois capitalism, leading with equal certainty to communist society,
appeared in this light. For from Marx's standpoint: 'the development of
the economic formation of society is viewed as a process of natural
history'.[44] Lewis Morgan (1818–81), one of the founders of American
anthropology, proposed a scientific explanation of history according to
which all societies passed from savagery to barbarism before attaining
civilization. Today's savage is thus 'our contemporary ancestor'.[45] Unlike
Rousseau, who made the state of nature the locus of authenticity,
Morgan regarded 'primitiveness' as a moment of incompletion.

---

41. Jean-Baptiste Say, *Cours complet d'économie politique* [1828], Brussels: Société
typographique belge, 1843, Part one, Chapter XIII, p. 74.

42. 'Order is the condition of all progress; progress is always the object of order.
Or, to penetrate the question still more deeply, progress may be regarded simply as
the development of order; for the order of nature necessarily contains within itself
the germ of all possible progress.' Auguste Comte, *System of Positive Polity* [1854], vol.
1, London: Longmans, Green & Co., 1875, pp. 83–4.

43. Karl Marx, 'Preface to the First Edition' [1867], *Capital Volume 1*,
Harmondsworth: Pelican/New Left Review, 1976, p. 91.

44. Ibid., p. 92. This, no doubt, is one reason why Marx should be considered
the last of the classical economists: not only because (like Adam Smith) he bases value
upon labour (or labour-power), but also because he, like his predecessors, asserts:
'Nature as it comes into being in human history – in the act of creation of human
society – is the *true* nature of man; hence nature as it comes into being through
industry, though in an *estranged* form, is true *anthropological* nature.' 'Economic and
Philosophical Manuscripts (1844)', in Karl Marx, *Early Writings*, Harmondsworth:
Pelican/New Left Review, 1975, p. 355.

45. 'Since mankind were one in origin, their career has been essentially one,
running in different but uniform channels upon all continents, and very similarly in
all the tribes and nations of mankind down to the same status of advancement. It
follows that the history and experience of the American Indian tribes represent, more
or less nearly, the history and experience of our own remote ancestors when in
corresponding conditions.' Lewis H. Morgan, *Archaic Society*, London: Macmillan &
Co., 1877, p. vii.

This social evolutionism should be carefully distinguished from the biological evolutionism associated with the work of Charles Darwin (who actually spoke of 'natural selection' rather than 'evolution'). Even before Darwin published his first studies on the adaptation of living species to their ecological niche and their social environment,[46] Herbert Spencer (1820–1903) had put forward his 'law of growing complexity' according to which living organisms, like social organisms, pass from homogeneity (a state of indefiniteness) to heterogeneity (a definite state), from lower to higher, and from formless to complex.[47] But it is not just that his theory came first; the difference has more to do with the fact that his social evolutionism is a *philosophy of history*, based upon an unverifiable teleological hypothesis (events follow one another according to a predetermined finality), whereas Darwin's biological evolutionism provides an explanation devoid of inner necessity, but supported by numerous observations, for the evolution of living species. Adaptation through trial and error does not correspond to a pre-established schema with the appearance of *Homo sapiens* as its end; nor does Darwin assume that the most recent species are necessarily superior to older ones. Despite these radical differences of approach, however, social evolutionism obviously did gain a certain scientific acceptance as a result of its (semantic!) proximity to Darwinism.[48] This useful confusion allowed two kinds of question to be answered in an apparently satisfactory manner.

1. At a theoretical level, social evolutionism could reconcile the diversity of societies with the unity of the human race. But this apparent respect for cultural identities was actually a sham, since 'the country that is more developed industrially only shows, to the less developed,

---

46. The role of the social environment is linked to the influence of R.T. Malthus on Darwin, whose *On the Origin of Species* first appeared in 1859. We know that Darwin discovered the principle of 'natural selection' at the same time as Alfred Russell Wallace, in 1858. The expression 'survival of the fittest' comes from Spencer. For Darwin, the one who survives is not necessarily the strongest but, rather, the best adapted.

47. See 'The Development Hypothesis' [1852] and, above all, 'Progress, Its Law and Causes' [1857], both in *Essays: Scientific, Political, and Speculative*, vol. 1, London: Williams & Norgate, 1868. Spencer argues that progress is a 'beneficent necessity'.

48. One is reminded of the convergence of myth and science in Antiquity. Among the footnotes of history, we know that Marx admired Darwin (and dedicated a copy of *Capital* to him), while Darwin showed scant interest in the social sciences. See Pierre Thuillier, 'La correspondance Darwin–Marx: une rectification', *La Recherche* 77, April 1977.

the image of its own future'.[49] This conclusion did away with any surprise at the strangeness of the other: one no longer saw; one merely compared. As a result, *non-Western societies were deprived both of their history* (reduced to imitating the Western epic) *and of their culture* (left only in vestiges that ought to be made rapidly to disappear). Belief in the natural and inevitable 'development' of societies prevented them from being considered for themselves, with their own specificities. Instead, they were simply judged in accordance with the Western reference.

2. At a political level, social evolutionism made it possible to legitimate the new wave of colonization (especially to Africa, Madagascar and Indochina) which was a feature of the late nineteenth century. By defining itself as the precursor of a history common to all, the West could treat colonization as a generous undertaking to 'help' more or less 'backward' societies along the road to civilization. Belief in a common 'human nature' – which also implied the same 'social nature' – meant that it could proclaim a *de facto* solidarity, now visible in the supposed benefits of colonial intervention.

CONCLUSION

It would be expecting too much to cover twenty-five centuries of Western philosophy in a few pages. The modest aim here has been simply to present the key moments in this history, so as to draw out the successive interpretations of the notion of 'growth/development'. After this overhasty review, a number of comments are in order.

1. There is both continuity and a break between Aristotle, Augustine and the moderns. The continuity lies, first, in the way of considering 'development' as natural and necessary; second, in the metaphorical application of the terms 'nature' and 'natural' to social institutions and history, with all the resulting confusion between image and reality; and, finally, in the proximity of science and myth, which, though distinct and treated as distinct, confer upon each other an extra degree of veracity that is favourable to the appearance of a shared belief (still resting upon a mixture of truth and falsehood). There is also a break, however, in the abandonment of the notion of decline or decay. This removes cyclical theories from the picture, promotes a linear reading of world history, and produces a new *episteme*, a new set of generally accepted values.

---

49. Marx, *Capital Volume 1*, p. 91.

2. What passes today for the truth of the history of humankind (that is, progressive access of every nation to the benefits of 'development') *is actually based upon the way in which Western society – to the exclusion of all others – has conceptualized its relationship to the past and the future.* For 'development' is also a 'prophetic' manner of envisaging history. This is what Latour calls 'particular universalism':[50] one society extends to all others the historically constructed values in which it believes. We have already noted that Ibn Khaldun saw history in a very different way, but the point may also apply to many other cultures which have no term for 'development', and imagine the 'good life' by, for example, associating material wealth not with its accumulation but with its distribution (within a large family or for the purposes of prestige). In every society, of course, people try to improve their conditions of existence, and it is not for anyone to question the legitimacy of their strivings. There is nothing to indicate, however, that 'development' is the only way of achieving them, or that every society wishes to have the same thing. The misunderstanding would not be so troublesome if 'development' discourse was not built into relationships of power. For when the pretence is made that everyone now believes in that discourse, the reason is doubtless that no one has the choice of doing otherwise and distancing themselves from the shared belief. Paradoxically, *'development' is becoming universal, but not transcultural.*

3. Given that belief combines truth and falsehood, what is the respective share of each? It will be readily agreed that over the last two centuries the total number of goods available to humanity has risen to a quite prodigious degree, that technological advances have eased the lives of those who benefit from them, and that average life expectancy has increased considerably. But at the heart of the 'development' system is a claim to be extended to the whole planet through endless growth, as a matter not of choice but of necessity – above all, for the countries already most 'developed'.[51] The fact is, however, that *this is not an achievable objective.* Today 20 per cent of humanity consumes 80 per cent of

---

50. *We Have Never Been Modern*, op. cit., p. 105.

51. In an article significantly entitled 'Croissance, l'impératif catégorique', Patrick Artus (*inter alia* a former OECD employee, scientific adviser to the Bank of France, and Associate Professor at the University of Paris-Dauphine) reviewed the various ways of reducing unemployment through work-sharing and service-job creation. He concluded: 'If we are to avoid both undesirable unemployment and the risks attached to an unprecedented level of work-sharing, *it is really indispensable for the French economy to become capable of greater medium-term growth.*' *Le Monde des Débats*, October 1994, p. 3 (emphasis added).

the planet's resources, and finds itself having to boost growth to keep the system going. But it is not possible to mobilize at least four times more extra resources: the environment simply could not sustain it. Still, one is required to act *as if* the belief were reasonable and the goal attainable. What the asymptotic growth curve indicates, then, is not what economics shows (increasing production and consumption) but what it conceals – that is, growing entropy, the conversion of free energy into bound energy, the exhaustion of non-renewable resources, the pollution of air and water, the greenhouse effect, and so on. In order to survive, the belief needs signs that everyone can see; and economic 'miracles' and technological 'wonders' play their part to perfection. In a more modest way, all manner of fairs (motor, home, aerospace) also do their bit. But the truth of the situation lies elsewhere, in what does not appear so directly: shrinking biodiversity, climatic changes, radioactive effects. There is thus a contradiction between the mechanistic paradigm of equilibrium economics, for which 'development is life', and the growing disequilibrium bound up with irreversible phenomena pointing to the possibility of imminent catastrophe. It is a peculiar feature of modern belief to have a constantly ambivalent relationship to time: on the one hand, the present is banalized and only future growth counts – you are here, but only to run somewhere else; on the other, because economic theory is incapable of seriously anticipating the 'market needs' of future generations, only the immediate dimension of 'economic reality' is held in view. *By dint of believing in 'the meaning of history', one ends up conjuring history away.*

4. It is contradictory to cling simultaneously to an evolutionist view of history (in which everyone has to attain the same 'development' in the end) and to an asymptotic representation of growth as the foundation of 'development'. Since time measured by the calendar passes at the same rate for everyone, it is by definition impossible for countries at the bottom to 'catch up' those at the top; the gap can only go on widening. And this is what is happening: the disparity was one to two around the year 1700, one to five at the end of the nineteenth century, one to fifteen in 1960, and one to forty-five in 1980.[52] And although the 'time is money' principle in reverse led some to believe that massive investment in the 'backward' countries would enable them to catch up more quickly, this was evidently a delusion. If the engine of

52. Gilbert Rist, Majid Rahnema and Gustavo Esteva, *Le Nord perdu. Repères pour l'après-développement*, Lausanne: Editions d'En Bas, 1992, p. 44.

'development' is growth, the engine of growth is belief – and it is far from being shared by everyone.

5. *It appears that the presuppositions of growth may be more important than growth itself, for in the end it is they which mean that it goes on being reproduced.*[53] In the epoch of 'real socialism' and dogmatic planning, economic failures were regularly attributed to defects in the plan. When the citizens rebel against a strong-arm government, it is not supposed to be because they are oppressed by those in charge, but because there are evil people or 'foreign agents' trying to sow disorder. If a problem is posed within the terms of a given system, the solutions on offer cannot but reinforce the system – for the elimination of abuses will only be aimed at making it function better. The same holds for 'development'. Once its presuppositions and sense-giving belief are accepted, the only course is to feed a kind of retrospective effect which widens the problem instead of solving it. This is why *'development', which is always presented as a solution, is itself actually a problem (as well as creating problems)*. To make a comparison: today's 'developers' are like the alchemists of old who vainly tried to transmute lead into gold, in the firm belief that they would then have the key to wealth. The alchemists disappeared once it was realized that true wealth came from elsewhere – from people and from trade. When will we realize that well-being does not come from growth?

---

53. A presupposition is that which is implicit in discourse. It is bound up with the fact that 'everything which is said can also be gainsaid.... It is therefore necessary that any fundamental belief, if expressed, ... should find a means of expression that does not lay it on the table where it can be fixed and contested. [The idea is to allow the speaker] to arouse certain opinions in the person addressed, without taking the risk of formulating them oneself [... and] hence to have something believed without saying it.' Oswald Ducrot, *Dire et ne pas dire. Principes de sémantique linguistique*, Paris: Herrmann, 1991, pp. 6, 15.

CHAPTER 3

THE MAKING OF A
WORLD SYSTEM

This chapter will focus on certain aspects of late-nineteenth-century colonialism, and then on the League of Nations, which was created at the end of the First World War. Our aim will be to throw light upon a fairly brief period of history – from 1870 to 1940 – when the 'great powers' put the then dominant ideas into practice and, in a sense, opened the way to 'development'. As we saw in the last chapter, the Western belief in 'development' has ancient roots, and by the late nineteenth century everything seemed in place, in terms of ideas, to embark upon the great adventure. In the cases of France, Britain, Belgium and Germany, this intervention 'outside Europe' was made in the register of colonization. It was also during this period – when the colonial powers were facing new problems in the conquered territories – that a number of practices which still persist under cover of 'development' had their origin. It was a transitional period, then, one in which brutal power relations existed alongside paternalist feelings of responsibility towards 'natives' who needed to be 'civilized'.

One might think that 'development' was already there, with only the word itself still lacking. But as we shall see, the situation was a little different, for the reality of colonialism made its mark even on the most generous-seeming practices.

There can be no question here of writing a history of colonization. Rather, we shall simply examine the sequence of discourses and practices which led to the 'development era', and note the similarities and differences between the two periods. We shall also be asking how it was that the enterprise proceeded with such a good conscience. For this is one of those cases in history where today we find it hard to understand that certain collective practices were unanimously advocated and accepted. Slavery in the ancient world or the Enlightenment, human sacrifice among the Aztecs, and European colonization belong to one and the same category. How could people have thought what has since become unthinkable, and legitimated what has become intolerable? Of course, history always requires us to place things in their context and to avoid judging the past through the eyes of the present. But apart from this methodological concern, a call to modesty would also be in order. For how will future generations view practices that today enjoy the favour and admiration of a huge majority of people? Such 'intertemporal decentring' is badly needed to convince ourselves of the shakiness of the things we consider most evident. Today's verities are always in danger of becoming tomorrow's lies.

COLONIZATION[1]

Towards the end of the last century, with a long history already behind it, European colonization branched out in quite different forms according to the place and the interests of the metropolis. France, for its part, had two groups of territories: (a) the 'historic' colonies of Guiana, Guadeloupe, Martinique and Saint Pierre and Miquelon in the Americas; Saint-Louis and Gorée in Senegal, the island of Réunion, and trading stations in Gabon and India; (b) the more recent possessions of Algeria (1830), the Marquesas Islands and Tahiti (1845), New Caledonia (1853), Cambodia (1865), Cochin-China (1867) and Senegal (1854–65). Settlers

---

1. In what follows, we shall mainly deal with French colonial history from the late nineteenth century on. The main sources are: Raoul Girardet, *L'idée coloniale en France, 1871–1962*, Paris: La Table Ronde, 1972; Bouda Etemad, *Le débat colonial. Tendances récentes de l'histoire de la colonisation*, University of Geneva, Faculty of Social and Economic Sciences, 1987; Jacques Marseille, *Empire colonial et capitalisme français. Histoire d'un divorce*, Paris: Le Seuil, 1984; Pierre Aubry, *La Colonisation et les colonies*, Paris: Octave Doin & Fils, 1909; Georges Hardy, *Nos grands problèmes coloniaux*, Paris: A. Colin, 1929; Paul Leroy-Beaulieu, *De la colonisation chez les peuples modernes* [1874], Paris: Félix Alcan, 6th edn, 1908, 2 vols; Albert Sarraut, *La Mise en valeur des colonies françaises*, Paris: Payot, 1923; Marc-Henri Piault, 'La colonisation: pour une nouvelle appréciation', *Cahiers ORSTOM*, série sciences humaines, XXI (1), 1985; Jacques Valette, 'Note sur l'idée coloniale vers 1871', *Revue d'histoire moderne et contemporaine*, vol. 14, April–June 1967, pp. 157–72; Pierre Larousse, ed., *Grand Dictionnaire universel du XIXᵉ siècle*, Paris, vol. XVII, second part, second supplement, 1866–72, article 'colonies'; 'Economic Achievements of the Colonizers: An Assessment', in Peter Duignan and L.H. Gann, eds, *Colonialism in Africa 1870–1960*, London: Cambridge University Press, 1975.

of French origin were not there in great number, except in the Americas and, more recently, Algeria – for the colonial system of the time very largely rested upon commercial interests, symbolized by the 'colonial pact' that assured the metropolis exclusive trading rights.

Despite the new colonial acquisitions of Louis-Philippe and Napoleon III, public opinion took little interest in these distant lands, except perhaps to denounce the evils of the colonial pact (in the name of free trade) or of slavery (in the name of human rights). In fact, these two controversies went back to the eighteenth century. Rousseau, Abbé Raynal, Montesquieu, Adam Smith, the Manchester School and Jean-Baptiste Say had all maintained that free trade was much more advantageous than a commercial monopoly, because it created a large market and allowed industry to develop both in the metropolis and overseas.[2] This position was widely shared by economists at the time, even though governments persisted in maintaining the principle of exclusiveness. As to the opposition to slavery, this began to be organized in 1788 with the creation of the *Société des Amis des Noirs*, whose members included Condorcet, Mirabeau and Necker.[3] In the teeth of opposition from supporters of the *colons*, the Convention declared 'Negro slavery abolished in all the colonies' on 4 February 1794. It was re-established by Bonaparte on 12 May 1802. But in 1834 a Society for the Abolition of Slavery came into being in Paris, and after a long public campaign the French Parliament definitively abolished it on 27 April 1848.

The Third Republic, declared after the defeat by Prussia in 1871, therefore unfolded in a climate of relative indifference towards the colonies. Yet in 1881 France launched into the conquest of a huge colonial empire. It is this turnaround that has to be explained.

Devising a Doctrine of Intervention

The new colonial adventure of the late nineteenth century began without a clear doctrine. Humiliated by defeat, France had as its main aim to keep its standing among the great powers. And since the other

---

2. 'The monopoly of the colony trade ... depresses the industry of all other countries, but chiefly that of the colonies, without in the least increasing, but on the contrary diminishing, that of the country in whose favour it is established.' Adam Smith, *The Wealth of Nations*, vol. 2, p. 126.

3. This *Société des Amis des Noirs* was the French counterpart of the Society for the Abolition of the Slave Trade, founded in London in 1787. See Jean-François Zorn, *Emancipation et colonisation*, unpublished paper presented to the seminar 'L'émancipation comme problème', Paris, 18–20 September 1989.

European nations – mainly Britain, but also Germany, Italy and Belgium – were increasing their strength by colonizing new areas, the national interest made it imperative to do likewise. All the same, there was strong resistance: liberal economists criticized colonial protectionism, and calculated that the costs of the new wars and the administration of the new territories would greatly outweigh the benefits to be derived from them; nationalists, on the other hand, insisted that the recapture of Alsace-Lorraine was a more urgent task than expeditions to faraway lands.[4] What was the point of wasting 'France's gold and blood' instead of looking to 'the blue line of the Vosges'? As for the Socialists, they kept to a humanist middle course, mainly criticizing the injustices of colonization and the frenzied pursuit of profit. But this led them into rather ambivalent positions:[5] while Clemenceau first criticized colonization and eventually rallied to it, Jaurès followed the opposite trajectory. Paul Louis was one of the very few who consistently denounced an undertaking launched only to satisfy the interests of the capitalists.[6]

On the other side were a series of actors whose disparate positions provided arguments capable of rallying the most varied milieux. First – and hardly surprisingly – the armed forces were calling for more naval supply ports,[7] and hoping to use the colonial wars to perfect new weaponry for a revenge match against the Germans. Next, the merchants – especially those of great ports such as Marseilles or Bordeaux, who banded together in the French Colonial Union – could look forward to

---

4. 'I have lost two sisters [Alsace and Lorraine] and you offer me twenty domestics!' exclaimed Paul Déroulède. Quoted in Girardet, p. 63.

5. The same ambivalence can be found in the '*colonies*' article in the *Grand Dictionnaire universel du XIX*e *siècle*: 'Colonization should be peaceful. To grab a territory by expelling those who own it, or by subjecting them to force, is not to colonize but to conquer, and the time is gone when one regarded as heroes those who – without provocation, with no other motive than ambition, no other right than that of the strongest – landed on a shore, declared themselves masters of it and took the land as it suited them, under the protection of bayonets. It may happen, nevertheless, that the colonizing powers are compelled to resort to force, but this extreme measure should be taken only in cases of legitimate self-defence' (p. 863).

6. The ambivalence of the Socialists is partly to be explained by Marx's earlier positions. For although he criticized the costs in money and human lives of colonial enterprises, he rejoiced in the progress they were bringing: 'England has to fulfil a double mission in India: one destructive, the other regenerating – the annihilation of the old Asiatic society, and the laying of the material foundations of Western society in Asia.' 'Letter of 22 July 1853', in Karl Marx and Friedrich Engels, *On Colonialism*, Moscow: Foreign Languages Publishing House, n.d., p. 77.

7. The Navy Ministry was responsible for colonial administration until a special ministry was set up in 1894. At the time, the best ships had a range of fifteen days, after which they had to take on fresh coal supplies.

new sources of profit. But the missionaries were also to be found in the same camp,[8] and – rather remarkably – the opponents of slavery, who argued, in the name of human rights and philanthropy, that colonization would allow human commodities to be converted into workers, for the greater good of the conquered territories. In other words, colonization was presented not only as an alternative to slavery but even as a way of redressing the wrongs of the slave trade. Victor Hugo, at a banquet commemorating the abolition of slavery, put it like this:[9]

> Men's destiny lies in the South.... The moment has come to make Europe realize that it has Africa alongside it.... In the nineteenth century, the White made a man of the Black; in the twentieth century, Europe will make a world of Africa. To fashion a new Africa, to make the old Africa amenable to civilization – that is the problem. And Europe will solve it.
>
> Go forward, the nations! Grasp this land! Take it! From whom? From no one. Take this land from God! God gives the earth to men. God offers Africa to Europe. Take it! Where the kings brought war, bring concord! Take it, not for the cannon but for the plough! Not for the sabre but for commerce! Not for battle but for industry! Not for conquest but for fraternity! Pour out everything you have in this Africa, and at the same stroke solve your own social questions! Change your proletarians into property-owners! Go on, do it! Make roads, make ports, make towns! Grow, cultivate, colonize, multiply! And on this land, ever clearer of priests and princes, may the divine spirit assert itself through peace and the human spirit through liberty!

In this extraordinary synthesis, the *philanthropic* case for colonization is that it holds a worldwide promise of civilization for all, and is the expression 'of the growing solidarity, the community of feelings and interests that unites the metropolis to its overseas possessions'.[10]

Jules Ferry took responsibility not only for the work of colonization[11] but, above all, for the elaboration of a doctrine which he presented to

---

8. It was in 1868 that the Bishop of Algiers, Mgr Lavigerie, founded the Society of White Fathers.

9. Quoted in Zorn, p. 6.

10. *Almanach Hachette, Petite encyclopédie populaire de la vie pratique*, Paris, 1931, p. 4 (under the entry 'Why We Have Colonies'). In the same period Albert Bayet wrote: 'The country which proclaimed the Rights of Man, which brilliantly contributed to the advancement of science, which made education secular, and which is the great champion of liberty in front of the nations, has by virtue of its past the mission to spread wherever it can the ideas that made it great' (quoted in Girardet, p. 183).

11. This involved the conquest of Tunisia (1881–84), Tonkin and Annam (1881–83), the Congo (1880–86), Niger and Dahomey (1882–94), Cambodia and Laos (1893), Madagascar (1883–94) and Morocco (1912). Jules Ferry was President of the Council from 23 September 1880 to 14 November 1881, and again from 21 February 1883 to 30 March 1885.

the Chamber of Deputies on 28 July 1885, and which acquired a quasi-official status. What was known then as the 'turning to account [*mise en valeur*] of the colonies' was said to rest upon three pillars:

1. Colonial expansion follows an economic objective: 'colonial policy is the daughter of industrial policy'. The continual growth of production and the accumulation of capital require new outlets, especially as international competition is intense and everyone has to increase their economic area.
2. The 'higher races' have rights and duties towards the 'lower races', and must share with them the benefits of science and progress. Colonial administration makes it possible to impose 'more light, order and private and public virtues', especially by prohibiting, where it still exists, 'the Negro trade, that horrible traffic, and slavery, that loathsome practice'.[12]
3. Colonization is necessary if France is to keep its place in the concert of nations and avoid the 'highroad to decay'. If it withdraws into itself and refrains from colonization, other nations will do it instead, but in the name of less noble values and with less talent.

It was thus in the name of three principles (economic, philanthropic and political) that a 'Greater France with a population of 100 million' was constructed. The force of the argument was connected with its variety of registers. Possible conflicts between them were less important than their unity within one and the same discourse, so that each interest group could feel that it was being taken seriously. One laid the stress on economic imperatives, control of raw materials, or the need to find new outlets for an industry fettered by European customs duties; another preached the spread of civilization and republican values, the improvement of native living conditions; yet another saw itself as upholding the national interest, the power of the State, territorial expansion, and the creation of bases for the naval and merchant fleet.

12. Jules Ferry, speech of 28 July 1885, quoted in G. Guenin, *L'Epopée coloniale de la France racontée par nos contemporains*, Paris: Larose, 1932, pp. 307 f. Paradoxically, having practised it themselves for so long, the Europeans now posed as the critics of slavery, whose prohibition figured in the 1885 Treaty of Berlin that shared out Africa. Now, however, the slavery marked out for international opprobrium was the one that the Arabs were accused of!

Winning Over the Public

It was necessary to work hard at convincing an indifferent public – both to have a base of popular support for colonization, and to ensure that enough people 'enlisted for the colonies' and settled down there.[13] This explains the importance of the Geographical Societies (whose membership increased from 780 to 2,000 in Paris between 1873 and 1880, and reached 9,500 in France in 1881), but also of new journals like *L'Explorateur* (which presented itself as 'the journal for the conquest of civilization at every point of the globe') or the *Revue des Deux Mondes* or, after 1877, the youth-oriented *Journal des Voyages*.[14] The Church, not to be outdone, increased the number of its missionary societies. And finally, we should not underestimate the importance of Jules Verne, whose *Voyages extraordinaires* helped to spread both the ideology of progress and the charms of exoticism.[15] Meanwhile, the colonial lobby was becoming organized politically. A 'colonial group' in the Chamber of Deputies rose from a membership of 91 in 1892 to 202 in 1902, and French companies moved to defend their common interests by founding in 1893 the *Union coloniale française*, which published the lavishly illustrated *Quinzaine coloniale* to celebrate the 'turning to account' of the colonies. By 1894 a Colonial Ministry existed, with all the formal rights and powers.

One sector of public opinion still had to be persuaded of the usefulness of colonization: the liberal economists, with whom a trade monopoly did not go down at all well. The task was taken up by Paul Leroy-Beaulieu, whose *De la colonisation chez les peuples modernes* was a bestseller, going through six editions between 1874 and 1908. Without

---

13. For the whole of this paragraph, see Girardet.

14. Already in 1863 the *Revue des Deux Mondes* declared: 'Colonization is one of the great enterprises of our time, and the modern spirit can be proud of the new sentiments for which it has gained acceptance in accomplishing the civilizing mission bequeathed to it by previous generations.' Quoted in Valette, p. 159.

15. *Five Weeks in a Balloon* (Stroud: Alan Sutton, 1995), first published in 1862, already contains the colonial project *in toto*: 'Then Africa will offer to new races the treasures accumulated for centuries in her bosom; those climes, fatal to foreigners, will have been purified by tillage and drainage; those scattered streams will unite in one common bed to form a great navigable artery. And this country over which we float, richer, more fertile, and more endowed with life than the others, will become some great kingdom, where discoveries will be made more astounding than electricity or steam' (pp. 44–5). See also Jean Chesnaux, 'Science, machines et progrès chez Jules Verne', *La Pensée, Revue du rationalisme moderne*, 133, June 1967, pp. 62–85; and Michel Serres, 'Le savoir, la guerre et le sacrifice', *Critique*, vol. 33 (367), December 1977, pp. 1067–77.

denying the costs of the venture, Leroy-Beaulieu showed that it would be profitable in the long term, and that there was anyway a duty to carry it out. This extract from the Preface gives a good idea of his thinking:

> Colonization is one of the highest functions of societies that have reached an advanced stage of civilization.... A society colonizes when, having itself reached a high degree of maturity and strength, it procreates, protects, places in good conditions for development, and leads on to virility, a new society that has emerged from its entrails. Colonization is one of the most complex and most delicate phenomena in the social physiology.... The merit of a colonizing people is to place the young society it has brought forth in the most suitable conditions for the development of its natural faculties; to smooth its path without hampering its initiative; to give it the means and tools that are necessary or useful for its growth.

This new avatar of the biological metaphor rehearsed the analogy between 'development' of a nation and the successive ages of human life.[16] But Leroy-Beaulieu completed his 'social physiology' with a new idea, that of the 'metropolis' (etymologically, the 'mother city') which brings forth the colonized societies to lead them to maturity. History does not repeat itself, but constantly reinvents everything. *On the basis of the old conceptual frameworks, together with snatches of ancient mythological discourse, the present was reinterpreted in such a way as to give it unchallengeable legitimacy.* By making colonization out to be 'natural', it was possible to disguise the political decisions and economic interests lying behind it, and thus render any debate about its wisdom superfluous.

By the last decade of the nineteenth century – thanks to these efforts coming from the most varied quarters, French public opinion was largely behind the principle of colonization. Some twenty years was all that had been necessary to overcome indifference and win round the sceptics. It is true that a few diehards were still holding out – people like Paul Louis[17] or Charles Maurras[18] – but on the whole, any doubts had succumbed to two main arguments.

---

16. See Charles Gide's assertion that colonization has 'all the characteristics by which one recognizes the forces of nature', quoted in *Encyclopaedia universalis*, in the article '*colonisation*'.

17. See Paul Louis, *Le Colonialisme*, Paris: Société nouvelle de librairie de l'idiom, 1905. Of course, after the Bolshevik Revolution of 1917 and Lenin's attacks on imperialism, the French Communist Party remained anti-colonialist until 1935. It should be noted that the French terms '*colonialiste*' and '*colonialisme*' came into being with a pejorative connotation (first being used by Gustave de Molinari in 1895), and that it was 1927 before they made it into the *Larousse* dictionary.

1. *Colonization is not a matter of choice but a matter of duty*:

Colonization is not a question of interest but a question of duty. It is necessary to colonize because there is a moral obligation, for both nations and
individuals, to employ the strengths and advantages they have received from
Providence for the general good of humanity. It is necessary to colonize
because colonization is one of the duties incumbent upon great nations, which
they cannot evade without failing in their mission and falling into moral
dereliction.[19]

As well as once more using the metaphor of individual recapitulation
of the destiny of society, this quotation issues a moral imperative that
taxes any opposition with the opprobrium of 'moral degeneracy'. Any
critic of the colonial enterprise must be a bad citizen or, worse still, an
egoist indifferent to the fate of humanity and ungrateful towards Providence.

2. The other argument, even more difficult to brush aside, was the
one of the *fait accompli*:

It might be thought, of course, that a country such as France would have an
advantage in giving up its colonial empire, but in fact it would be shirking
a responsibility that it has assumed in the course of its history, and acting in
the manner of a person who, having blundered into something, escaped its
consequences by displacing them onto others. Since France has colonies, it
has a duty to preserve them, to make security prevail there, and to guarantee
the liberty of the inhabitants, settler and native, as it does in the home country;
it must have a colonial policy.... If colonization is understood as the exploitation and civilization of every region on earth, it is evidently a quite legitimate enterprise ... in the interests of mankind.[20]

Since the colonies exist, it is necessary to administer them – even if it
is thought that they were 'blundered into'. It is too late for discussions,

---

18. We should add, later, the Surrealist group, including André Breton, Paul Eluard,
Louis Aragon and René Char. On the occasion of the Colonial Exhibition of 1931,
they denounced 'colonial brigandage' and refused to accept that there could be such
a thing as 'good colonization': 'Whether the scandalous Socialist Party and the jesuitical
League of the Rights of Man agree or not, it would be a bit much for us to distinguish
between a good and a bad way of colonizing. Immediate withdrawal from the colonies [should therefore be demanded].' *Tracts surréalistes et déclarations collectives 1922–
1939*, vol. 1, Paris: Le Terrain vague, 1980.

19. Charles Gide, 'Conférence sur le devoir colonial' [1897], quoted in Aubry,
p. 78.

20. Quoted in Aubry, pp. 76–7, 78. 'The domination of France in Indochina,
West Africa and Madagascar – whatever our evaluation of the government's policy
which has brought about this great colonial empire – is a definitive fact whose legitimacy can no longer be placed in question.' Ibid., p. 226.

even if the interest that the metropolis draws from its overseas territories is not as high as people would have it. *On top of the moral obligation, there is a moral responsibility.* The past cannot be changed, so one must follow it through logically and convince oneself that this serves the interests of mankind.

'Colonial Policy' and the Invention of New Practices

The forms of colonial intervention varied widely according to the metropolitan power concerned. The differences between the two largest, Britain and France, are usually summarized by saying that the former favoured *indirect rule* (in which the traditional authorities were used to keep law and order) while the latter, in the name of lofty republican principles, had a policy of assimilating the 'natives' as future citizens with the same Gallic ancestors as the French. The reality was doubtless more complex, and what was known at the time as 'colonial policy' (that is, the policy for 'turning the colonies to account') cannot be reduced to such straightforward guidelines.

If this history is reread in the light of the principles gradually laid down for 'development' co-operation,[21] it will be seen that *many practices presented today as new were actually thought up long ago.* Real novelty is a rare thing. What is really surprising, on the other hand, is the amnesia affecting this period. It is as if the 'developers' wanted people to believe in the originality of current policies, and thus forget the long-term trajectory into which those policies are inserted. Here we can do no more than give a few examples.

(a) So that the recruitment of administrative personnel should not be left to chance, a Colonial School was set up on 23 November 1889 'for the teaching of colonial sciences', and in the early years of the twentieth century this was complemented by a two-hours-a-week 'free course in colonial studies' at the Sorbonne, with an annual prize of 20,000 francs for the best student donated by the Union coloniale. The institutes of development studies have now taken over, but the rewards they offer are less alluring.

(b) The importance of what is now called the 'cultural dimension' was understood at a very early date. Even when it was thought necessary to reform them, there was a recognition that 'the natives'' political, legal and economic institutions are not arbitrary schemas due to chance

---

21. It should be pointed out again that this overview mainly concerns French policy.

or individual fantasy, but the necessary result of a set of local, natural, psychological circumstances'.[22] It was by no means the intention, then, to foster assimilation through straightforward imitation of metropolitan institutions.

(c) 'Primary health care', nowadays official WHO doctrine, was in large part already recommended by Colonial Minister Albert Sarraut:

> It is necessary to develop general hygiene and prophylaxis; therefore necessary to increase everywhere the number of medical training centres, clinics, maternity homes and ambulances, and to organize the 'mobile' assistance that will carry medical care from the big centres into the remote bush where the deprived sections of the population are scattered.[23]

Although such initiatives were sometimes described as a 'health dictatorship', they clearly anticipate measures taken in the second half of the twentieth century.

(d) In the field of education, particular attention was paid to vocational training, problems connected with career openings, and the early 'pedagogic disaster' of imitating the European model.[24] A case was already being made for programmes adapted to local circumstances in which traditional methods would be combined with the practice of nursery schools;[25] for textbooks that referred to something other than the daily experience of little Europeans; and for the spreading of agricultural knowledge through the establishment of 'pilot farms' or 'school farms', as they were also known.[26] In many respects, the broad themes constantly taken up by UNESCO were already defined here, and it may be regretted that some educational policies of now independent countries have not taken more account of mistakes committed during the colonial period.

To these examples could be added a number of others: the establishment of village credit banks financed by their own members and backed by the colonial administration;[27] a special concern for the situation of

---

22. Aubry, p. 124. 'In each colony, the flexible variety of education programmes and pedagogical methods must be adapted to the special character of the milieu, to local needs and the mentalities of very different races. To apply them everywhere identically and uniformly would be a grave error, one already condemned by experience' (Sarraut, pp. 96–7).

23. Sarraut, pp. 94–5.

24. Hardy, pp. 74 f.

25. 'Huge gardens, or even veritable plantations, are attached to the rural schools, and school time is divided into two parts: one for general education, itself geared to agriculture; and one for practical exercises.' Hardy, pp. 20, 79.

26. Ibid., p. 19.

27. Ibid., p. 33.

women, popular participation, and so on.[28] As for the great current debates on structural adjustment or balanced budgets and trade, they can be traced back to what used to be called the need for the colonies to be economically and financially self-supporting.

These similarities in good intentions should not, however, blind us to other characteristics of the colonial system – forced labour, and the like; the raising of taxes, population displacement, the imposition of cash crops; as well as all manner of abuses linked to the feelings of superiority with which Europeans were imbued. Even if these things, too, have perhaps not changed as radically as one might hope, the big difference lies in the fact that the colonizer was incapable of seeing the native population as real and true subjects. The more generous initiatives did aim at their 'emancipation', because, as Turgot put it, 'the colonies are like fruits that cling to the tree only until they are ripe'. But that day seemed an extremely long way off. For:

> it should not be forgotten that we are centuries ahead of them, long centuries during which – slowly and painfully, through a lengthy effort of research, invention, meditation and intellectual progress aided by the very influence of our temperate climate – a magnificent heritage of science, experience and moral superiority has taken shape, which makes us eminently entitled to protect and lead the races lagging behind us.[29]

The initiative in turning the colonies 'to account' could thus be taken only by the metropolitan countries, and this openly asymmetrical, hierarchical and non-egalitarian relationship compromised the entire colonial enterprise.

THE LEAGUE OF NATIONS AND THE MANDATE SYSTEM

If colonization threw up an array of arguments justifying intervention outside Europe to serve the national interest, the League of Nations legitimated the *internationalization* of this intervention in the name of civilization itself, considered as the common heritage of the European countries.

---

28.   See Jean-Pierre Chauveau, 'Participation paysanne et populisme bureaucratique. Essai d'histoire et de sociologie de la culture du développement', in Jean-Pierre Jacob and Philippe Lavigne-Delville, eds, *Les Associations paysannes en Afrique. Organisation et dynamiques*, Marseilles: APAD/Karthala: IUED, 1994, pp. 25–60.

29.   Sarraut, pp. 118–19.

Annexation Internationalized

In putting an end to the First World War, the Treaty of Versailles (signed on 28 June 1919) was preceded by the adoption of the Covenant of the League of Nations, the first permanent international political institution. As far as the history of 'development' is concerned, this text is important because of its Articles 22 and 23, which established the mandate system and conferred upon certain League members administrative responsibility for the territorial possessions of countries on the losing side in the war.

Without going into the detailed negotiations that resulted in the text of the Covenant, we should note that it involved a compromise worked out by the South African General Jan Smuts. Opinions had been divided about what should be done with the German colonies and the debris of the Ottoman Empire. On the one side, President Woodrow Wilson of the United States, whose armies had played a decisive role in the Allied victory, resolutely invoked his country's anti-colonial tradition and the principles of free trade to oppose any extension of the colonial empires of Great Britain and France. On the other side, the Europeans clearly intended to become masters of the former German colonies, especially in Africa, and to consolidate the positions they had gained during the war in the Near East (Iraq, Trans-Jordan and Palestine in the case of Britain; Syria and Lebanon in that of France).[30] Between these two positions, the Socialists (especially the Labour Party) and the philanthropic movements did not really oppose colonial administration of the former possessions of the defeated empires, but they wanted it to be entrusted to an international authority (the League of Nations), not to the colonizing States.

The compromise was that the colonial powers received League 'mandates' over the newly 'available' territories, but had to account for their administrative practices to a Permanent Mandates Commission (PMC) and its secretariat, headed by a Swiss, William Rappard. The United States won a victory because the territories in question were free from colonial protectionism ('open door policy'); the colonial powers were satisfied with what was in effect disguised annexation or colonization legitimated by an international organization; and the opponents of direct colonial administration could console themselves with the idea that all

---

30. These territorial 'acquisitions' had already been the subject of agreement among the victors (e.g. the Sykes–Picot Agreement of 1916), of public declarations (the Balfour Declaration of 2 November 1917 on the creation of a 'Jewish National Home' in Palestine), and of secret negotiations with the Arabs to assist their independence – all of which would singularly complicate the political situation in the region.

the operations would be supervised by an international agency. Agreement was thus eventually reached to insert the following Article 22 into the Covenant:

1. To those colonies and territories which as a consequence of the late war have ceased to be under the sovereignty of the States which formerly governed them and which are inhabited by peoples not yet able to stand by themselves under the strenuous conditions of the modern world, there should be applied the principle that the well-being and development of such peoples form a sacred trust of civilization and that securities for the performance of this trust should be embodied in this Covenant.

2. The best method of giving practical effect to this principle is that the tutelage of such peoples should be entrusted to advanced nations who by reason of their resources, their experience or their geographical position can best undertake this responsibility, and who are willing to accept it, and that this tutelage should be exercised by them as Mandatories on behalf of the League.

3. The character of the mandate must differ according to the stage of the development of the people, the geographical situation of the territory, its economic conditions and other similar circumstances.

4. Certain communities formerly belonging to the Turkish Empire have reached a stage of development where their existence as independent nations can be provisionally recognized subject to the rendering of administration advice and assistance by a Mandatory until such time as they are able to stand alone. The wishes of these communities must be a principled consideration in the selection of the Mandatory.[31]

5. Other peoples, especially those of Central Africa,[32] are at such a stage that the Mandatory must be responsible for the administration of the territory under conditions which will guarantee freedom of conscience and religion, subject only to the maintenance of public order and morals, the prohibition of abuses such as the slave trade,[33] the arms traffic and the liquor

---

31. At issue here are the 'A' mandates, recognized to hold 'communities' – that is, structured societies. It was no doubt claiming too much to say that they could express 'wishes' about the selection of a mandatory (which, in reality, imposed itself during the war against the Ottoman Empire), but their independence was gradually recognized: for Iraq in 1932, Syria and Lebanon in 1941 (the latter already formally recognized by France in 1936). As for Jordan – or Trans-Jordan, as it was known – it had been included in the Palestine mandate while enjoying autonomous administration. It became independent in 1946.

32. These were the 'B' mandates, inhabited only by 'peoples', which comprised the former German colonies of Togo and Cameroun (both shared out between France and Britain), Tanganyika (allocated to Britain), and Ruanda-Urundi (assigned to Belgium). Geographical continuity with other colonies was the key criterion of apportionment.

33. Already in the Berlin Act of 26 February 1885, the signatory powers had undertaken 'to be vigilant in preserving the native populations and improving their moral and material conditions of existence, and to work for the suppression of slavery and, in particular, the negro trade'.

traffic, and the prevention of the establishment of fortifications or military and naval bases and of military training of the natives for other than police purposes and the defence of the territory, and will also secure equal opportunities for the trade and commerce of other Members of the League.[34]

6. There are territories,[35] such as South West Africa and certain of the South Pacific Islands, which, owing to the sparseness of their population, or their small size, or their remoteness from the centres of civilization, or their geographic continuity to the territory of the Mandatory, or other circumstances, can best be administered under the laws of the Mandatory as integral portions of its territory, subject to the safeguards above mentioned in the interests of the indigenous population.

7. In every case of mandate, the Mandatory should refer to the Council an annual report in reference to the territory committed to its charge.

8. The degree of authority, control, or administration to be exercised by the Mandatory shall, if not previously agreed upon by the Members of the League, be explicitly defined in each case by the Council.

9. A permanent Commission shall be constituted to receive and examine the annual reports of the Mandatories and to advise the Council on all matters relating to the observance of the mandate.[36]

This text is interesting in a number of respects. *First, it introduced the concept of 'stage of development' into the literature of international organizations, thereby justifying a classification system according to which there were 'developed' nations at the top of the ladder.* Of course, this way of seeing things corresponded to the dominant evolutionism,[37] so that for the various peoples 'not yet able to stand by themselves under the strenuous conditions of the modern world', a day would come when they would lead an independent existence (even though this was formally mentioned only in relation to the 'A' mandates). Secondly, the justification

---

34. This 'open door policy' was introduced to satisfy the United States, even though it never joined the League of Nations.

35. The main one of these 'C' mandates, defined merely as 'territories', was the former German colony of South West Africa/Namibia; it was assigned to South Africa, which kept it – despite judgements handed down by the International Court of Justice in 1966 and 1971 – until 21 March 1990. New Guinea, New Ireland, New Britain and the Solomon Islands were allocated to Australia, which also administered Nauru on behalf of the British Empire. The Mariana, Caroline and Marshall Islands went to Japan, and Western Samoa to New Zealand. The 'C' mandates had no legislation of their own.

36. [Quoted from F.P. Walters, *A History of the League of Nations*, London: OUP, 1969, pp. 56–7. – *Trans. note.*]

37. 'The opinion appears to be growing that the people inhabiting the tropical and subtropical regions are in the "adolescent" stage of development reached by the white peoples thousands of years ago.' Raymond Leslie Buell, 'Backward Peoples under the Mandate System', *Current History*, XX, June 1924, p. 393.

for these disguised annexations was couched in a humanitarian–religious language that suggested a 'sacred trust of civilization' for the colonial powers. Beyond the economic and political interests, there were supposed to be universal values – 'civilization', 'material and moral well-being', 'social progress'[38] – which could be legitimately invoked to justify intervening in the existence of other peoples. Henceforth, the colonial enterprise would be conducted in the name of this unchallengeable 'sacred trust'.[39] Finally, this universalism was itself underwritten by an international authority that played the role of a kind of family counsellor, mediating between a 'minor' native population and the 'adult' mandatory power.

This ideology had the finishing touches given to it by the India-born Sir Frederick Lugard who, having retired from a long career in the British Army in Africa, sat as a member of the Permanent Mandates Commission. According to Lugard's doctrine of the 'dual mandate', the mandatory power had a responsibility both towards the natives – whom it had to 'emancipate' by taking account of their interests ('trust for the benefit of the native population') – and towards the whole of mankind ('trust for the benefit of world development'), since the immense resources had to be exploited for the benefit of all.[40] This was a subtle use indeed of humanitarian ideology to evade the question of the direct interests of the home country – and it came from a man with a lifetime's service to British imperialism behind him, a constant champion of 'Greater Britain' against the 'Little Englanders' who wanted to get rid of the Empire on the grounds that it was too expensive! This, no doubt, was why his new interpretation of the mandates was rapidly accepted by the League of Nations.

---

38. These terms figure in the official texts of the mandates.

39. 'Colonization became a national endeavour in France only by taking on the character of a generous enterprise motivated by a concern for humanity. Public opinion would not have accepted it in any other form.' Victor Chazelas, *Territoires africains sous mandat de la France: Cameroun et Togo*, Paris: Société d'éditions géographiques, maritimes et coloniales, 1931.

40. See Frederick Lugard, *The Dual Mandate in British Tropical Africa*, Edinburgh/London: W. Blackwood & Sons, 1922. 'In carrying out this trust they [the mandatory powers] exercise a "dual mandate" – as trustees on the one hand for the development of the resources of these lands, on behalf of the congested populations whose lives and industries depend on a share of the bounties with which nature has so abundantly endowed the tropics. On the other hand they exercise a "sacred trust" on behalf of the peoples who inhabit the tropics and who are so pathetically dependent on their guidance.' (Frederick Lugard, 'The White Man's Task in Tropical Africa', *Foreign Affairs*, V, 1926, p. 58.)

The Impossibility of International Control

Because of its institutional weakness, the League of Nations could not play the political role for which it had been created, nor head off the Sino–Japanese conflict or the Italian aggression in Ethiopia – not to speak of the outbreak of the Second World War. The mandates system, though it was supposed to establish international control over the activities of the mandatory powers, reflected this institutional impotence and operated largely for the benefit of the colonial States.

Most of the mandatory powers were anyway *de facto* members of the Permanent Mandates Commission,[41] which discussed the annual reports of activity to 'increase the well-being of the natives' but did not have the right to make investigations of its own. Its impartiality was therefore doubtful right from the beginning. Moreover, this (consultative) Commission could only make recommendations or observations, which were simply passed on to the mandatory powers and to the Council of the League. Here too the colonial powers had a seat – a fact which shackled any criticism and, *a fortiori*, any initiative contrary to their policy on the matter – all the more so as the Council itself could act only in the form of recommendations. After 1923, the Commission allowed a right of petition to the populations under mandate, but this could be exercised only through the mandatory power, not through direct appeal to the Commission.[42] Not surprisingly, such petitions were dismissed more often than not.[43]

---

41. The PMC initially consisted of nine members: one British, one French, one Belgian, one Japanese, one Italian, one Dutch, one Portuguese, one Spanish and one Swedish. With the exception of the last of these, all belonged to states which then had (or had previously had) colonial interests. Officially, however, it could be said that a majority of members were citizens of non-mandatory powers. They were also appointed in a personal capacity, and did not formally represent their respective countries. In 1924 the size of the PMC was increased to ten, and from 1927 it included a German among its members.

42. In 1926 there was a long debate on the Council about whether petitioners should, in exceptional cases, have the right to be heard by the PMC. But the mandatory powers sided with the British representative, who argued that 'the Commission was displaying an inclination to extend its authority to the point where it would no longer be the Mandatory but the Mandates Commission which administered the territories'. League of Nations, *Rapport à l'Assemblée*, 1 June 1927, p. 45.

43. Most of the petitions concerned Palestine. They were much rarer in the case of 'B' and 'C' mandates, and then were most often brushed aside. For instance, the PMC turned down four petitions submitted between 1923 and 1924 by the Adjigo clan in Togo (and again in 1928 via the *Bund der Deutsch-Togoländer*) against measures taken by the French authorities to reduce its power. An attempt was made to get round the problem by allowing a right of petition to associations established outside

In short, the work of the Commission was limited to the preparation of ever more detailed questionnaires on the situation in the mandated territories, and the recording of answers supplied by the mandatory powers, together with a sprinkling of prudent remarks or the expression of wishes that were not expected to be granted.[44] It should be stressed that in many ways the Commission did its best to promote the 'material and moral well-being of the natives', by posing very precise questions about the social situation of the local population, the measures taken against slavery, working and health conditions, the safeguarding of land-ownership rights, and so on.[45] But apart from the fact that the system gave almost discretionary powers to the Mandatories, the Commission could do nothing to challenge the self-satisfaction they manifested in their annual reports. Two examples will suffice here. In 1938 Belgium congratulated itself on advances in hygiene in Ruanda-Urundi and puffed up the statistics relating to sales of soap, adding that 'the case may be mentioned of the chief Baranyanka, who possesses a cemented bathroom with an enamelled bath'.[46] In the same year, France noted that 'evolution is proceeding rapidly among the natives [in the Cameroons]'; the

> evidence takes many forms, from the installation of houses and communities to expenditure on luxuries – bicycles and even automobiles. The native dwelling is undergoing transformation; it is larger, more solidly built, better lighted and ventilated by the fitting of windows; animals are no longer kept in them; the inhabitants possess furniture which, though scanty, demonstrates

---

the mandated territories and acting on behalf of the indigenous population. (In 1928, for example, the International Native Bureau drew the attention of the PMC to working conditions in the African territories under mandate.) Such petitions were also dismissed.

44. For example, in connection with Togo, 'the Commission wondered whether the so-called tax in services did not constitute forced labour whose conditions were not exactly those authorized by the mandate'. Or concerning Cameroun: 'Returning to a question it has dealt with [before], the Commission earnestly repeats its wish that the next annual report shall contain full and precise information about the conditions of workers employed on construction of the Central Railway, ... for among the 6,000 or so natives employed on the sites, ... the mortality rate reached a high level during the period from December 1923 to August 1924.' (CPM, 6ᵉ session, 10 juillet 1925, Doc. A.14.1925 VI, pp. 3, 5.) To which the French representative replied on 6 August 1925 (Doc. A.21.1925 VI) that the tax in services was 'fiscal labour not forced labour', because the taxpayer had a choice whether to render it in money or 'by performing a specific task for a limited period of time'. As for the mortality of railway construction workers, the discussion ended with a statement that it was higher still under German colonial rule.

45. For a systematic (official) review of the questions dealt with by the PMC, see *The Mandates Systems: Origin, Principles, Application*, Geneva: League of Nations, 1945.

46. Quoted in the official balance sheet, *The Mandates System*, ibid., p. 68.

a certain idea of comfort. Very often, the house has a small flower-garden, and is screened from the road by a hedge.... In the most remote regions, clothing has become customary.... By the force of circumstances, all these factors, slowly, surely, but inevitably, lead to the disintegration of the local primitive society which had preserved itself intact until our day.[47]

There could hardly be a more touching evaluation of the 'sacred trust of civilization'.

The Beginnings of International Co-operation

A little-known episode in the history of the League of Nations casts a surprising light upon the beginnings of international co-operation. China, a full member of the League, expressed a wish after the Paris Conference that the international organization should assist its modernization effort by providing both knowledge and capital – an initiative which finally bore some fruit only in the early 1930s.[48] The first Chinese request concerned health and hygiene, and proposed the sending of experts to China, a trip by Chinese experts to Europe and the United States, and the establishment of a group of experts under the auspices of the League's health organization. Gradually the collaboration extended to education, transport and the organization of rural co-operatives. Between 1929 and 1941, the League provided China with some thirty experts.

It should be stressed that these initiatives were taken in the tense political climate of war between China and Japan. The League therefore took considerable care to explain that the allocation of experts had a purely 'technical' character (even if, in practice, it raised the prestige of the Kuomintang). It was also clear that the experts did not infringe Chinese sovereignty in any way; they could only advise, not make decisions.

This was the setting in which the forerunner of the UNDP 'resident representatives' was appointed on 18 July 1933 – that is to say, a 'technical representative' whose task was 'to liaise with China's National Economic Council for the purposes of technical collaboration with the competent bodies of the League of Nations'.[49] This 'liaison officer' had

47. Quoted in ibid., pp. 70–71.
48. See Norbert Meienberger, *Entwicklungshilfe unter dem Völkerbund. Ein Beitrag zur Geschichte der internationalen Zusammenarbeit in der Zwischenkriegzeit unter besonderer Berücksichtigung der technischen Hilfe in China*, Winterthur: P.G. Keller, 1965.
49. Document C.474.M.241.1933.VII, p. 2.

a duty to inform the Chinese about the functioning of the League's technical agencies, to pass on to the League any Chinese requests for co-operation, and to co-ordinate on the spot the activities of experts belonging to the technical agencies of the League. The basic difference from today's 'resident representatives' was that the Chinese had clearly indicated 'that the length of his mandate would be one year, and that his travelling expenses, as well as his upkeep, would be payable by the Chinese government'.[50]

At the time, of course, China was in the midst of reconstruction and could pass for what was known as a 'backward country'. But it is significant that the initiative for international co-operation did not arise within the framework of the mandates system, dominated as it was by the national interests of the Mandatory Powers. Equally important is the fact that technical co-operation did not originate in the form of 'assistance' financed by the international institution, but as an equal relationship between the League and a member State (one too jealous of its independence not to pay itself for the services it had requested).

CONCLUSION

Colonization and the mandates system occupied the same temporal, geographic and ideological space. Both were conducted without the United States and formed an integral part of European history (involving, in some cases, the illusion that the conquered areas were only extensions of the national territory). *But although the similarities were great, it would be wrong simply to conflate the two experiences; indeed, each illuminates the other by exposing to view what it tried to conceal.*

First, as regards the *conquest of geographical space*, the colonial expeditions of the late nineteenth century were inseparable from 'discoveries', voyages of exploration, the meeting of Livingstone and Stanley. Lands hitherto unknown (to Europeans) were visited, and cartographers were able to fill the empty regions formerly thought to be inhabited by lions [*hic sunt leones*] or monsters. Before exploitation could begin, it was necessary to demarcate, to draw up inventories, to grade and classify. No region on earth would now be free from curiosity or plunder. The blue or red of Europe was everywhere – or almost – on the world maps; even the oceans were controlled. So much for concrete space

---

50. Letter of 14 July 1933 from the Chinese Representative, Wellington Koo, to the Secretary-General.

visible to the senses. But beyond the furious campaigns to occupy territory still untouched by whites, and beyond the conflicts waged in the name of the national interests of the colonizers, *a political and symbolic space*, revealed by the internationalism of the League of Nations, was already taking shape. Though torn apart, the world had to appear united. The powerful States discussed together even as they clashed on the ground; they could not really settle the world's problems, but at least they agreed to recognize one another's right to profit from their conquests. These two distinct spaces, far from being counterposed, actually complemented each other – for both asserted a kind of mastery. The first grabbed hold of places and living people, while the second exerted its sway over minds in the name of universalism and humanity.

Then there was the *conquest of public opinion*. At the start of the colonial wars, most people in the metropolitan countries had no really firm views and could scarcely imagine what might be expected from such far-flung expeditions so costly in men and money.[51] But within a mere twenty years – in France, anyway – there was a complete turn-around. Even if everyone did not become an ardent supporter of colonization, no one (except a few anarcho-communists) opposed it in any real sense. True, abuses and excesses were known about, and they never failed to be denounced. But as always when a declining paradigm continues to dominate 'normal science', appeals were made to well-advised colonization against ill-advised colonization, so that exceptions (or 'unfortunate mistakes') could be placed within a nobler framework. The League of Nations showed the way in this. Far from sacrificing the native populations to the national interest, was not colonization

---

51. The debate over whether the colonial powers actually profited from colonization is still open. (See Jacques Marseille.) No doubt the balance sheet varies according to the period and region – and the basis of calculation – but it is impossible to accept the extreme position that the enrichment of the metropolitan countries was due entirely to colonial pillage. In any event, the modest scale of private capital investment in the colonies, and the relatively small share represented by colonial trade, do not allow final conclusions to be drawn – especially as account must also be taken of the huge costs of public investment in the building of roads, ports and railways, not to speak of the human cost of wars and epidemics. At most, we can say that some private companies made considerable profits, and that in hard times the protective shelter of trade with the colonies allowed some branches of industry to survive. 'Africa did not return to its investors and traders what earlier imperialists and promoters had hoped for.' (Peter Duignan and L.H. Gann, p, 677; see also Bouda Etemad.) Moreover, if colonization provided the large gains sometimes claimed, it is not easy to see why capitalists preferred to invest in the Russian railways and state loans rather than in the colonies. Of course, this does not in any way excuse the devastating effects of colonial policy in the countries affected: while the profits to the colonizers can be (and are) disputed, the losses to the colonized are not.

entirely geared to their 'material and moral well-being' as part of the general progress of humanity? *There could be no question of exploitation, only of sharing out.* Since the land – a common heritage – was bursting with so many riches that would be useful to everyone, why leave them buried away where no one profited from them? It was a doctrine that went back a long way, proclaiming the coincidence of private and general interests, or the compatibility of private vice and public benefit.

A final argument gave added legitimacy to all the others. Just as Christopher Colon (or Columbus[52]) conquered America in the name of Christ and evangelism – which offered him cast-iron justification in those times – so did colonization now present itself, through the League of Nations, as a 'sacred trust of civilization'. This was not just an innocent form of words, for it placed the final objective in the realm of religion and the sacred. And, as is often the case, the end was thought to justify the means, to excuse errors, abuses and failures. *Everyone can make mistakes, but the cause itself is above all suspicion.* The late-nineteenth-century colonialists, with Jules Ferry at their head, had tried to make a case for their policy that did not exclude economic profit and political prestige – to which they added a number of humanitarian arguments, doubtless in completely good faith but also with the rhetorical intent of persuading doubters. The League of Nations did not trouble itself with such scruples. Conquest could not be justified on grounds of self-interest. No problem; one just had to keep quiet about them and substitute a virtuous, sacred objective, a sacred trust that no one could question. At a stroke, the accomplished fact of conquest took on a positive value, and one was at liberty to destroy whole societies for their own good.

Just as colonization revealed the basic project of the League of Nations mandate system to be disguised annexation of territories taken from the enemy, so did the League justify the colonial enterprise by giving it a quasi-religious objective, excusing its aberrations and blowing up its successes out of all proportion. The 'international community' now seemed to embrace all the peoples of the world, and its belief – or its good conscience – looked as if it rested upon a general consensus. But there was still one actor missing from it all: the United States. And one concept still needed to be invented: 'development'.

---

52. The name Colon ('settler' or 'colonizer' in French) should really be preferred, because it is the one that the person most directly concerned chose for himself to show that he was colonizing as the 'bearer of Christ' (which is the etymological meaning of Christopher).

CHAPTER 4

THE INVENTION OF
DEVELOPMENT

The Second World War turned everything upside down. Europe, in order to free itself from Nazism, had to place itself in the hands of the new powers, the United States and the Soviet Union, which – for their different reasons – had no interest in protecting colonial empires. Even before hostilities were over, the defunct League had been replaced by the United Nations Organization, whose headquarters, significantly enough, were to be in New York rather than Geneva. The discovery of the Nazi concentration camps – which certainly came late in the day – had shown the atrocities that followed when one race claimed to dominate others, and the general condemnation of racism placed a question mark over the very concept of race. A new Universal Declaration of Human Rights reaffirmed that everyone was equal, emancipating at a stroke all those peoples who had for so long been treated as wards or minors. Besides, had they not participated *en masse* in the battles waged by the European powers? And this time, had it not been necessary to make them a few promises which victory now required to be kept?

Nevertheless, in the immediate postwar period, the most urgent problems seemed to be in the North rather than the South. First, there was the reconstruction of ruined Europe. On 5 June 1947, the Marshall Plan was launched to help the European economy and to provide America's huge production capacity with the markets it needed for postwar conversion. But there were also the looming breach between the wartime Allies, and Stalin's claims in Europe as Poland (1947), Romania (1948), Czechoslovakia (1948) and Hungary (1949) became 'people's democracies' – not forgetting the civil war in Greece between 1946 and 1949. By 1948 the Soviets were blockading Berlin, and the Cold War called for serious preventive measures that led to the creation of NATO. The major powers were thus mainly preoccupied with events transforming political relations in Europe, while the changes in the South tended to be pushed into the background.[1] It was in this hardly propitious context, however, that the concept of 'development' entered the arena.

PRESIDENT TRUMAN'S POINT FOUR

By the end of 1948, American foreign policy was in ferment as it was compelled to face the major changes taking place more or less everywhere in the world. At the same time, the presidential speech-writer was trying to define a few clear points that could structure the Inaugural Address that President Truman was due to make on 20 January 1949. An initial meeting came up with three ideas that soon won unanimous support: the United States would continue to back the new United Nations Organization; it would keep up the European reconstruction effort by means of the Marshall Plan; and it would create a joint defence organization (NATO) to meet the Soviet threat. Then a civil servant suggested adding that the technical assistance already granted to parts of Latin America would be extended to the poorer countries of the world. After some hesitation, the idea was taken on board as a public relations gimmick, contrasting with the rather conventional first three points. As one might have expected, the main headlines the next morning were all about 'Point Four', although nobody – not even the President or the Secretary of State – could say more about it than what everyone read.[2]

---

1. These changes were far from trivial, however: the League of Arab States was formed in 1945; India became independent in 1947; the ending of the British mandate in Palestine in 1947 was followed the next year by the creation of the State of Israel; the Chinese civil war ended in 1949 with the coming to power of Mao Tsetung; and Sukarno's Indonesia declared independence in 1945, and became a united republic in 1950.

2. The story is told in Louis J. Halle, 'On Teaching International Relations', *The Virginia Quarterly Review*, 40 (1), Winter 1964, pp. 11–25. On 27 January 1949, a week after his speech was delivered, Truman replied to press questions: 'The origin of point four has been in my mind, and in the minds of members of the Government, for the past 2 or 3 years, ever since the Marshall plan was inaugurated.' (In fact, the Marshall Plan was launched in June 1947, a year and a half before Point Four!) 'It originated', he went on, 'with the Greece and Turkey proposition. Been studying it ever since. I spent most of my time going over to that globe back there, trying to figure out ways to make peace in the world.' *Public Papers of the Presidents of the United States, Harry S. Truman*, Year 1949, 5, United States Government Printing Office, 1964 (January 27), p. 118. This is a fine example of opportunist deception, because in reality there had been no advance planning, and it would take nearly two years for the Administration to start implementing Point Four.

Despite the anecdotal character of this episode, *Point Four inaugurated the 'development age'*, and significantly enough, it was first proclaimed by a president of the United States. Here is the text of this key document.[3]

Fourth, we must embark on a bold new program for making the benefits of our scientific advances and industrial progress available for the improvement and growth of underdeveloped areas.

More than half the people of the world are living in conditions approaching misery. Their food is inadequate. They are victims of disease. Their economic life is primitive and stagnant. Their poverty is a handicap and a threat both to them and to more prosperous areas.

For the first time in history, humanity possesses the knowledge and skill to relieve the suffering of these people.

The United States is pre-eminent among nations in the development of industrial and scientific techniques. The material resources which we can afford to use for assistance of other peoples is limited. But our imponderable resources in technical knowledge are constantly growing and are inexhaustible.

I believe that we should make available to peace-loving peoples[4] the benefits of our store of technical knowledge in order to help them realize their aspirations for a better life.

And, in cooperation with other nations, we should foster capital investment in areas needing development.

Our main aim should be to help the free peoples of the world, through their own efforts, to produce more food, more clothing, more materials for housing, and more mechanical power to lighten their burdens.

We invite other countries to pool their technological resources in this undertaking. Their contributions will be warmly welcomed. This should be a cooperative enterprise in which all nations work together through the United Nations and its specialized agencies whenever practicable. It must be a world-wide effort for the achievement of peace, plenty, and freedom.

With the cooperation of business, private capital, agriculture, and labor in this country, this program can greatly increase the industrial activity in other nations and can raise substantially their standards of living.

Such new economic developments must be devised and controlled to the benefit of the peoples of the areas in which they are established. Guarantees to the investor must be balanced by guarantees in the interest of the people whose resources and whose labor go into these developments.

The old imperialism – exploitation for foreign profit – has no place in our plans. What we envisage is a program of development based on the concepts of democratic fair-dealing.

---

3. *Public Papers of the Presidents* (January 20), pp. 114–15.

4. In the United Nations Charter, the 'peace-loving peoples' are the victors of the Second World War. In this context, however, they are the non-Communist countries. Compare the concept of 'free peoples' in the next paragraph.

All countries, including our own, will greatly benefit from a constant program for the better use of the world's human and natural resources. Experience shows that our commerce with other countries expands as they progress industrially and economically.

Greater production is the key to prosperity and peace. And the key to greater production is a wider and more vigorous application of modern scientific and technical knowledge.

Only by helping the least fortunate of its members to help themselves can the human family achieve the decent, satisfying life that is the right of all people.

Democracy alone can supply the vitalizing force to stir the peoples of the world into triumphant action, not only against their human oppressor, but also against their ancient enemies – hunger, misery, and despair.

On the basis of these four major courses of action we hope to help create the conditions that will lead eventually to personal freedom and happiness for all mankind.

At first sight, there is nothing too out-of-the-ordinary in this short list of good intentions; it seems to limit itself to hopes about what might be done, and anyway offers no commitment. The circumstances in which it saw the light of day explain, no doubt, why this 'bold new program' merely talks of mobilizing non-material resources (science and technology), North American social actors (capitalists, farmers and workers) and the international community. For the US Administration itself makes no promises but simply points out that it is prepared to take charge of operations, while diplomatically referring to the role that might be played by the UN. Yet this text is, in its way, a minor masterpiece. For in synthesizing a number of ideas that were obviously in line with the Zeitgeist, it puts forward *a new way of conceiving international relations*.

A NEW WORLD-VIEW: 'UNDERDEVELOPMENT'

The adjective 'underdeveloped' appears at the end of the opening paragraph of Point Four. This was the first time it had been used in a text intended for such wide circulation,[5] as a synonym for 'economically backward' areas. Subsequently, the noun 'underdevelopment' was introduced. It was this *terminological innovation* which altered the meaning of 'development' itself, by relating it in a new way to 'underdevelopment'.

---

5. According to Peter Praxmarer (*Development: On the Sociogenesis, Political Usage and Theoretical Possibilities of a Concept*, Institut universitaire de hautes études internationales, University of Geneva, 1984, mimeo, 421 pp.), the term was first used

Of course, the use of the word 'development' in a socioeconomic context was not new. Both Marx and Leroy-Beaulieu employed it, and as we have seen, it figured – together with 'stages of development' – in Article 22 of the Covenant of the League of Nations. Lenin wrote a work called *The Development of Capitalism in Russia* in 1899; Schumpeter composed his *Theory of Economic Development* in 1911; and Rosenstein and Rodan submitted *The International Development of Economically Backward Areas* in 1944. And most recently, in December 1948, the UN General Assembly had adopted a pair of resolutions: 'Economic Development of Underdeveloped Countries' (198-III) and 'Technical Assistance for Economic Development' (200-III).[6] What all these examples have in common is that, in keeping with Western tradition, they present 'development' as an intransitive phenomenon which simply 'happens'; nothing can be done to change things.

The appearance of the term 'underdevelopment' evoked not only the idea of change in the direction of a final state but, above all, the possibility of bringing about such change. No longer was it just a question of things 'developing'; now it was possible to 'develop' a region. Thus *'development' took on a transitive meaning* (an action performed by one agent upon another) which corresponded to a principle of social organization, while 'underdevelopment' became a 'naturally' occurring (that is, seemingly causeless) state of things.[7]

Nor were these changes merely semantic; they radically altered the way the world was seen. Until then, North–South relations had been organized largely in accordance with the colonizer/colonized opposition. The new 'developed'/'underdeveloped' dichotomy proposed a different relationship, in keeping with the new Universal Declaration of Human Rights and the progressive globalization of the system of States. In place of the hierarchical subordination of colony to metropolis, every State was equal *de jure*, even if it was not (yet) *de facto*. Colonized and colonizer had belonged to two different and opposed universes, so that confron-

---

in 1942 by an ILO functionary, William Benson, in an article entitled 'The Economic Advancement of Underdeveloped Areas' (in *The Economic Basis for Peace*, London: National Peace Council, 1942) – although obviously it was in current use in other fields such as biology, psychology or photography. This section has drawn much of its inspiration from Praxmarer's work. See also Wolfgang Sachs, 'L'Archéologie du concept de "développement"', *Interculture* (Montreal), XXIII (4), Autumn 1990, Cahier 109.

6. The two resolutions based themselves on Art. 55 §a of the Charter, whereby the United Nations was to promote 'higher standards of living, full employment, and conditions of economic and social progress and development'.

7. Accordingly, the verb 'to underdevelop' is rarely used in its active mode.

tation between them (in the form of national liberation struggles) had appeared unavoidable as a way of reducing the difference. Now, however, *'underdeveloped' and 'developed' were members of a single family*:[8] the one might be lagging a little behind the other, but they could always hope to catch up – rather as a 'deputy manager' can always dream of becoming a manager himself ... so long as he continues to play the same game and his conception of managing is not too different.

Conceptually, *the 'development'/'underdevelopment' contrast introduced the idea of a continuity of substance*, so that now the two terms of the binomial differed only relatively. 'Underdevelopment' was not the opposite of 'development', only its incomplete or (to stay with biological metaphors) its 'embryonic' form; an acceleration of growth was thus the only logical way of bridging the gap. The relationship more or less established itself in a quantitative mode, with a fundamental unity assumed between the two phenomena. In this comparison, moreover, each nation was considered for itself: its 'development' was very largely an internal, self-generated, self-dynamizing phenomenon, even if it could be 'assisted' from outside.[9] Once more, the naturalization of history empties history of its content. The historical conditions that would explain the 'lead' of some countries over others cannot enter into the argument, since the 'laws of development' are supposedly the same for all, and 'win their way through with iron necessity';[10] what happened in Europe between the eighteenth and nineteenth centuries must therefore be reproduced elsewhere. Not only does this bracket out the effects of conquest, colonization, the slave trade, the dismantling of craft production in India, the breaking up of social structures, and so on; it also presents things as if the existence of industrial countries did not radically alter the context in which candidates for industrialization

---

8. Simplifying somewhat, one might say that the relationship to the Other moved from extermination during the sixteenth-century Conquest, through exploitation (and contempt) during the nineteenth-century colonization, to end in integration within the framework of 'development'. There are several ways of denying the Other: rejection, eating as symbolic appropriation, and expropriation.

9. These presuppositions may be found in the view of economic theory that actors seek to maximize their profit within a self-regulating market. Already Marx noted: '[Value] is constantly changing from one form into another, without becoming lost in this movement; it thus becomes transformed into an automatic subject ... of a process in which, while constantly assuming the form in turn of money and commodities, it changes its own magnitude, throws off surplus-value from itself considered as original value, and thus valorizes itself independently.' *Capital Volume 1*, p. 255.

10. Ibid., p. 91.

have to operate.[11] The world is conceived not as a structure in which each element depends upon the others, but as a collection of formally equal 'individual' nations. One recognizes here the ideology of equal opportunities and the 'self-made man'. Through hard work and perseverance, a worker can become the boss, a lift boy the director, and a movie actor the head of state.

US HEGEMONY

This new way of dividing up the world was remarkably attuned to North American interests. It showed just how much the exercise of power is bound up with word usage: rhetoric is always preferable to force if it serves its purpose of persuading people. Let us see how this worked.

First of all, the new dichotomy was much more effective in discrediting colonialism than was the mandates system (which rested on the idea of the better-off having a mission to spread civilization). With the whole of mankind now included in the 'development' paradigm, legitimacy was 'naturalized' and rooted in a universality much less open to question than the political intrigues of a so-called international organization. What President Wilson failed to accomplish at the end of the First World War, President Truman achieved at the end of the Second by imposing a new vocabulary that would be used to justify the process of decolonization.[12] In fact, decolonization may be seen as the price that France, Belgium and Britain had to pay for US involvement in the Second World War. Critiques based on the old concept of 'imperialism' are thus at once both true and false: true, because the United States had an evident interest in dismantling the colonial empires to gain access to new markets;[13] false, because the 'development programme' allowed it to deploy a new anti-colonial imperialism.

---

11. In fact, England's 'lead' already posed problems for the countries of continental Europe, which had to build up their industrial strength in different ways. Faced with free-trade regulations that favoured Britain, Friedrich List responded with protectionism based upon the 'infant industry argument'.

12. The 'anti-colonial tradition' of the United States goes back, of course, to the War of Independence of the thirteen British colonies of North America in the late eighteenth century. But it is possible to argue that the United States – like the Soviet Union – had 'internal colonies' whose fate was no more enviable than that of the Europeans' 'external colonies', even if international law did not allow this to become apparent.

13. The 'development path' proposed by the United States – and taken over by the UN bureaucracy – made it possible to keep the various liberation movements under control.

Secondly, the 'development'/'underdevelopment' couplet maintained a gap between different parts of the world, but justified the possibility – or the necessity – of intervention on the grounds that one cannot remain passive when one is confronted with extreme need. On the one hand, 'underdevelopment' appears to exist without a cause, as a state of 'poverty' that is a 'handicap' and produces 'victims' oppressed by 'hunger, disease and despair'. On the other, 'development' is a state characterized by affluence, by wealth 'that keeps growing and is never exhausted', by resources that have only to be mobilized and brought into play. In the face of this, *it is impossible to do nothing*. But unlike in the colonial period, the action required is not a transfer of values or a pedagogical programme in which people from outside have the initiative but, rather, an 'international effort', a 'collective enterprise' based upon an increase in production and better use of the world's natural and human resources. Now, to intervene is 'to make resources available', 'to help others help themselves' (a jackpot-winning formula!), 'to encourage everyone to produce more'. And from the great share-out, almost as an added bonus, everyone will emerge richer and more prosperous.[14]

Finally, the Americans asserted their hegemony by means of a generous proposal that claimed to be beyond the ideological divide between capitalism and communism. The key to prosperity and happiness was increased production, not endless debate about the organization of society, ownership of the means of production or the role of the State.[15] Without questioning the existence of a hierarchical ladder along which societies could be placed (the basis of all forms of evolutionism), Point Four simply imposed a new standard whereby the United States stood at the top: namely, Gross National Product. Notions of primacy linked to 'civilization' appeared rather dubious, because they willy-nilly placed the West in competition with other civilizations or cultures. But national statistics, with their mathematical aura of objectivity, seemed to offer a much more acceptable basis of comparison.[16] *The proposed solution was genuinely hegemonic, because it appeared to be not only the best but the only possible one.*

---

14. In accordance with the 'time is money' motto, it is implied that the injection of capital into 'underdeveloped' economies will enable them to 'gain time' and 'bridge the gap'.

15. The values of democracy were, of course, celebrated, but in this case more for the ears of colonial peoples seeking independence than for those of supporters of the so-called 'people's democracies'.

16. The calculation of GNP was a new economic instrument, first established in the 1940s.

A NEW PARADIGM

The interest of Point Four also lies in the way it is structured. It can be broken down into four parts of unequal length. The first recalls the desperate straits – the horror of hunger and want – in which more than half the world's population live. Then the good news is given that, 'for the first time in history', something is at hand that will bring happiness and make it possible for their lives to be transformed. This will not come unless energies are mobilized to produce more, to invest, to get down to work, to expand trade. But in the end, if the chance is seized and people agree to the efforts required, an era of happiness, peace and prosperity will dawn from which everyone stands to benefit.

An American evangelist would have said much the same thing. Jesus Christ offers salvation to those abandoned to sin and death, provided that they fall in with what the faith demands of them; for that is how they will attain eternal life, and enjoy the bliss promised to the elect.

Truman's speech was intended first and foremost for his fellow-countrymen, who could not be insensitive to such a way of presenting history, and the fact that it corresponded (in a secular mode) to the truth proclaimed by the Church made it sound all the more convincing. But the audience went far beyond the United States, and the underlying belief was shared not only by the Christian world but, in a way, by everyone who belonged to a salvationist religion.[17] *Taking advantage of this structural homology with religious discourse, the new belief in 'development' had its credibility further strengthened by a naturalist metaphor so long part of the Western collective consciousness.* This, no doubt, is why the same style of speech was used again and again in declarations affirming the necessity of 'development' as the only solution to the problems of humanity.[18]

By the same token, it became impossible to question 'development' as such. One was quite free to debate its forms, the ways of accelerating growth or distributing its effects more equitably, but the transitive character of 'development' – that is, the intervention it represented into the internal affairs of a nation – was not to be challenged. That would have been to attack the underlying belief of a programme designed for universal happiness. You don't argue about the obvious; the most you can do is try to improve it.

---

17. See Marie-Dominique Perrot, Gilbert Rist and Fabrizio Sabelli, *La Mythologie programmée. L'économie des croyances dans la société moderne*, Paris: PUF, 1992, pp. 195 f.
18. Ibid., pp. 196–7.

THE 'DEVELOPMENT' AGE

These, then, are the reasons why Point Four should be considered the opening act of a new era – not because reality is created by words, but because certain forms of discourse express more accurately than others a reality in the making, because certain texts bring out more clearly than others the episteme of an epoch, and finally – this is the performative aspect of the text – because *power does not necessarily involve changing reality, but, rather, inserting it into a different problematic*, proposing a new interpretation to kindle the illusion of change. All this is contained in Point Four, which is thus an important moment in the ceaseless reinterpretation of the metaphor of change. Power always belongs to the one who can make himself the master of words.

Of course, it took time to transcribe into the real world the implicit meaning borne by this new interpretation of history. Just as twenty years had been needed to convince French public opinion of the merits of colonization, so was the same length of time required to make 'development' appear as the collective project of humanity. Decolonization was the occasion of stubborn conflicts which were often resolved by weapons rather than words. New international organizations (e.g. the Expanded Programme of the United Nations, later the UNDP), as well as new forms of economic management, would be necessary for production to become transnational and the market worldwide. Only then did the idea of an interdependence of nations win through.

Nevertheless, in just a few paragraphs, Point Four managed to chart a global strategy. Although it primarily served the interests of the world's most powerful nation, it made out that it had only the common good at heart, and presented 'development' as a set of technical measures outside the realm of political debate[19] (utilization of scientific knowledge, growth of productivity, expansion of international trade). It thereby became possible – according to the time and place – to give such measures either a conservative or a revolutionary interpretation.[20]

---

19. As if technology were ever ideologically neutral! As if it could ever be acquired without financial compensation! As if it had no cultural cost! As if it did not carry within itself the genetic code of the society that produced it!

20. 'Development policies' could serve various functions, according to whether they were used within the domestic order (to do something for 'the poor'), as an element in foreign policy (public aid or military assistance), or to put together a consensus within international organizations. When political contradictions came too much to the fore, it was always possible to put 'development' on the agenda. Thus the various manifestations of the Cold War, which deprived the UN of any possibility of intervening in military conflicts, were by no means unimportant in the promotion of 'development'.

Moreover, by defining 'underdevelopment' as a lack rather than the result of historical circumstances, and by treating the 'underdeveloped' simply as poor without seeking the reasons for their destitution, 'development policy' made of growth and aid[21] (conceived in techno-cratic, quantitative terms[22]) the only possible answer.

From 1949 onwards, often without realizing it, more than two billion in-habitants of the planet found themselves changing their name, being 'officially' regarded as they appeared in the eyes of others, called upon to deepen their Westernization by repudiating their own values. No longer African, Latin American or Asian (not to speak of Bambara, Shona, Berber, Quechua, Aymara, Balinese or Mongol), they were now simply 'underdeveloped'. This new 'definition' was accepted by those who headed the independ-ent States, because it was a way of asserting their claim to benefit from the 'aid' that was supposed to lead to 'development'. For the colonized, it was a way of affirming the legal equality that was refused them. It looked as if they had everything to gain – respectability and prosper-ity.[23] But *their right to self-determination had been acquired in exchange for a right to self-definition.* In gaining political independence, they forfeited their identity and their economic autonomy, and were now forced to travel the 'development path' mapped out for them by others. Whereas the world of colonization had been seen mainly as a political space to encompass ever larger empires, the 'development age' was the period when economic space spread everywhere, with the raising of GNP as the number one imperative.[24]

---

21. The notion of 'aid' or 'giving' was obviously conceived in different ways in different cultures. Outside the West, to receive without giving anything in return means to lose face and (unless one dies) to place oneself in a relationship of depend-ency upon the donor. The gift thus enters into a process of domination of which the (Western) donor, who attributes to it a positive value, is all the less aware.

22. In a way, the United States was proposing to wage 'war on poverty' with the same weapons that had won it victory over Germany and Japan: that is to say, a superior productive capacity, and the mobilization of scientists. Sometimes this trig-gered the same military logic: to liberate a town you've got to destroy it...

23. To avoid any misunderstanding, we should remember that 'external' coloni-alism (the 'first type') has all too often been replaced by internal colonization (bene-fiting local 'elites') and external dependency (or 'colonialism of the second type').

24. In defining 'underdevelopment' as a mere lack, economism imposed an order of its own. Scarcity – the basis of economic 'science' – was thus a 'naturally given fact' (rather than a social construct), which had to be combated even if the 'unlim-ited' character of human needs (as of growth) meant that in the end there was no prospect of victory.

CHAPTER 5

THE INTERNATIONAL DOCTRINE AND INSTITUTIONS TAKE ROOT

Point Four caused considerable surprise, but the authority of the man who pronounced it meant that it was at once taken seriously. As there could be no doubting America's commitment to the first three points in Truman's speech – the Marshall Plan, the United Nations and NATO – there was good reason to believe in the future of 'development assistance'. But everything remained to be done: the institutions directing the project had to be created, and the future beneficiaries had to organize themselves and seize the opportunity being offered them.

In international policy, the 1950s were evidently dominated by the Cold War. Let us then start by just mentioning a few of the major events: the Korean War (1950–53), involving military intervention by UN member States under a 'unified command' entrusted to General MacArthur;[1] the death of Stalin on 5 March 1953 and his replacement by the Khrushchev–Malenkov–Bulganin 'troika'; the French defeat at Dien Bien Phu in 1954, followed by the Geneva Accords in July 1955, a year after the beginning of the Algerian war of independence; the Franco–British–Israeli Suez operation in 1956, following Nasser's nationalization of the Canal; and simultaneously, the Soviet intervention in Hungary. The Cold War had at least two consequences. First, it constituted the 'Third World' as an ideological battleground of the major powers,[2] so that new States or national liberation movements were able

---

1. The scenario was rather similar to the intervention against Iraq in 1993.
2. The term 'Third World' [*Tiers Monde*] was first used by Alfred Sauvy in an article entitled 'Tiers Monde, une planète' (*L'Observateur*, 14 August 1952), which compared the colonial or ex-colonial countries to the Third Estate of the *ancien régime*

to benefit from the support of influential protectors (sometimes switching from one to another). Second, it blocked the UN decision-making system, because the veto of the permanent members of the Security Council could be used to prevent any action under Chapter VII of the Charter 'with respect to threats to the peace, breaches of the peace, and acts of aggression'.[3] The organization was thus forced to occupy itself with matters on which there was more of a consensus, 'development' being one of the most important of these.

This chapter will now examine the new principles of 'development' co-operation formulated both by Third World countries and by international organizations.

THE BANDUNG CONFERENCE

The demands of the colonial peoples went back a long way and had been expressed in many places after the Russian Revolution of 1917. When Lenin convened the Baku Congress of the Peoples of the East in 1920, he already showed the advantage he intended to draw from the anti-colonial struggle. Congresses for the Advancement of the Oppressed Peoples were held in Paris in 1920 and London in 1923. In 1924, a League against Imperialism organized the first Congress of the Oppressed Peoples in Moscow, then a second in 1927 in Brussels which was attended by Sukarno and Nehru. Finally, just a few months before India's independence, twenty-five countries took up Nehru's invitation to an Asian Relations Conference, held in New Delhi from 23 March to 2 April 1947.

It was against this historical background, and with the aim of developing a common 'development' policy, that the governments of Burma, Ceylon, India, Indonesia and Pakistan called a conference in

in France. In a short book called *Qu'est-ce que le Tiers État*, published in 1789, Abbé Sieyès had launched his famous formula: 'What is the Third Estate? Everything. What has it been so far within the political order? Nothing. What does it ask? To be something.' In the expression 'Third World', the sense of 'third' is thus political, not mathematical; as if the world were divided into three parts, of which the first is capitalist and the second communist.

3. The UN intervention in Korea had been formally 'recommended' on 27 June 1950 by the Security Council (in the absence of the Soviet representative), but the conduct of operations drew its authority from the General Assembly, which, in Resolution 377/V of 3 November 1950 – the so-called 'Uniting for Peace' or 'Acheson' Resolution – substituted itself for a Security Council again paralysed by the return of the Soviet delegate. This episode, legally murky as it was, demonstrated the UN's incapacity to act in accordance with the provisions of the Charter.

Bandung, Indonesia, which marked the beginning of the 'Non-Aligned' movement and of Third World demands within international organizations.[4] The conference took place in a Cold War setting, of course: many of the participants were militarily tied to the Western powers;[5] others (People's China, Afghanistan, Burma, Yemen, North Vietnam) belonged to the other camp; while India, Saudi Arabia and Indonesia were trying hard to preserve their neutrality.

A political analysis of the proceedings at Bandung would doubtless emphasize the sharp criticism of colonialism (sometimes including Soviet colonialism), the support given to Indonesia's claims in Western New Guinea, the demand for the independence of all colonial countries (especially Tunisia, Algeria and Morocco), the request for UN membership for participating countries not yet admitted,[6] and the creation of a platform on which the People's Republic of China could assert its status as a major power. A further important aspect was that most of the participants came from Asia, and although the continuation of colonialism explains why the Africans were so thin on the ground, it seems more difficult today to understand the absence of Latin America. At any event, Bandung marked the beginning of collective demands by the Third World in the fields of politics (decolonization) and 'development'; most of its demands were repeatedly taken up in UN resolutions, and gradually won acceptance.

One is immediately struck by the fact that the ten principles which conclude the final communiqué scarcely go beyond existing international law or the provisions of the UN Charter: that is to say, respect for basic human rights, sovereignty and territorial integrity, equality of

---

4. The following countries participated in the conference: Afghanistan, Cambodia, China (People's Republic), Egypt, Ethiopia, Gold Coast (Ghana), Iran, Iraq, Japan, Jordan, Laos, Lebanon, Liberia, Libya, Nepal, Pakistan, the Philippines, Saudi Arabia, Siam (Thailand), Sudan, Turkey, Vietnam (Democratic Republic), Vietnam (Republic of), Yemen. It should be noted that neither Ghana nor Sudan was independent at the time.

5. The relevant alliances were (a) the South-East Asia Treaty Organization (SEATO, founded in 1954), which comprised Great Britain, the United States, France, Australia, New Zealand, Thailand and Pakistan, and guaranteed Laos, Cambodia and South Vietnam; and (b) the Baghdad Pact (1955), which consisted of Britain, Turkey (also a NATO member since 1952), Iran, Iraq (which withdrew in 1959) and Pakistan.

6. To protect its majority in the General Assembly, the United States systematically blocked the admission of new countries whose government was on bad terms with it. The USSR retaliated by doing the same. But the business seemed to be settled when 16 countries (including Cambodia, Ceylon, Jordan, Libya and Nepal) joined in 1955, Japan, Morocco, Sudan and Tunisia in 1956, Ghana and Malaysia in 1957, and Guinea in 1958.

races and nations, non-interference in internal affairs, the right of
national or collective self-defence, abstention from acts or threats of
aggression or the use of force, peaceful settlement of disputes, international co-operation based upon mutual interests, respect for justice
and international obligations, and 'abstention from the use of arrangements of collective defence to serve the particular interests of any of
the big powers'.[7]

In the section of the communiqué on 'human rights and self-
determination', reference was naturally made to the right of peoples to
self-determination and, in particular, to the racial discrimination in
South Africa and the 'rights of the Arab people of Palestine'. These
references, too, would later be taken up in a ritualistic manner in countless resolutions of the UN General Assembly.

As for 'development', this was seen in terms of economic co-
operation, which was envisaged as follows in the first section of the
final communiqué.

1. The Asian–African Conference recognized the urgency of promoting
economic development in the Asian–African region. There was general desire
for economic cooperation among the participating countries on the basis of
mutual interest and respect for national sovereignty. The proposals with regard
to economic cooperation within the participating countries do not preclude
either the desirability or the need for cooperation with countries outside the
region, including the investment of foreign capital. It was further recognized
that the assistance being received by certain participating countries from outside the region, through international or under bilateral arrangements, had
made a valuable contribution to the implementation of their development
programmes.

2. The participating countries agreed to provide technical assistance to
one another, to the maximum extent practicable, in the form of: experts,
trainees, pilot projects and equipment for demonstration purposes; exchange
of know-how and establishment of national, and where possible, regional
training and research institutes for imparting technical knowledge and skills
in cooperation with the existing international agencies.

3. The Asian–African Conference recommended: the early establishment
of the Special United Nations Fund for Economic Development; the allocation by the International Bank for Reconstruction and Development of a
greater part of its resources to Asian–African countries; the early establishment of the International Finance Corporation which should include in its

---

7. The last of these principles was debated at length and gave rise to contradictory drafts. It did not prohibit military alliances except in so far as these served the
'particular interests' of a big power, and it could always be said of the struggle against
communism that a collective interest was at stake. Non-alignment, then, was not as
strict as one might have supposed.

activities the undertaking of equity investment, and encouragement to the promotion of joint ventures among Asian–African countries in so far as this will promote their common interest.

4. The Asian–African Conference recognized the vital need for stabilizing commodity trade in the region. The principle of enlarging the scope of multilateral trade and payments was accepted. However, it was recognized that some countries would have to take recourse to bilateral trade arrangements in view of their prevailing economic conditions.

5. The Asian–African Conference recommended that collective action be taken by participating countries for stabilizing the international prices of and demand for primary commodities through bilateral and multilateral arrangements, and that as far as practicable and desirable, they should adopt a unified approach on the subject in the United Nations Permanent Advisory Commission on International Commodity Trade and other international forums.

6. The Asian–African Conference further recommended that: Asian–African countries should diversify their export trade by processing their raw material, wherever economically feasible, before export; intraregional trade fairs should be promoted and encouragement given to the exchange of trade delegations and groups of businessmen; exchange of information and of samples should be encouraged with a view to promoting intraregional trade and normal facilities should be provided for transit trade of land-locked countries.

7. The Asian–African Conference attached considerable importance to Shipping and expressed concern that shipping lines reviewed from time to time their freight rates, often to the detriment of participating countries. It recommended a study of this problem, and collective action thereafter, to induce the shipping lines to adopt a more reasonable attitude. It was suggested that a study of railway freight of transit trade be made.

8. The Asian–African Conference agreed that encouragement should be given to the establishment of national and regional banks and insurance companies.

9. The Asian–African Conference felt that exchange of information on matters relating to oil, such as remittance of profits and taxation, might eventually lead to the formulation of common policies.

10. The Asian–African Conference emphasized the particular significance of the development of nuclear energy for peaceful purposes, for the Asian–African countries. The Conference welcomed the initiative of the Powers principally concerned in offering to make available information regarding the use of atomic energy for peaceful purposes; urged the speedy establishment of the International Atomic Energy Agency which should provide for adequate representation of the Asian–African countries on the executive authority of the Agency; and recommended to the Asian and African Governments to take full advantage of the training and other facilities in the peaceful uses of atomic energy offered by the countries sponsoring such programmes.

11. The Asian–African Conference agreed to the appointment of Liaison Officers in participating countries, to be nominated by their respective national Governments, for the exchange of information and ideas on matters of mutual interest....

12. The Asian–African Conference recommended that there should be prior consultation of participating countries in international forums with a view, as far as possible, to furthering their mutual economic interest. It is, however, not intended to form a regional bloc.[8]

The tone is set straight away: *'development' is necessary and should take place within a perspective of integration into the world economy.* The diplomatic language often produces a limiting clause to leave options open ('as far as practicable and desirable', etc.). But there is essential agreement that 'development' is above all an economic matter of production and accumulation, based upon private investment and external assistance;[9] industrialization will allow raw materials to be processed on the spot in the Third World, and a major role will be played in this by modern technology (nuclear energy). Finally, the freedom of multilateral trade is grounded upon supposedly 'mutual interests' between partners, even if this means wishing for a stabilization of commodity prices,[10] as well as appropriate measures relating to transport and various privileges for land-locked countries.

At the same time, a number of new institutions or political orientations were sketched out.[11] In 1958 the UN would create SUNFED, the Special United Nations Fund for Economic Development (later merged with the Expanded Programme of Technical Assistance – established in 1949 – to form the UNDP). The World Bank would gradually come to allocate nearly all its funds to the Third World, and in 1956 it set up the International Finance Corporation (IFC) to promote private investment. The International Atomic Energy Agency came into being in 1957, and regional development banks were created for Africa (1964) and Asia (1966).[12] As to the stabilization of raw materials prices and the problems of transport, these were among the reasons for the creation of UNCTAD in 1964.

---

8. 'Final Communiqué', reprinted in George McTurnan Kahin, *The Asian–African Conference: Bandung, Indonesia, April 1955*, Ithaca, NY: Cornell University Press, pp. 76–8.

9. These highly conventional formulations should be compared with the violent denunciation of 'dollar imperialism' at the Conference on Asian Relations convened by Nehru in 1947.

10. This point was not new – in 1954 the UN Economic and Social Council had created a Commission dealing with international trade in primary products, with a brief 'to study measures that will avoid excessive fluctuations in primary product prices and trade volumes'. See Charles Chaumont, *L'ONU*, Paris: PUF, 1962, p. 102.

11. It should be recalled that the Bretton Woods institutions (International Monetary Fund and World Bank) had been created in 1944, and that GATT had been in existence since 1947.

12. The Inter-American Bank had already existed since 1954.

A careful reading of the 'Economic Cooperation' section of the Bandung communiqué allows us to identify two further themes that would have contrasting fortunes in subsequent years. The first, contained in the opening two paragraphs, concerns the co-operation that participating countries envisaged among themselves to elude the pitfalls of economic imperialism resulting from foreign aid. It is true that the principle is rather timidly asserted, and accompanied by references to the 'valuable contribution' made from 'outside the region' to the development of participating countries.[13] Nevertheless, this was the first allusion to what the New International Economic Order (NIEO) would sanctify as 'collective self-reliance', later to be known as 'South–South co-operation'.[14] The second theme concerns the special role of oil which, according to the hopes expressed in paragraph 9, 'might eventually lead to the formulation of common policies'. This early recognition of the strategic importance of 'black gold' carried through to the creation of OPEC, which played a considerable role in the aftermath of the Israeli–Egyptian conflict of October 1973.[15]

The Bandung Conference has remained in the collective memory as the launching pad for Third World demands, where the countries of the South resolved to set a distance between themselves and the big powers seeking to lay down the law. Some have even characterized the debates at the conference as 'inverted racism'.[16] What is certain is that the final communiqué – in its section on 'cultural cooperation' – strongly condemned colonialism, and asserted that 'these policies amount to a denial of the fundamental rights of man' and constitute 'a means of cultural suppression'. It is also clear that this kind of statement (and, in the case of some delegates, the condemnation of internal colonialism in the USSR) was not displeasing to the United States, which used the same arguments in its efforts to end colonialism.[17] As many of the

---

13. The allusion is to the Colombo Plan, which made it possible (with mainly American and British help) to finance new development projects in the non-communist countries of Asia.

14. See the resolutions on the NIEO of 1 May 1974: nos 3201 and, above all, 3202 S-VII.

15. The Iranian Prime Minister, Muhammed Mossadeq, nationalized the Anglo–Iranian Oil Company in 1951, but was subsequently disavowed by the Shah. The presence of Iran at Bandung prevented this point from being developed further.

16. Richard Wright – quoted in Pierre Gerbet, *Les Organisations internationales*, Paris: PUF, 1960, p. 122.

17. It should also be noted that Chapters XI and XII of the UN Charter ('Declaration Regarding Non-Self-Governing Territories' and 'International Trusteeship System'), which took over some formulations from Article 22 of the Covenant of the League of Nations, had in a way 'programmed' decolonization.

participating countries were also members of US-dominated military alliances, this strong language did not necessarily reflect an autonomous political line. Thus, although Nasser tried to regain the initiative in late 1957 by organizing an 'Afro–Asian Solidarity Conference' (a 'Peoples' Bandung'), its results can be termed 'revolutionary' only with serious qualifications. In any event, the ritualistic condemnations of 'colonialism, neo-colonialism and imperialism' did not make their debut at Bandung.

The same conclusions apply with regard to 'development'. It was seen as a universal necessity that would come everywhere at the end of a major economic effort, to be stimulated by foreign capital and the introduction of modern technology. This optimistic vision suited all the main actors, whether in the American or the Soviet camp, and all referred to models which, except on the role of foreign capital, bore a considerable resemblance to each other. Significantly, culture was invoked in its most 'idealist' form. For example:

> Asia and Africa have been the cradle of great religions and civilizations which have enriched other cultures and civilizations while themselves being enriched in the process. Thus the cultures of Asia and Africa are based on spiritual and universal foundations. Unfortunately contacts among Asian and African countries were interrupted during the past centuries.[18]

Although the final communiqué insisted that 'all nations should have the right freely to choose their own political and economic systems and their own way of life',[19] this remained no more than a pious wish. For elections might well establish a particular political regime or determine a particular economic policy, but they could not offer a choice between several ways of life. Real innovation with regard to 'development' would have meant focusing on the actual practices of Asian and African societies, and contrasting them with the changes that 'development' could not fail to bring in its wake. But the participants at Bandung did not think of themselves as breaking new ground in that domain – especially as for most of them the choice had already been made.[20]

---

18. 'Final Communiqué', p. 79.

19. Ibid., p. 84.

20. The only real debate on the Western 'development' model had taken place in India in 1947, when Nehru's first development plan (which had the support of both industrialists and Communists) was opposed by Gandhi. Too often it has been thought that Gandhi was bent on turning the clock back and reducing Indian industry to use of the craftsman's wheel. It is true that his economic system was largely based upon ethical principles of justice and self-sufficiency, but he offered an original 'bottom-up' approach that proceeded via concentric circles, so that the largest circle did not lay

Bandung's main contribution on 'development' was *to hasten the advent of new international institutions (or to inflect the policy of existing ones) charged with promoting the 'development' model of the industrial countries, and especially the United States*. Politically, an impetus was also given to Third World diplomatic activity, as the various countries in the region met more often to harmonize their points of view. This led to the definition of 'non-alignment' at the Belgrade Conference of 1961 (which was dominated by Tito, Nasser and Nehru), and a year later to the creation of the 'Group of 77' on the occasion of the Economic Conference of Developing Countries in Cairo. As for the more 'revolutionary' countries, Castro's victory in Cuba in 1959 allowed them to find an expression in the Tricontinental.

THE NEW INTERNATIONAL 'DEVELOPMENT' AGENCIES

As we have already seen, Article 55a of the Charter required the United Nations to promote 'higher standards of living, full employment, and conditions of economic and social progress and development', and the General Assembly had concerned itself with 'development' since the end of 1948.[21] There was no special structure for this new area, however, and the UN Secretary-General – together with the Economic and Social Council and other UN institutions – was responsible for implementation of these provisions.

Truman's Point Four eventually gave the impetus to establish a series of special agencies for the promotion of 'development'. Thus, on 16 November 1949, the General Assembly approved the creation of an 'Expanded Programme of Technical Assistance', with voluntary contributions from member States, the main aim of which was to finance the sending of technical experts, the granting of scholarships to Third World citizens, and the training of managerial personnel. Requests for assistance had to be made by governments, and a Technical Assistance

---

down the law for the smallest. Consciously opting for simplicity, Gandhi sought to limit accumulation, the job-destroying division of labour, and the dependence resulting from foreign trade. Such ideas were quickly forgotten by the ruling classes of India after his assassination on 30 January 1948.

21. Compare Article 25 of the Universal Declaration of Human Rights: 'Everyone has the right to a standard of living adequate for the health and well-being of himself and of his family, including food, clothing, housing and medical care and necessary social services.' See also Articles 22, 23 and 26.

Board, comprising the specialized agency directors, set up the programmes and monitored them to ensure that the funds were being distributed in an impartial manner. A Standing Technical Assistance Committee (TAC), drawn from members of the Economic and Social Council, examined draft projects and made sure they were not a form of interference. This was still simple machinery, but as Truman had hoped, *it did internationalize Third World aid by drawing in countries that had no colonial responsibilities.*

Important though it was, the technical assistance was not enough and had to be complemented by capital transfers. At first, the Economic and Social Council tried to solve the problem through the World Bank, but the Bank refused to act when it judged the return on capital to be too low. Other ways had to be found, then, of funding unprofitable ventures in such areas as infrastructure. After an initial attempt to create a Special United Nations Fund for Economic Development ended in failure in 1953, two other approaches eventually led to a solution. On the one hand, the World Bank founded in 1956 an International Finance Corporation (IFC), and then in 1960 an International Development Association (IDA), whose task was to make loans at better than market rates to the poorest countries. On the other hand, a Special Fund was established by the General Assembly (Resolution 1240/XII of 14 October 1958) to collect voluntary contributions for the financing of major projects in the most impoverished countries. Later, in 1965, this Special Fund was merged with the Expanded Programme of Technical Assistance to form the United Nations Development Programme.[22]

The 1950s thus appear as a time when 'development' was still 'incubating'. *In order to carry out the strategy envisaged in Point Four, it was necessary both to complete decolonization and to convince international public opinion that 'development' really depended upon a concerted effort by one and all.*[23] Paradoxically, this twofold objective was admirably served by the consequences of the Cold War. Paralysed by the veto, and incapable of preventing the many conflicts that the major powers waged through Third World proxies, the United Nations built its agenda for action around three closely related issues: human rights, decolonization and 'development'.

----

22. See Resolution 2029/XX of 22 November 1965, 'Serving Progress'.
23. In a faithful reflection of the dominant concerns, the Organization for European Economic Cooperation (OEEC), which had been set up in 1948 in the wake of the Marshall Plan, turned itself into an Organization for Economic Cooperation and Development (OECD) in 1961.

The strategic conditions for 'development' were therefore present when all the countries of French West and Equatorial Africa, plus Nigeria, Togo, Madagascar and Somalia, gained independence in 1960, to be followed a year later by Mauritania, Outer Mongolia and Tanzania. In 1962 the Acting Secretary-General, U Thant (who had taken over after the death of Dag Hammarskjöld in the Congo), submitted proposals for the United Nations Development Decade, proclaimed the previous December following a speech by President Kennedy, which were substantively endorsed by the General Assembly and the Economic and Social Council.[24]

In his *Proposals for Action* U Thant did not, of course, promise that the problems of underdevelopment would be solved within ten years, but he introduced a number of themes which would later be constantly repeated and become the basis of all discourse on 'development'.[25] Let us briefly mention a few of these.

- 'Development is not just economic growth, it is growth plus change.' Clearly this is directed against economic reductionism, but without denying the determining character of the economy. *The hard core of 'development' is still growth* – to be complemented by (unspecified) 'change'. Thirty years later, the UNDP would maintain: 'Just as economic growth is necessary for human development, human development is critical to economic growth.'[26]

- 'During the past decade we have not only gained greatly in understanding of the development process and what it requires, but we have also achieved much.' The actual resolution on the Development Decade noted – in what would also become a sad ritualistic formula – that 'in spite of the efforts made in recent years the gap in *per caput* incomes between the economically developed and the less developed countries has increased'.[27] But above all, *it was necessary to keep hopes alive; people's efforts must not be discouraged.* In 1991 the UNDP echoed: 'The first *Human Development Report* stressed that human develop-

---

24. The idea of a development decade actually originated with a speech to the US Congress ('Act for International Development') by President Kennedy, who then raised it in a speech to the UN General Assembly on 25 September 1961.

25. 'Foreword to the United Nations Development Decade', in U Thant, *Public Papers of the Secretaries-General of the United Nations, 1961–1964*, vol. VI, ed. Andrew W. Cordier and Max Harrelson, New York: Columbia University Press, 1976, pp. 140–45.

26. *Human Development Report 1991*, p. 2.

27. Resolution 1710 (XVI): 'United Nations Development Decade'.

ment is clearly possible. This much is evident from the progress of the past three decades.'[28]

- 'The acceptance of the principle of capital assistance to developing countries is one of the most striking expressions of international solidarity as well as enlightened self-interest.' This yoking together of solidarity and self-interest became one of the basic elements in 'development' discourse, as a way of convincing both those who emphasized the 'humanitarian imperative' and those who focused on national interests. On the one hand, it asserted that solidarity was disinterested, and on the other that it was a matter of self-interest – which was obviously contradictory.[29] *To say that one has an interest in being disinterested is to place oneself in a double bind.* It would appear that the antinomy contained in such thinking gradually faded by dint of repetition, as if one could get used to any nonsense in the end.

- 'The disappointing foreign trade record of the developing countries is due in part to obstacles hindering the entry of their products into industrial markets.' And the UNDP in counterpoint: 'Trade barriers in industrial countries protect national markets from a whole range of countries – rich and poor. Non-tariff measures, for example, are imposed mostly on products in which developing countries are more competitive.'[30] Implicitly the idea is the same: it is by developing trade that each country will earn more and itself 'develop'. *Trade is always considered in general as one of the engines of growth, with no distinction between different situations.*

This list is far from exhaustive. We could add 'the importance of the human factor' and 'the urgent need to mobilize human resources' (U Thant), or what the Resolution on the Development Decade calls 'the utilization of resources released by disarmament for the purpose of economic and social development'. This corresponds to the expression 'peace dividend' now used by the UNDP, as if peace were a marketable security with a variable return. The biblical prophets had already dreamed of turning swords into ploughshares!

---

28. Ibid., p. 1.

29. On this point, see Marie-Dominique Perrot, Gilbert Rist and Fabrizio Sabelli, *La Mythologie programmée. L'Économie des croyances dans la société moderne*, Paris: PUF, 1992, pp. 183 f. This coincidence of opposites, so beloved of the Schoolmen, already formed part of the discourse of colonialism, which sought to reconcile 'heart and mind, duty and interest' as two elements without which 'no policy can ever become popular'. Albert Sarraut, *La mise en valeur des colonies françaises*, Paris: Payot, 1923, p. 87.

30. *Human Development Report 1992*, pp. 5–6.

It is not being suggested, of course, that current discourse simply reproduces what was around in the past. In some respects, the ambitions used to be greater, since the UN once expected that 'public development assistance' would reach 1 per cent of income in the advanced countries, whereas today the target has fallen to 0.7 per cent and is still rarely achieved. In other respects, the perspectives of the early 1960s were based upon a simplistic analysis that annual GNP growth of 5 per cent would by itself enable the problems to be solved. Since then, and on the basis of (often inconclusive) experience, we have learnt to put forward more nuanced positions.

That said, the general framework for the 'development' adventure was in place by the early sixties. The core of the doctrine had been clearly stated, the international organizations had managed to arouse widespread interest and to mobilize growing resources, decolonization was well under way,[31] and the rulers of the new Third World States had discovered ways in which they could themselves benefit from offers of international aid. The political preliminaries were over, we might say, so that economics was able to sweep onto centre-stage.

---

31. Of course, in Africa a solution still had to be found – not without considerable difficulty – in the Portuguese colonies, Rhodesia (Zimbabwe), South-West Africa (Namibia) and South Africa itself.

CHAPTER 6

MODERNIZATION
POISED BETWEEN HISTORY
AND PROPHECY

Nowadays it is thought quite proper to criticize Rostow and his evolutionist theory.[1] Such criticism, though doubtless justified, requires some qualification, for it is always easy to marvel at the past while claiming that it is over and done with.

In a way, Rostow's role in 'development' theory has been comparable to that of Leroy-Beaulieu in the theory of European colonialism. Both were economists – even if Rostow calls himself an 'economic historian' – and both published a work for 'an intelligent non-professional audience' which had a massive and lasting impact on public opinion. Each was writing at the threshold of a new period, when it was felt that political decisions (colonization and decolonization respectively) were challenging the industrial countries' relations with the South, but it was not really known what could be expected from them. The merit of both Rostow and Leroy-Beaulieu is that they offered a clear line from which policies could take their inspiration. The first question to be asked, then, is not whether they were essentially right or wrong, but how broad was their influence.

Rostow's first draft of *The Stages of Economic Growth* was a series of lectures delivered at Cambridge University in 1958.[2] (The book itself appeared in 1960.) These set out to answer the 'central challenge of our time', that of 'creating, in association with the non-Communist

---

1. Walt W. Rostow, *The Stages of Economic Growth: A Non-Communist Manifesto*, Cambridge: Cambridge University Press, 1960.
2. Before that, in 1952, Rostow had published another work entitled *The Processes of Economic Growth*.

politicians and peoples of the preconditions and early take-off areas, a partnership which will see them through into sustained growth on a political and social basis which keeps open the possibilities of progressive, democratic development'.[3] The problem was twofold: it had to be shown, mainly by reference to European economic history, how the recently decolonized countries might in turn promote growth leading to 'development'; and it had to be explained why communism, far from making it possible to achieve this objective, was actually 'a kind of disease which can befall a transitional society if it fails to organize effectively those elements within it which are prepared to get on with the job of modernization'.[4] Hence the subtitle: 'A Non-Communist Manifesto'. The book's huge success was no doubt due to the fact that it convincingly addressed these two concerns, even if the conviction it sought to share often hinged upon a dubious line of argument. At a historical moment when the field of 'development' was taking shape, Rostow showed how it could be of interest not only for theoretical reflection but also for the race to keep ahead in economics and politics. But before we examine the reasons for its cult status, we should outline the content of the new doctrine.

A PHILOSOPHY OF HISTORY: ROSTOW'S STAGES OF ECONOMIC GROWTH

The excellent summary that Rostow himself provides of his general thesis opens as follows: 'It is possible to identify all societies, in their economic dimensions, as lying within one of five categories: the traditional society, the preconditions for take-off, the take-off, the drive to maturity, and the age of high mass-consumption.'[5] This announces the extremely general level of the whole argument, with its small number of 'laws' applying to 'all societies'.[6] On the other hand, the use of such terms as 'degree of development', 'stages' or 'maturity' suggests the

---

3. *Stages of Economic Growth*, p. 164.
4. Ibid.
5. Ibid., p. 4.
6. In his introduction, however, Rostow remarks: 'I cannot emphasize too strongly at the outset, that the stages-of-growth are an arbitrary and limited way of looking at the sequence of modern history: and they are, in no absolute sense, a correct way. They are designed, in fact, to dramatize not merely the uniformities in the sequence of modernization but also – and equally – the uniqueness of each nation's experience' (p. 1).

strong influence of an organicist metaphor of 'development', especially as Rostow himself talks of 'the essentially biological field of economic growth'.[7]

Alongside this, there is the aeronautical metaphor of 'taking off', rapidly incorporated into 'development' jargon, which partly accounted for the book's success.[8] By depicting the future of societies in the manner of an aeroplane that speeds to the end of a runway and climbs rapidly skyward above all earthbound obstacles, Rostow also seemed to be conjuring up the asymptotic graph of every company's ideal performance. At least this is what is suggested by his constant references throughout the book to 'the powerful arithmetic of compound interest',[9] seen as 'a major independent variable in the stages-of-growth'.[10] It is this almost-divine force, appearing as the engine of growth, which is supposed to ensure that 'the age of high mass-consumption becomes universal'.[11]

After these preliminaries, Rostow proceeds to build his argument around copiously documented historical comparisons between the evolution of industrial societies in Europe, North America, India, China and Japan, with a few incursions into Latin America and Australia. Without following him into this level of detail, we may still question the pertinence of some of his arguments.

(a) For Rostow, *traditional society is a kind of degree zero of history corresponding to a natural state of 'underdevelopment'*. Seen from the special viewpoint of industrial society, its distinguishing feature is a low level of productivity due to ignorance of the modern technology that allows nature to be rationally exploited. Hence, the progress registered from one generation to the next is extremely limited. Although Rostow does not consider 'primitive' societies to be static, he yields to the

---

7. Ibid., p. 36.

8. The 'take-off' metaphor originated with Rosenstein-Rodan's formulation in 1957: 'Launching a country into self-sustaining growth is a little like getting an airplane off the ground. There is a critical ground speed which must be passed before the craft can become airborne.' *The Objectives of United States Economic Assistance Programs*, Cambridge, MA: MIT Center for International Studies, 1957, p. 70; quoted in Gerald M. Meier, 'From Colonial Economics to Development Economics', in Gerald M. Meier, ed., *From Classical Economics to Development Economics*, New York: Saint Martin's Press, 1994, p. 179.

9. Ibid., p. 10. 'This phrase is used as a shorthand way of suggesting that growth normally proceeds by geometric progression, much as a savings account if interest is left to compound with principal' (p. 2, note). The occasions are certainly many on which the phrase occurs in the book.

10. Ibid., p. 154.

11. Ibid., p. 167.

ordinary conception of them as largely shaped by a ceaseless struggle against scarcity.[12] This implies that such societies should gratefully welcome the technological means that allow them to produce more. For those who are happy to have a lot, it may seem logical enough that those who have little should wish to have more. But the anthropological evidence shows that it has not always been so. In many societies, it is not low productivity but a rejection of accumulation which is the factor limiting production.[13] *The economic historian who thinks that all societies behave alike and harbour the same desires is therefore guilty of a kind of socio-centrism.* For *Homo oeconomicus*, frustrated by the scarcity that forces a choice between unlimited desires, is not a universal phenomenon. Unwittingly Rostow himself has to admit this, for in his view the passage from traditional society to market society cannot take place gradually and involves a solution of continuity.

(b) During the stage when the 'preconditions of take-off' are taking shape, 'the idea spreads not merely that economic progress is possible, but that economic progress is a necessary condition for some other purpose, judged to be good: be it national dignity, private profit, the general welfare, or a better life for the children'.[14] This demonstration effect, stemming from the most advanced societies, triggers or hastens the disintegration of traditional societies, until a 'modern alternative is constructed out of the old culture'.[15] *For Rostow, the main thing is to move from tradition to modernity.* He seems to suggest that the one can be 'constructed' out of the other, but in reality he recognizes that in contemporary societies – unlike in Britain in the early nineteenth century – the change comes about as a result of external circumstances. This allows him, in his own way, to justify colonialism:

> Colonies were often established initially not to execute a major objective of national policy, nor even to exclude a rival economic power, but to fill a vacuum; that is, to organize a traditional society incapable of self-organization

---

12. 'The central fact about the traditional society was that a ceiling existed on the level of attainable output per head. This ceiling resulted from the fact that the potentialities which flow from modern science and technology were either not available or not regularly and systematically applied' (ibid., p. 4). Or again: 'After all, the life of most human beings since the beginning of time has been mainly taken up with gaining food, shelter and clothing for themselves and their families' (p. 91).

13. See, for example, Marshall Sahlins, *Stone Age Economics*, Chicago: Aldine–Atherton, 1972; or Jacques Lizot, 'Économie primitive et subsistance', in *Libre*, Paris: Petite Bibliothèque Payot, 1976, pp. 69–118.

14. *Stages of Economic Growth*, p. 6.

15. Ibid.

(or unwilling to organize itself) for modern import and export activity, including production for export.[16]

Thus, everything is linked together for the best in the best of worlds,
and 'development' would not be so close if the societies of the South
had not been a little 'shaken up' by the North. The other positive
effect of this 'intrusion' was the arousal of the nationalism of people in
the colonies – that is, the formation of a new elite moved by an entrepreneurial spirit, open to science and eager to raise productivity.

(c) Take-off is 'the interval when the old blocks and resistances to
steady growth are finally overcome.... Growth becomes [the] normal
condition [of the economy]. Compound interest becomes built, as it
were, into its habits and institutional structures.'[17] *We find ourselves here
with a naturalistic interpretation of 'development' or growth*: the bud opens
out, the chick breaks through its shell, the butterfly emerges from its
chrysalis – and an irresistible force removes all the obstacles to growth.
Even people's habits incorporate the notion of compound interest –
which for Rostow probably means that a new tradition of accumulation
is bringing about a global change in the ethos of the society.[18] During
this period, investment rises from 5 to 10 per cent of GNP, agriculture
is commercialized, new industries spring up and deploy modern technology. It really is a 'great watershed',[19] one dominated by a ruling class
eager to push through modernization as the antithesis of all things
traditional.

(d) The next stage, continuing the analogy, is the 'drive to maturity',
which covers the forty years or so between the end of take-off and the
achievement of maturity. During this period, 'the society makes such
terms as it will with the requirements of modern efficient production'.[20]

---

16. Ibid., p. 109. 'Some colonials were drawn into those minimum modern economic activities necessary to conduct trade to produce what the colonial power wished
to export and what could profitably be produced locally for the expanding urban and
commercialized agricultural markets' (pp. 27–8). 'There is no doubt that without the
affront to human and national dignity caused by the intrusion of more advanced
powers, the rate of modernization of traditional societies would have been much
slower' (p. 28).

17. Ibid., p. 7.

18. This focus on accumulation is not peculiar to Rostow; it could already be
found in 1954 in the writings of W. Arthur Lewis. For example: 'The central fact of
economic development is rapid capital accumulation (including knowledge and skills
with capital).' 'Economic Development with Unlimited Supply of Labour', *Manchester
School*, 22 (2), p. 139; quoted in Meier, p. 176.

19. The expression recalls the famous 'for the first time in history' in Truman's
Point Four.

20. Ibid., p. 9.

his is Rostow's muffled way of describing, in semi-Darwinian language, the inevitable structural and cultural upheavals that make it possible to 'overcome' the values and institutions of traditional society, thanks to technology, the entrepreneurial spirit, and major investments (in railways and other infrastructure, for example) rising from 10 to 20 per cent of GNP.

(e) The fifth stage is 'the age of high mass-consumption' characterized by American Fordism. Here, productivity gains are distributed to the workers in order to raise consumption, and the Welfare State is put in place. It is the period that Europe and Japan were entering in the 1960s, and towards which the Soviet Union was striving.

Three problems arise from Rostow's marvellous fresco of humanity marching towards greater happiness. The first has to do with the nature of the historian's work, which, however many precautions are taken, is always a reinvention of the past. *Starting from a contemporary situation defined as 'modernity', there is a great temptation to identify certain values or behaviour as preconditions of modernization, and thus to mix up cause and effect.* For example, is individualism prior to the quest for maximum profit, or does the accumulation imperative shape egoistic behaviour? Does the entrepreneurial spirit precede industrialization, or does the prospect of industrial profits stir entrepreneurs into action? As the two aspects are in practice inextricably intertwined, it seems rash indeed to distinguish between what comes before and after, in the manner of Rostow.

Furthermore, by presenting modernization as a way of increasing the range of people's choices, *one always runs the risk of keeping only what is valued today and forgetting what has been lost in the process of modernization.*[21] Modern technology evidently makes it possible to increase the goods on the market, but it also does away with the old know-how. Similarly, the nation's wealth grows as a result of accumulation, but so do inequalities; industrialization creates new jobs but makes it harder to work creatively and to gain social recognition. At the extreme, consumers are 'free' to choose from a huge range of cars, but pollution puts them off walking down the road. It is not a question of systematically idealizing the past, but simply of recognizing that the 'gains of progress' also claim many casualties. *It is too facile to dismiss what has disappeared as being of no account.*

21. See Frédérique Apffel Marglin and Stephen A. Marglin, eds, *Dominating Knowledge: Development, Culture and Resistance*, Oxford: Clarendon Press, 1990.

Finally Rostow, like all evolutionists, is confronted with the problem of defining the 'final stage' – a task all the more difficult in that growth is supposed to have no limits. He begins by saying that it is 'impossible to predict' how things will work out, but then raises the question of what lies 'beyond consumption'.[22] Will it be boredom or 'spiritual stagnation'? Or will a continuation of high birth rates (as in America in the 1950s) bring a shift towards different values, which might eventually allow growth to be pursued? To be frank, Rostow does not give a definite answer; he merely raises a number of possible scenarios. Anyway, around the end of the fifties, everything turned on whether the Cold War and the arms race would lead to a major world conflict, or whether peace would come to be based upon arms control and a decision by nationalist movements to lead their countries, once mature, towards the age of mass consumption. The latter was clearly Rostow's way, and he prophesied that 'in its essence Communism is likely to wither in the age of high mass-consumption'.[23] Methodologically, this places a question mark over the whole of Rostow's construction, for it is hard to see why – if the general history of societies has unfolded so uniformly and (in retrospect) so predictably over the last few centuries – the present moment should suddenly be considered as a crossroads leading towards unknown destinations.[24] Why was it necessary for history to wait until the middle of the twentieth century before claiming back its rights? Rostow gives no explanation, but contents himself with the optimistic thought that – despite all the vicissitudes of history – the future should fall within the trajectory defined by the past.

ANTI-COMMUNISM OR MARXISM WITHOUT MARX?

Throughout the second part of his work, Rostow tries to show that the late-fifties situation of the USSR (which he always calls Russia) represents a kind of 'deviation' from the general theory of modernization. Having reached 'maturity', the USSR should 'logically' enter the age of mass consumption for which its people avidly long, but

---

22. *Stages of Economic Growth*, pp. 11–12.
23. Ibid., p. 133.
24. 'Historians are thus likely to recognize the existence of a watershed in the early 1950s.' Ibid., p. 121.

instead it is going astray in an effort to impose communism. This leads it to ruin itself by investing 20 per cent of GNP in the arms race, to maintain a police state, and to force upon its citizens an austerity akin to the pauperization that Marx forecast for workers in capitalist countries. This, for Rostow, is one of the consequences of 'the reactive nationalism which helped create modern Russia',[25] and which tends to show the 'un-Marxist character of Communism'.[26] Hence the importance, for the Western countries, of standing up to communism,[27] not only through military deterrence but also by persuading the USSR to give up its hegemonic ambitions and accept arms control. In the end: 'the Russians [must] accept that their only rational destiny is to join the great mature powers of the north in a common effort to ensure that the arrival at maturity of the south and of China will not wreck the world'.[28] Meanwhile, the threat should be parried through a rising standard of living for the peoples of the West and of the 'underdeveloped countries'.

Looking back some thirty-five years later, one cannot but recognize a certain foresight on Rostow's part – even if Russia's replacement of the USSR and return to the international arena have more to do with the defection of the East European countries than with the aspirations of the Russian people themselves. In any event, Rostow's primal anti-communism always carries with it an evolutionist premiss which makes him see a direct continuity from Marx to Lenin and from Lenin to Stalin – a continuity also repeatedly affirmed in the wooden language of Soviet Communism. Indeed, Rostow sets about the originator in order to strike down the self-styled heirs more effectively, without realizing that his own argument bears a curious resemblance to the one he is attacking.

To begin with, Rostow's 'anti-Marxism' rests upon a conviction that 'economic forces and motives are not a unique and overriding deter-

---

25. Ibid., p. 120.

26. Ibid., p. 162. This is not such a grave judgement, after all. Marx himself is reported by Engels as having said: 'All I know is that I am not a Marxist.' Engels to Conrad Schmidt, 5 August 1890, in Marx and Engels, *Selected Correspondence*, Moscow: Progress Publishers, 1975, p. 393.

27. 'And this effort is wholly justified: in my view it is not sufficiently large.' *Stages of Economic Growth*, p. 125. Rostow, who was born in 1916, became a White House adviser between 1961 and 1968, and played a considerable role, under President Nixon, in the American involvement in Vietnam. Subsequently he returned to being an economics professor, at the University of Texas in Austin.

28. Ibid., p. 134.

minant of the course of history';[29] that human motives are in reality much more complex. His argument here rests upon an oversimple reading of Marx. For unlike some of his successors, Marx never proclaimed 'economic determination of social life' in the last instance as some kind of dogma.[30] Rostow does, it is true, freely admit that his own theory resembles Marx's in focusing upon social change linked to economic change, and in setting 'genuine abundance' (defined according to productivist criteria) as the 'ultimate goal'. However, Rostow seems incapable of seeing that they also have a common evolutionist basis. He accuses Marx of illegitimately projecting the English situation into the future of other countries,[31] but he does not realize that he follows the same faulty procedure by anticipating that the sequence of changes which took place in today's industrial societies will also occur in the nations of the South. His 'end of history' is as idyllic as Marx's classless society (in which the State withers away and wealth is distributed by the principle 'to each according to their needs'). For 'the end of all this is not compound interest for ever; it is the adventure of seeing what man can and will do when the pressure of scarcity is substantially lifted from him'.[32] In this vast utopian prospect, society is like a child trying to leap over its own shadow. And when Rostow asserts that the sequence of 'these stages [has] an inner logic and continuity', and that they 'are rooted in a dynamic theory of production',[33] he speaks a language that the author of *Capital* would not have disowned.

Paradoxically, Rostow's theory of modernization appears as a kind of 'Marxism without Marx'. It is based upon a similar evolutionist view of history, and that, as we have seen, rests in turn upon the Western

---

29. Ibid., p. 121; see also pp. xi, 149.

30. Such a reading was denounced long ago by Engels: 'According to the materialist conception of history, the *ultimately* determining factor in history is the production and reproduction of real life. Neither Marx nor I have ever asserted more than this. Hence if somebody twists this into saying that the economic factor is the *only* determining one, he transforms that proposition into a meaningless, abstract, absurd phrase. The economic situation is the basis, but the various elements of the superstructure − ... especially the reflections of all these real struggles in the brains of the participants, political, legal, philosophical theories, religious views and their further development into systems of dogmas − also exercise their influence upon the course of the historical struggles and in many cases determine their *form* in particular' (Engels to Joseph Bloch, 21 September 1890, in *Selected Correspondence*, pp. 394−5).

31. *Stages of Economic Growth*, p. 157. Rostow adds that 'the British case of transition was unique in the sense that it appeared to have been brought about by the internal dynamics of a single society, without external intervention' (ibid.).

32. Ibid., p. 166.

33. Ibid., pp. 12−13.

myth of growth conceived according to a biological paradigm. *Blinded by their own presuppositions, both authors replace history with a philosophy of history, which prevents today's 'underdevelopment' from being understood as historical in origin.* And when Rostow revels in listing Marx's errors (for example, the theory that declining profits will lead to pauperization of the working class), he does not realize that his own 'predictions' about the 'take-off' of countries in the South are open to the same criticisms, and for the same reasons.[34]

For Rostow, each country is like any other. Despite his qualifications about Britain and the positive aspects of colonialism,[35] the 'natural' evolution of all countries – or, as Guy Kouassigan puts it, their 'way of the cross' – necessarily passes through the five-stage programme that Rostow has defined for them. This comes down to saying that *modernization is only a form of Westernization.*[36] But what is certain is that the so-called traditional societies have been subjected by the industrial societies to a massive demonstration effect, and that they are changing and have to change. It would be absurd to deny this, and no one does. But the change does not occur everywhere in the same direction, or at the same speed. While modernization gains ground here and there among certain ruling classes of certain countries, the phenomenon is far from general. There is, rather, a 'hybridization of development', which is accepted at the level of consumption products but ignored when it is supposed to spur an increase in production.[37] Whereas Rostow foresaw the worldwide substitution of modernity for tradition, what we see emerging today are a syncretism that produces societies quite unlike anything before, and whole peoples which, though certainly modernized, are not at all modern.

---

34. André Gunder Frank gives a remarkable summary of Rostow's 'errors' in his 'Sociology of Development and Underdevelopment of Sociology', part of an essay collection, *Latin America: Underdevelopment or Revolution*, New York: Monthly Review Press, 1969, pp. 39 ff. He shows, among other things, that for Rostow there is no stage prior to underdevelopment, and all today's 'developed' societies used to be 'underdeveloped' – which is contrary to the facts, and robs the societies of the South of their own history.

35. See Notes 16 and 31 above.

36. Compare Lévi-Strauss's remark that the Third World blames the industrial countries not for having Westernized it, but for not having given it the means to Westernize fast enough. 'Race et histoire' [1952], in *Le Racisme devant la science*, Paris: UNESCO, 1973, p. 31.

37. See Gilbert Rist, 'Des sphinx, des licornes et autres chimères… Trois approches des relations entre culture et "développement"', in G. Rist, ed., *La Culture, otage du développement?*, Paris: L'Harmattan, 1994, pp. 49–68.

The success of Rostow's book was thus due not to its originality but, on the contrary, to its roots in a tradition that assured for it a certain legitimacy. Far from renewing 'development theory', it established it within the continuity of Western intellectual history, from Aristotle to Marx via Fontenelle and Condorcet. Only in this light does Rostow's evolutionary schema become plausible – or rather, comforting, because it justified the dominant practices and made it seem likely that they would succeed. It is certainly no accident that *The Stages of Economic Growth* ended with a creed, for it was based upon *faith* that the age of mass consumption would spread throughout the world. This reassuring promise encouraged the Western world to continue its aid, not in the name of 'civilization' but in that of a more ancient belief in 'growth', symbolized by the ineffable virtue of compound interest that nothing could resist.

But Rostow's success was not limited to the 1960s. Whether one likes it or not, his conception of modernization has not ceased to nourish the hopes as well as the illusions of the rulers of both North and South.[38] The final goal has remained the same, and the means towards it (spread of technology, industrialization, exploitation of nature) have not changed. Every belief feeds on doubts. Today people are raising questions about the generalizability of the stages-of-growth model, the schedule keeps being pushed back, and its effects on the environment are a source of concern. But essentially everyone acts as if it were true – that is, as if it were desirable, possible and achievable. Any other view would endanger the dearly won consensus that makes it possible to soothe bad consciences and to justify the measures supposed to bring about the radiant future. Since, according to Rostow, sixty years or three generations are always needed for ways of thinking to change, we may have to wait until the year 2020 before his theory ceases to be seen as the pinnacle of the history common to earth's inhabitants.

---

38. A purely Rostowian style informs the Chinese *Resolution of the Central Committee of the CPC on the Guiding Principles for Building a Socialist Society with an Advanced Culture and Technology, 28 September 1986* (Beijing: Foreign Languages Press, 1986), drafted in the context of the so-called four modernizations policy. It states, for example: 'By the end of the century we should have brought the Chinese economy to a level of relative affluence, and around the middle of the next century to a level close to that of the developed countries in the world.' Or again: 'In today's world, science appears more and more as a revolutionary force working for historical progress, as an important criterion of a nation's degree of civilization.' [Translated from the French text (pp. v and vii), as several pages were missing from the misprinted English-language edition – *Trans. note*.] In many respects, the policies of countries that have emerged from the debris of the Soviet empire are still inspired by modernization theory.

DISSIDENT VOICES

The enormous popularity of *The Stages of Growth* should not make us overlook the existence of different perspectives, even if they have remained largely unrecognized. Here we can only briefly mention the work of two authors who, each in his way, have made a mark on the history of 'development'.

François Perroux

Founder of the Institut de Sciences Économiques Appliquées in 1943, professor at the Universities of Lyons and Paris and from 1955 at the Collège de France, François Perroux exerted a major influence on theories of 'development', especially in France.[39] We cannot here give a systematic account of his thought, which is anyway dispersed over a large number of books, articles and lectures none of which can be said to condense the whole of his work.[40] Nor is the task of summary made any easier by Perroux's expansive style of writing, which is closer to oratory (in which he excelled) than to methodical description of 'economic facts'. Nevertheless, his oeuvre reveals to us an original, if not really heterodox, thinker, who poses problems within a perspective unlike that of the dominant theoretical models.

In many ways, then, Perroux is impossible to classify. He criticizes classical and neo-classical (as well as marginalist) economics on the grounds that their mechanistic concept of equilibrium disregards the inequality between actors. He is also known for his masterly preface to the collection of Marx's economic writings edited by Maximilien Rubel. But this is by no means to say that he is a Marxist. In reality, he occupies a position between institutionalism, with its stress upon 'extra-economic factors',[41] and a personalist humanism that allows him to look beyond 'development' and to define growth as 'the combination of mental and social changes in a people that make it fit to increase its

---

39. Jean Weiller and Bruno Carrier, *L'Économie non conformiste en France du XXᵉ siècle*, Paris: PUF, 1994, pp. 85–128.

40. Here we shall focus on two books published in the early 1960s: a collection of articles entitled *L'Économie au XXᵉ siècle* [1961], Paris: PUF, 1964; and *L'Économie des jeunes nations: Industrialisation et groupements de nations*, Paris: PUF, 1962.

41. For example, he writes in his preface to Marx's work: 'Economic life today may be understood as the interaction of science, technology and industry.' 'Dialectiques et socialisation', in Karl Marx, *Oeuvres: Économie*, vol. 1, 1965, p. ix.

total real product, cumulatively and durably'.[42] Perroux is thus clearly in favour of growth, understood as full employment of all human and material resources both present and potential,[43] but only on condition that it is harmonious and leads to 'the development of the whole man within each man', to all-round socialization that allows everyone to flourish.[44] This high-minded vision helped to moralize the 'development debate', without really clarifying it. But it is not there that we should look for what is original in Perroux.

His main contribution is a method which always investigates the real economy, instead of trusting in abstract models whose assumptions obscure our vision. Thus, Perroux wants to see the creation of a world market as 'the exploitation of all the earth's human and material resources to satisfy the needs of all',[45] but he concentrates on the asymmetrical 'domination effects' resulting from the existence of big monopolies and powerful nations which lay down the law for the rest.[46] This explains his sharp condemnation – new at the time – of attempts to pursue colonialism beyond independence:

> Since the beginnings of modern industry, Western societies have been structures based upon domination.... As much as they could, they have denied workers and colonial peoples the right to speak, seeing them respectively as 'the dangerous classes' and 'infant peoples'. When the right to speak was conceded, it was so that everything could be discussed *except the essentials*.... Political rights and colonial parliaments were not originally meant to challenge colonialist domination. The granting of the right to speak is itself a means of struggle: it maintains the forms of inequality and domination bound up with the social order.[47]

There can indeed be no dialogue worthy of the name between 'real nations' and 'apparent nations'.

This focus on history and economic facts led Perroux to define the economies of the 'young nations' as disjointed, dominated, and incapable of meeting the 'human costs'.[48] Nations, in his view, often recede into

---

42. *L'Économie au XXe siècle*, p. 155. This humanism explains the links between Perroux and P. Lebret.

43. Ibid., pp. 163, 277.

44. 'Dialectiques et socialisation', p. xv.

45. *L'Économie au XXe siècle*, p. 281.

46. Although Perroux sometimes writes of 'centre' and 'periphery' (e.g. *L'Économie au XXe siècle*, p. 21), he does not try to impose these as new concepts, and prefers to use the terms 'home country' and 'affiliated country'. But his focus on domination effects makes him a forerunner of the Latin American *dependentistas*.

47. 'Dialectiques et socialisation', pp. xliii–xliv.

48. *L'Économie au XXe siècle*, pp. 156 f.

the background of economic spaces (not necessarily the same as political spaces) within which the 'big units' play a determining role and set up the fields of force. Beyond technical discussions about 'growth poles' or 'centres of progress', Perroux is concerned to challenge the simplistic idea of a 'nation' current in economic theory – that is, of a tightly knit unit within an international system, each of whose parts is at once autonomous and equal to all the others. We can see that questions are being asked here about the complexities of the real world, instead of abstract models being constructed through oversimplification.

Dudley Seers

Dudley Seers – who was director of the Institute for Development Studies at Sussex University – has left us one contribution whose importance is equalled only by the near-total obscurity in which it has been kept. In this little article first published in 1963, 'The Limitations of the Special Case',[49] Seers shows that the dominant economics taught in universities is based upon phenomena in today's 'developed' countries (the 'special case'), and that it is therefore generally inapplicable to the 'underdeveloped' countries (which are the 'general case'). What he disputes, then – on the basis of empirical-historical evidence – is the claim of economics to universal validity:

> A book is not called 'Principles of Astronomy' if it refers only to the earth or the solar system or even the local galaxy. We justifiably expect a lecture course on geology to deal with other continents besides the one on which the author happens to live, unless the title is duly qualified.[50]

When economists assert that certain 'principles' or 'laws' are valid everywhere and for everyone, they are engaging in a piece of deception, because it is illegitimate to deduce a 'general theory' from particular cases. This, no doubt, is why most economists come to grief when they talk about 'development'; they could be successful only if they 'unlearnt' what they have been taught.

Without going over Seers's demonstration, we can simply note that he lists the fundamental differences which exist in nearly every respect between the industrial nations and the rest. Factors of production, struc-

---

49. In *Bulletin of the Oxford Institute of Economics and Statistics*, 25 (2), May 1963, pp. 77–98; reprinted in Gerald Meier, *Leading Issues in Economic Development*, New York: Oxford University Press, 3rd edn, 1976, pp. 53–8.
50. Ibid., p. 54.

ture of the economy, public finances, foreign trade, household expenditure, structure of savings, investment capacity, population growth – all these differ radically from one group of countries to the next. It is therefore impossible to think that each will behave in the same way. Indeed, the various aggregates used by economists (labour force, full employment, savings) are themselves inadequate when they are applied to 'underdeveloped' countries, and what happens there is incomprehensible unless it is placed in the general context of the (commercial and financial) world economy, which has a much greater influence on them than on the industrial countries. The task, Seers concludes, is no less than *to reconstruct economics* – for which the slogan is: 'Economics is the study of Economies' (rather than of economic models).[51]

There could be no clearer rejection of academic theories in general (and Rostow in particular), as well as of the mass of advice coming from national and international 'experts' attached to the planning, agriculture and foreign-trade ministries in the countries of the South. Seers implies that it is necessary to found a new discipline, which he might perhaps have called 'development economics', but which would actually have been more of an economics of the non-industrialized or dominated countries. Having much in common with economic anthropology, its aim would not have been to keep the South in a state of blissful poverty but, rather, to tackle the special problems posed by the entry of 'traditional' societies into an international system with quite different rules. This idea was fraught with theoretical implications, the most important of which was that economics would become a 'local' discipline, not a 'science' with universal pretensions. Or – which comes to the same thing – there was to be a 'general economics' within which the industrial countries formed a 'special case' or 'atypical area', where particular rules applied. In both cases, the aim was to do justice to the diversity of historical situations (*vis-à-vis* the international system) and of autochthonous practices. Clearly Seers failed to recognize the force – or the symbolic violence – exerted by the dominant paradigm, which henceforth limited the autonomy of development economics and forced it to work within the neo-classical or Keynesian traditions.[52]

---

51. Ibid., p. 58.
52. If I may add a personal note here, I remember that around this time I told a professor with an international reputation that I was interested in the economics of 'developing countries'. He looked at me with commiseration and said he did not understand what I was talking about. In his view, every country in the world – including my own – was 'developing'.

At most, it could be allowed some interest in those strange phenomena with the generic title 'development co-operation' which do not come under the province of the market (or under autochthonous practices of exchange, for that matter).

Seers's critique, then, questioned too much to be heard. To protect its credibility, the corporation of economists preferred silence to debate, oblivion to controversy. But the problem had been posed, and in many respects it continues to be posed thirty years later. For there are still very few economists who are really aware of the limits to their 'science' stemming from its Western origins.

CHAPTER 7

THE PERIPHERY AND THE UNDERSTANDING OF HISTORY

The seductiveness of modernization theory has been explained in two ways. For the countries of the North, it justified the continuation of existing policies that emphasized domestic growth and foreign aid as ways of countering communist designs. For the countries of the South, it entrusted the promise of a better future to the new ruling classes that were accumulating tokens of Westernization as they lined their own pockets.

The counteroffensive was organized from two ends – by North American Marxists or neo-Marxists, and by Latin American intellectuals. The latter soon concluded from their own observation that the international system, far from guaranteeing the South's prosperity, brought domination effects to bear upon it and locked it in dependence. Before presenting their argument more precisely, we should make three remarks.

1. The 'dependency school', as we shall call it, was a loosely defined grouping of intellectuals from various disciplines who shared a common sensibility. It had clear roots in the United States (Paul Baran and Paul Sweezy), in Chile (the United Nations Economic Commission for Latin America, or CEPAL, headed by Raúl Prebisch, as well as Osvaldo Sunkel), in Brazil (Fernando Cardoso, Enzo Faletto and Celso Furtado), in Colombia (Orlando Fals Borda), and in Mexico (Rodolfo Stavenhagen). Later it opened out to include researchers from other continents: for example, Samir Amin in Africa, André Gunder Frank, Pierre Jalée, Dieter Senghaas and Johan Galtung in Europe – all strong personalities who never came together behind a leader or spokesperson.[1]

2. While Rostow's theory permeated the North American and international establishment and was reflected in the practice of international relations, the arguments of the dependency school were gradually adopted by everyone opposed to US policy, and by what are known as 'Third Worldists'. The movement – if that is the right word – had a characteristic sympathy for the Cuban Revolution, Fidel Castro and Che Guevara, and for Third World liberation struggles in general. All those associated with it had a similar critique of the activity of transnational companies, and denounced in similar terms the US intervention in Vietnam. There was also a particular attraction to the Chinese Cultural Revolution, which appeared to symbolize the revenge of the masses over a corrupt bureaucracy. Despite the popular appeal of the dependency school, however, scarcely any concrete policies were inspired by it (the two very special cases being Cuba, and Chile from 1970 to 1973, under Salvador Allende). The heaviness of reality called for the challenge of ideas.

3. *The main propositions of the* dependentistas *can often be counterposed point by point to Rostow's theory.* Whereas he based himself on a philosophy of history, they focused on the study of real history made by men and women in definite social circumstances; whereas he treated countries as relatively autonomous entities, they approached them within the global structure of international relations; whereas he gave a favourable account of colonialism as the occasion of an 'awakening' to modernity, they saw it as synonymous with things falling apart; whereas he considered that internal inequalities played a positive role by

---

1. The literature has taken on sizeable proportions, and we can do no more than give a very limited selection: Paul A. Baran and Paul M. Sweezy, *Monopoly Capital: An Essay on the American Economic and Social Order* [1966], Harmondsworth: Pelican, 1968; Fernando Henrique Cardoso and Enzo Faletto, *Dependency and Development in Latin America* [1969], Berkeley: University of California Press, 1973; Fernando Henrique Cardoso, *As idéias e seu lugar, ensaios sobre as teorias do desenvolvimento*, Petrópolis: Vozes, 1980 – quoted and translated here from the French edition, *Les idées à leur place*, Paris: PUF, 1984; Samir Amin, *Unequal Development: An Essay on the Social Formations of Peripheral Capitalism* [1973], Hassocks: Harvester Press, 1976; Samir Amin, *Imperialism and Unequal Development* [1976], Hassocks: Harvester Press, 1977; Samir Amin, *Accumulation on a World Scale: A Critique of the Theory of Underdevelopment* [1970], Hassocks: Harvester Press, 1974; Orlando Fals-Borda, *Ciencia propia y colonialismo intelectual*, Bogotá: Editorial Oveja Negra, 1971; Rodolfo Stavenhagen, *Las clases sociales en las sociedades agrarias*, 7th edn, Mexico City: Siglo XXI, 1975, and Stavenhagen, ed., *Agrarian Problems and Peasant Movements in Latin America*, Garden City, NY: Doubleday & Co., 1970; Arghiri Emmanuel, *Unequal Exchange: A Study of the Imperialism of Trade* [1969], London: New Left Books, 1972; Pierre Jalée, *The Pillage of the Third World* [1967], New York: Monthly Review Press, 1967; André Gunder Frank, *Latin America: Underdevelopment or Revolution*.

encouraging competition that would eventually balance things out, they saw them as the root of the whole problem and demanded corrective intervention by the State. Finally, for Rostow 'development' implied strategies of association (progressive inclusion of the 'young' economies in the world market), while for the dependency school it required dissociation from the structure of exploitation. In this seesaw conflict, each side counterbalanced the other. And it is this which explains why the antithesis was less perfect than it might first appear.

NEO-MARXISM IN THE UNITED STATES

Marx himself had taken only a moderate interest in colonialism, except on the occasions when he was writing articles for the *New York Daily Tribune*. But the theories of imperialism of Lenin[2] and Rosa Luxemburg were an important legacy for neo-Marxist writers, which alerted them to the importance of monopolies or – as we say today – of trans-national companies.

In 1966 Baran and Sweezy published their *Monopoly Capital*, a work designed to explain the economic evolution of the United States from 1900 to 1960, using a huge amount of historical material and placing it within its international context.[3] The twentieth century was, in their view, characterized by the progressive establishment of North American hegemony in place of the European colonial empires. In the shadow of US power, competitive capitalism gave way to monopoly capitalism, in which, as Lenin had predicted, industrial capital was intertwined with finance capital and concentration created giant corporations that were able to control the market. These corporations could prevent prices from falling in line with the major productivity increases, and were thus able to build up a massive surplus.[4] The main problem then became how to absorb this surplus: for monopoly capitalism is incapable of generating sufficient effective demand to assure the full employment of

---

2. 'Imperialism, the Highest Stage of Capitalism' [1917], in Lenin, *Selected Works*, vol. 1, London: Lawrence & Wishart, 1947, pp. 630–725.

3. In fact Baran died on 26 March 1964, but Sweezy tells us that by then the contents of the book had already been comprehensively discussed and partly drafted. Much of their research was also published in various issues of *Monthly Review*.

4. For Baran and Sweezy, rates of profit have a tendency to decline in competitive capitalism because firms are under pressure to lower prices, but in monopoly capital-ism rates of profit tend to rise because firms are able to fix prices, so that a large part of the surplus (corresponding to Marx's surplus-value) is absorbed by the state.

labour and capital;[5] and left to itself, the system would sink into stagnation, producing in an ever less profitable manner goods that give off
ever greater profit. As neither consumption nor investment is enough
to stimulate demand,[6] recourse must be had to other means: advertising
and the 'sales effort' in general, all the more necessary because an en-
trepreneur in a situation of monopoly does not think of lowering his
prices to boost demand; or state subsidies (e.g. the building of motorways to support the car industry, or the raising of transfer payments in
such forms as unemployment benefit). For Baran and Sweezy, however,
all these things together cannot prevent the system from collapsing
beneath the weight of its own contradictions. There remains the state
development of the military–industrial sector:

> If one assumes the permanence of monopoly capitalism, with its proved in-
> capacity to make rational use for peaceful and humane ends of its enormous
> productive potential, one must decide whether one prefers the mass unem-
> ployment and hopelessness characteristic of the Great Depression or the rela-
> tive job security and material well-being provided by the huge military budgets
> of the 1940s and 1950s.[7]

This military expenditure, ideologically justified by the Cold War, makes
it possible both to keep the system alive and to combat all those seeking the victory of socialism. But in the long run, the efforts are in
vain:

> For the threat to the [US] empire comes from revolutionary movements
> which … are sparked by a deep-seated yearning for national independence
> and fuelled by an increasingly urgent need for economic development,
> […which can] be achieved … only if their nationalist revolutions are also
> socialist revolutions.[8]

Thus, although *Monopoly Capital* is largely devoted to a description
– and denunciation – of the irrationality of the North American capitalist system, it ends by expressing a hope for *world revolution* as the
'drama of our time', with the countries of the South occupying a
similar position to that of the proletariat in Marx's writings.[9]

---

5. *Monopoly Capital*, pp. 87 ff., 115, etc.
6. Indeed, foreign investment adds to the surplus (pp. 110 f.).
7. Ibid., p. 208.
8. Ibid., pp. 204–5.
9. The subtitle, 'An Essay on the American Economic and Social Order', is clear
enough – but the book is dedicated 'For Che'.

The highest form of resistance is revolutionary war aimed at withdrawal from the world capitalist system and the initiation of social and economic reconstruction on a socialist basis.... It is no longer mere rhetoric to speak of the world revolution: the term describes what is already a reality and is certain to become increasingly the dominant characteristic of the historical epoch in which we live.[10]

The question we must ask ourselves is not whether Baran and Sweezy were wrong, or whether the current hegemony of capitalism is no more than an episode in history. Published at the height of the challenge to consumer society and the Vietnam War, their book offered an interpretation of North–South relations that was highly influential for two main reasons. First, it gave the dominated countries a role as subjects or actors in the course of history. And second, it argued that the only way of achieving genuine 'development' was to leave the system rather than to seek integration within it.[11]

THE LATIN AMERICAN *DEPENDENTISTAS*[12]

The origins of the Latin American movement lay in the UN Economic Commission for Latin America, which was founded in the 1950s in Santiago de Chile to promote 'development' in the region, and was headed by an Argentinian, Raúl Prebisch, later to become (in 1964) the first secretary-general of UNCTAD. The prevailing doctrine at the time (which has hardly changed since) based the 'development' of the non-industrial countries upon three pillars: massive transfers of (mainly private) capital, exports of raw materials, and the comparative advantage supposed to benefit all market traders.[13]

---

10. Ibid., p. 351.
11. Ibid., p. 25.
12. This section owes much to Fernando H. Cardoso's illuminating work *Les idées à leur place*.
13. The theory of comparative advantage should be briefly described here, because in the form of the 'Heckscher, Ohlin, Samuelson theorem' it continues to play a decisive role in justifying the inclusion of dominated countries in the system of world trade. The so-called 'law' of comparative advantage, first formulated by David Ricardo, states that each country can gain by exchange if the relative prices of the products put on the market differ from one country to another. (*The Principles of Political Economy and Taxation* [1817], London: J.M. Dent & Sons, 1978.) In a famous example (pp. 82–7), he defines as follows the relative price of two goods (wine and cloth) produced by Portugal and England.

[*note 13 contd.*]

	Portugal	England
cost in hours of labour per unit of wine	80	120
cost in hours of labour per unit of cloth	90	100

The first point is that Portugal has an *absolute advantage* in the production of both goods, because it produces them more cheaply than England does. But the *relative costs* are not the same. Thus in Portugal the relative cost of wine expressed in cloth is 80/90 or 0.88 – which means that one unit of wine procures only 0.88 of a unit of cloth. In England, on the other hand, the relative cost of wine in cloth is 120/100 or 1.2 – which means that one unit of wine procures 1.2 units of cloth. Ricardo concludes that free trade is of advantage to both countries. Portugal gains more from wine production because it produces a unit of wine in 80 hours as against England's 120 hours – that is, in 66 per cent of the time – whereas it takes 90 hours to produce a unit of cloth against England's 100 hours – that is, in 90 per cent of the time. The situation is the reverse for England, which is at *less of a disadvantage* in producing cloth (100 hours against 90, or a rate of 111 per cent) rather than wine (120 hours against 80 hours, or a rate of 150 per cent). Consequently, in order to gain by the exchange, each will specialize in the area more beneficial to it – that is to say, it will reallocate to production of the good in which it is more competitive the hours of labour given over to the other good. Then in Portugal the 90 hours formerly devoted to cloth production will create 1.125 extra units of wine, while in England the 120 hours formerly devoted to viticulture will create 1.2 extra units of cloth. In other words, before specialization, the production of 2 units of wine and 2 units of cloth required 170 hours in Portugal and 220 in England, or a total of 390 hours. Now the same work can be done in 360 hours (160 in Portugal and 200 in England). For each to gain by this, the 'international exchange relationship' must lie somewhere between the two relative costs in a situation of isolation: that is, >0.88 for Portugal and <1.2 for England. If it were to be exactly 1, Portugal would sell to England 100 units of wine that had cost it 8,000 hours of labour, in exchange for 100 units of cloth that would in isolation have cost it 9,000 hours. England, for its part, would sell 100 units of cloth that had cost it 10,000 hours, in exchange for 100 units of wine that it could have produced in isolation for 12,000 hours.

The mathematical reasoning cannot be faulted, but it assumes a number of hypothetical facts which rarely occur in reality. Here are just the main ones: (1) Each country is capable of producing both goods in isolation. (2) In calculating the cost of the products, only the cost of labour – excluding capital and technology – is taken into consideration. (3) The production costs are constant, remaining unaffected by economies of scale or changes in technology. (4) The goods in question can be reproduced *ad infinitum* without constituting stocks. (5) The factors of production are immobile: workers do not emigrate, nor does capital. (6) The workforce is homogeneous: every wine-grower in one country can become a clothmaker, and vice versa, earning the same wage in both sectors. (7) Wage rates are the same in the two countries. (8) Specialization is total. (9) No allowance is made for the elasticity of demand (would the English want as much wine and the Portuguese as much cloth as the other could produce?). (10) The economic actors have perfect information. (11) No customs duties are levied on either product. (12) Currency exchange rates are fixed. (13) There is full employment in both countries. It is enough to apply these points to the exchange of bananas for computers, or oil for weapons, to appreciate the gulf between theory and the concrete conditions in which it is applied.

CEPAL studies revealed discrepancies between these principles and concrete situations in history. Thus free trade (and the theory of comparative advantage) was favourable to the industrial economies because the difference between their structure and that of the dominated economies led to *unequal exchange*, and in addition the terms of trade worsened over time for the countries of the South. This set of characteristics allowed one to define relations between the two according to the model of *centre and periphery*.[14] And a number of conclusions followed from this: that the periphery should not specialize as a raw materials producer but develop forms of import-substitutionist industry, even if this meant appealing to foreign capital; that attempts should be made to build a regional economic grouping; and that the State should play a role in the prevention of inequalities, especially by carrying out land reform and ensuring a better distribution of investment.[15]

Innocuous though they may seem, these proposals triggered a two-fold reaction. The Right could not tolerate the 'politicization' of economics, the attacks on free trade, or the redefinition of the role of the State – all of which smacked of a kind of covert socialism.[16] But the Left was just as severe in its criticism, arguing that CEPAL was interested only in capital accumulation and not in the class relations that

---

14. This critique of international trade was also put forward by Gunnar Myrdal in 1956: 'If left to take its own course, economic development is a process of circular and cumulative causation which tends to award its favours to those who are already well endowed and even to thwart the efforts of those who happen to live in regions which are lagging behind.' *Development and Underdevelopment*, Cairo: National Bank of Egypt, 1956, p. 10; quoted in Gerald M. Meier, 'From Colonial Economies to Development Economics', in G.M. Meier, ed., *From Classical Economics to Development Economics*, New York: Saint Martin's Press, 1994, p. 178.

15. On the whole, there was nothing very new in these measures, which took their inspiration from the German Historical School (Friedrich List). A strategy of import-substitutionist industrialization (*desarrollismo*) had been widely pursued in Latin America in the 1950s. It corresponded to Nurske's theory of balanced growth, or Rosenstein-Rodan's 'big push', both of which advocated State-led multi-sector industrialization until a critical threshold was reached. These various measures were the focus of *dependentista* critiques, on the grounds that they played into the hands of the national bourgeoisies.

16. The opposition was especially strong in the United States, where the CEPAL had been an object of suspicion ever since it was created in 1948. Still, the Alliance for Progress, launched by Kennedy in 1960, put forward many proposals that were in line with CEPAL thinking, including the idea of 'development' based upon industrialization rather than exports of primary products.

were its underpinning. This was the real point of departure for the theses of the *dependentistas*.[17]

It should be stressed at this point that – contrary to a mechanistic view of the dependency school that is quite widespread – it did not mainly set out to denounce some manipulation of the peripheral national bourgeoisies by an imperialist centre symbolized by the transnational corporations. Its primary concern, rather, was to study historical phenomena within the Latin American countries themselves, in order to explain their relationship to the international capitalist system.[18] As Cardoso put it: 'the concept was born impure in the midst of a concrete struggle'.

Of course, the economic dependence of the peripheral countries upon the capitalist heartlands was a postulate shared by all those at issue here (including the CEPAL researchers), but the *dependentistas* proper were further interested in what this general phenomenon implied for the social structure.[19] By analysing the relationship between 'development' and 'underdevelopment' within a historical–structural perspective,[20] they thought they could show that foreign domination was passed on in internal domination, and that the classes (or class alliances) in power changed according to the internal structure of the economy (an enclave economy dominated by foreign capital, or national economy dominated now by *latifundistas* and agrarian exporters, now by the industrial bourgeoisie, etc.). As for the State, it played the role of arbiter among these various classes. A balance could be maintained up to the moment when a populist government dared to carry out a land reform that destabilized the *latifundistas* and triggered moves towards a military putsch. Moreover, 'associated dependent industrialization' caused the economy to be

---

17. Rather schematically, one could say that the *dependentistas* were mostly sociologists, whereas the CEPAL people were economists. The Chilean Faletto, for his part, was a historian.

18. It was chiefly Third Worldists within the industrial countries who practised a 'ceremonial consummation' of dependency theory (Cardoso), by amalgamating the work of the *dependentistas*, the conclusions of Baran and Sweezy's book regarding the 'messianic role' of the periphery, and Frank's idea that 'development' creates 'underdevelopment'.

19. 'We conceive the relationship between external and internal forces as forming a complex whole whose structural links are not based on mere external forms of exploitation and coercion, but are rooted in coincidences of interests between local dominant classes and international ones, and, on the other side, are challenged by local dominated groups and classes' (Cardoso and Faletto, p. xvi).

20. Structure is a matter of social regularities and social relations, history of the processes or changes that take place within specific social conditions.

penetrated by finance capitalism and metropolitian technology (inter-nationalization of the domestic market), which led to structural eco-nomic distortions and growing social inequality, as well as preventing the accumulation necessary for 'development'.[21] This forced the State to maintain social cohesion – including through a military takeover – and transformed it into 'a pivot of development based upon social exclusion, the concentration of incomes, and satisfaction of the needs of the well-off layers of the population'.[22]

Within this framework of analysis, some authors laid the stress on internal factors, others on external factors including unequal exchange;[23] some paid special attention to sectoral or regional disparities, others to problems connected with social classes. At times it was argued that the existing situation prevented all 'development' (Frank); at others that 'dependent development' was compatible with the foreign domination imposed by the international division of labour (Cardoso). These theo-retical differences were not exactly slight, and they were the stuff of debate until the end of the seventies. In the end, the question was whether it was possible to escape this carefully analysed state of dependence – and if so, how. Cardoso eventually became extremely critical of the dependency school that he himself had helped to found. He accepted, of course, that all the *dependentistas* claimed the inspiration of a 'socialist alternative', but

---

21. Either the national bourgeoisies invest in sectors of production that do not benefit the whole population, or they transfer their profits abroad, or the profits made by foreign companies are repatriated to the centre. In addition, there is the indebtedness linked to purchases of technology (control of surplus-value through innovation) and of sophisticated equipment.

22. Cardoso, *Les idées à leur place*, pp. 175–7.

23. The concept of unequal exchange ultimately refers to the difference in labour-power remuneration between the centre and the periphery, which leads to a worsening of the terms of trade. The periphery, so the argument goes, must pay more and more for what it gets in the centre, where there are regular wage increases. It is difficult, however, to demonstrate a cause-and-effect relationship between impoverishment in the periphery and enrichment in the centre. For it has not been during periods of greatest pillage (from the conquest of the Americas to colonialism) that the centre has most increased its wealth in comparison with the periphery.

The concept of 'unequal' exchange also presupposes one of 'equal' exchange defining the hypothetical price that would be formed if factor remuneration were the same everywhere in the world – which is hardly a possibility. Finally, it is not necessarily the countries most closely associated with international trade (even the peripheral ones) which are the least 'developed'. On the critique of this concept, see Serge Latouche, *Faut-il refuser le développement?*, Paris: PUF, 1987, p. 137; and *Critique de l'impérialisme*, Paris: Anthropos, 1979. (It should be noted that for Marx, of course, the capitalist exploits the labour force by offering wages which only cover its costs of reproduction.)

their political analysis of dependence becomes virtually devoid of reality, taking a kind of eschatological refuge in affirmations of the principle of Revolution without managing to light up the way towards it. The weakness of their propositions conceals itself behind the catastrophist picture of a situation for which there can be only a radical way out, even though the class or classes that might deal a final blow to the existing order are never really delineated.[24]

A NEW PARADIGM, BUT AGE-OLD PRESUPPOSITIONS

If a paradigm may be defined as a set of hypotheses which for a time provide a research community with typical problems and solutions that can be applied to different situations, then the dependency school produced a perfect paradigm. *Beyond individual variations were a body of concepts and a common theoretical perspective which posed a radical challenge to the other dominant paradigm: that of modernization.* Thanks to the dependency school, 'development' and 'underdevelopment' could be conceived in such a way as to replace the naturalness of stages of growth with a historical view of changes in the periphery that located them within the world capitalist system.

By arguing in terms of *international structure* (instead of individual national destiny), the *dependentistas* brought to light the national and international mechanisms for the appropriation of surplus by the central economies, and demonstrated that the accumulation regime in the old industrial countries could not be reproduced in the periphery. The peripheral countries were not doomed to export raw materials; they could themselves 'develop' in the Rostowian sense – that is, industrialize and, to some extent, modernize. But this 'associated dependent development'[25] could not benefit the whole population, for reasons that had to do as much with the internal political structure as with external domination. Such arguments greatly helped to reinsert the economic into the social-political order, so that it was no longer treated as an independent variable.

But although dependency theory made a major contribution to 'development' thinking, it presented a number of problems and led to a number of misunderstandings.

(a) Immoderate use of the term 'dependence' often gave rise to oversimplification by suggesting that the 'development' of the centre

---

24. Cardoso, p. 179.
25. This corresponds to what was known as 'industrial redeployment' in the 1970s.

was based entirely upon 'underdevelopment' of the periphery.[26] Relations of domination were thus conceived according to the model of blood transfusion or communicating vessels, so that the centre became a huge Ali Baba's cave continually replenished by thieves and swindlers bleeding the periphery dry.[27] Now, it is true that exchange between the two is unequal – one major reason for this being that labour is much less mobile than capital (which can be invested more or less freely anywhere). It is also true that some of the profits made in the periphery are repatriated to the centre. But this does not mean that the prosperity of the centre can be wholly attributed to exploitation of the periphery[28] – for the world capitalist system does not function everywhere in the same manner. Thus imperialism – supposedly made necessary by the outlets crisis – has turned out not to be a necessity at all. During the period from the end of the Second World War to the middle of the 1960s, the economic growth of the industrial countries owed very little to international trade (which anyway took place mainly between industrial countries); rather, it was based upon the Fordist mode of regulation, which permitted growth of the domestic market thanks to redistribution of productivity gains to the workers.[29]

(b) The degree of a country's (or a group of countries') external dependence is, in the end, rather difficult to identify. If we exclude very large nations such as the United States, which can theoretically be self-sufficient, the 'independent' or 'non-dependent' countries are few

---

26. Similarly, colonization had once been considered the main cause of the enrichment of the metropolis. Western ethnocentrism is thus present not only in modernization theory but also in versions of dependency theory that make the centre totally responsible for the process of 'development'/'underdevelopment', and convert the peripheral countries into passive victims of the expanding capitalist system.

27. See Latouche, *Faut-il refuser le développement?*, pp. 140–59.

28. A CEDETIM study (*L'Impérialisme français*, Paris: Maspero, 1976, pp. 72–5) quoted by Latouche (*Faut-il refuser*, p. 146) estimates that 4 per cent of the remuneration of France's productive capacity can be attributed to the surplus coming from the periphery. Alain Lipietz (*Mirages et miracles*) similarly puts at 4 per cent of GDP the amount that France 'draws' from the Third World.

29. In order to function properly, Fordism must be able to rely upon the generalization of wage-labour, a highly organized workforce in a position to impose collective agreements and a minimum wage, effective social protection, and so on. These conditions are not present in the South. Besides, wage-labourers form a relatively small part of the total population there, so that any increase in their purchasing power cannot significantly boost total demand – especially as wage income is spread among a large number of dependants. The history of capitalism is thus one of *decreasing* importance of foreign trade. (See Lipietz, p. 53.) It should be noted, however, that the phenomenon of globalization is now tending to assign an important role to foreign trade.

and far between. Most of them – beginning with the European countries – import technology, generally need to export or import, and imitate American consumption models, but they are not, for all that, 'underdeveloped'. Conversely, if it is maintained that the countries of the centre can enrich themselves only by drawing on the periphery, it must by the same token be admitted that they are dependent upon those they exploit. In the end, we can probably say that all today's 'developed' countries (with the exception of Britain?) were themselves once dependent. Some of the contradictions denounced by *dependentistas* have always existed, and – like it or not – are part of the 'normal' functioning of international trade.

(c) As Cardoso has noted, the *dependentistas* hardly offered any solution to the problem they posed – as if waiting for the revolutionary explosion were the first 'move' in any process of reflection. Nor were their political slogans at all clear, even if each Latin American country tried out one or another form of 'revolutionary' movement – from Che's Bolivian *maquis* through Camilo Torres and the Tupamaros to the election of Allende in Chile. The Marxist option certainly entailed a rejection of capitalism, but it did not succeed in identifying the forces that might be the bearer of a different model of society.

(d) The *dependentistas* 'are content to propose the same type of development for the benefit of *other classes*'.[30] And what if that really was the issue? No doubt the dependency school steeped itself in history and refused to think of 'underdevelopment' as a natural state: if the periphery was incapable of securing its material well-being, this was owing to historical circumstances bound up with colonialism and the effects of central capitalist domination. But the only conclusion they drew was that 'development' had been 'blocked', and that the periphery should have followed (or should now follow) its 'natural' course, were it not obstructed from doing so. We find here again the old idea of the natural goodness of nature, led astray by human turpitude and 'interference'. For reason to triumph in society, it is necessary either to 'free market forces' or to purify the system of injustice, inequality or private property. Either way, the principle is the same: to clean up a basically good system so that it can at last follow its 'natural bent'. Evil is only a form of deviance from a 'normal' path.

If one follows dependency theories, then, *one may know the origins of 'underdevelopment' but not much about 'development' itself*. And one is still in the dark about the radically new departure that ought to occur if

---

30. Cardoso, p. 180.

the 'obstacles to development', whether structural or historical, were removed. As we said at the beginning of this chapter, the dependency school opposes modernization theory point by point – so much so that one wonders whether the counterposition of centre and periphery is not just another variant of the dichotomy of tradition and modernity. By saying yes to capitalism and no to development,[31] the *dependentistas* shed greater light upon the mechanisms of underdevelopment and its links with class interests and the international system as a whole. On the other hand, they did not challenge the basic presuppositions of that system, which come down to the idea that growth is necessary to gain access to the Western mode of consumption. *Is not the final aim to modernize, to industrialize, and to capture foreign markets?* And to that end, are 'anti-capitalist' strategies not compelled to promote such bourgeois values as economic rationality, efficiency, utility, and hard work? Indeed, could things be otherwise once the theory was so deeply rooted in Marxism? It has often been pointed out that while Marx proposed a remarkable *internal critique* of the Western system, he did not succeed in making a critique *of* the Western system. 'Development of the productive forces' was the common objective of capitalism and socialism, even if, as Cardoso stressed, the benefits were not distributed to the same classes. This, no doubt, is why the dependency school did not consider the cultural aspects of 'development',[32] or the possibility of models resting upon different foundations, or the ecological consequences of treating industrialization as necessary to collective well-being.

According to one of its best-known representatives, dependency theory did not survive the crisis of the capitalist system that became apparent in the mid-seventies:

> The Achilles heel of these conceptions of development has always been the implicit, and sometimes explicit, notion of some sort of 'independent' alternative for the Third World. The theoretical alternative never existed, in fact – certainly not in the noncapitalist path and now apparently not even through so-called socialist revolutions. The new crisis of real world development now renders such partial development and parochial dependence theories and policy solutions invalid and inapplicable.[33]

---

31. Ibid.

32. Except, that is, to denounce 'cultural dependence' upon modes of thought and consumption imported from the centre.

33. André Gunder Frank, *Reflections on the World Economic Crisis*, New York: Monthly Review Press, 1981, p. 127; quoted in Björn Hettne, *Development Theory and*

The judgement is harsh, but it is on the mark. This is not to say that no alternative is possible; there are two reasons why one may be. First, theories resting upon a single paradigm – whether it be modernization or dependency – should be treated with suspicion. Second, the world is evolving: the international division of labour, international capitalism and the problems held to be urgent change in the course of time. All the countries of the periphery are not in the same position *vis-à-vis* the centre, and the centre itself has to adapt to new conditions. This was the case in the mid-seventies, for example, when a recession resulted from oil price rises and the stagnation of demand for goods that had long stimulated growth (cars, household appliances). To maintain its rate of profit – and to avoid a wage cut for the workforce still employed – the capitalist centre sought to relocate production in low-wage countries with an authoritarian regime, especially in Southern Europe and South-East Asia. This permitted the emergence of new industrial countries.[34]

Those who belonged to the nebula of the dependency school when they were criticizing modernization theory have learnt that history does not conform to the abstractions of theory, or to stereotyped schemas. But nor is there an evil genie who organizes the system, loading the dice and making sure the same people win all the time. There are only various actors who use the system opportunistically according to the changing situation. This is why it is always possible, in the interstices of historical constraints, to invent different ways of conceptualizing the present.

---

the Third World, Helsingborg: SAREC, 1992, p. 53. The best recent proof of the end of the dependency paradigm is Cardoso's election as President of Brazil in 1994, having practically abandoned his old theories.

34. If the costs of industrial relocation or redeployment were analysed in terms of jobs gained or lost, it would become clear that this time 'unequal exchange' penalized the workers of the centre.

8

SELF-RELIANCE:
THE COMMUNAL PAST
AS A MODEL FOR
THE FUTURE

Towards the end of the 1960s, debate was raging between modernizers and *dependentistas*, independence was raising people's hopes in a whole series of countries, new agencies had been created and new measures taken within the framework of the first Development Decade. Yet for most countries of the South there were still hardly any signs of improvement.

It was at this difficult time that the Tanzanian President, Julius Nyerere, decided to tackle the problem of 'underdevelopment' by urging his fellow-citizens to rely upon their own forces. The Arusha Declaration – which spelt out this new way of escaping poverty – was adopted by the Tanganyika African National Union (TANU) on 5 February 1967. Suddenly the concept of self-reliance (or autonomy, or 'autocentred development') entered the vocabulary of 'development'.[1]

Opinions are divided about the precise origins of the concept. The list of countries that had charted a course of their own obviously included Cuba, isolated since 1960 by the US blockade, and Guinea-Conakry, where Sékou Touré had refused to join the French Community in 1958. But these two countries, though prevented from being

---

1. The Arusha Declaration was published in a selection of Nyerere's writings, *Freedom and Socialism*, Dar Es Salaam: Oxford University Press, 1968, pp. 231–50, as well as in Johan Galtung, Peter O'Brien and Roy Preiswerk, eds, *Self-Reliance, A Strategy for Development*, Geneva: IUED, and London: Bogle-L'Ouverture Publications, 1980, pp. 387–400. The latter work contains a number of contributions that afford a clearer grasp of the notion of 'self-reliance', including the Cocoyoc Declaration, which was drafted by a group of intellectuals (among whom Samir Amin, Marc Nerfin and Johan Galtung played a key role) for a joint UNEP–UNCTAD seminar held in Mexico City between 8 and 12 October 1974.

part of the international system, did not really set themselves the goal of 'autocentred development' and survived largely by counting on the support of the Soviet Union.[2]

The trail leading to Gandhi is more sure.[3] For he advocated village self-sufficiency on the basis of the principles of *swadeshi* (interiority or endogenousness) and *sarvodaya* (improving everyone's living conditions). The whole of Gandhian thought is built upon a form of non-exploitative 'moral economics' in which everyone works for the common good without seeking to accumulate any more than they need. From individual to nation (through family, village, region, etc.), each level is supposed to obtain what it needs in a self-supporting manner – but if necessary, it can have recourse to the level above it (by way of concentric circles) in order to acquire what it cannot produce itself.[4] In this system, industry is tolerated if it is publicly owned and does not reduce the number of job possibilities; bureaucracy must be kept to a strict minimum, as it always threatens to impose its own way of seeing things and to brush aside initiatives from the grass roots; and international trade should be reserved for indispensable goods that cannot be produced within the national framework. In short, the lower levels should be given as much power as possible, to ensure that they are not subject to domination. It is a populist strategy which – as everyone knows – was never put into practice, because independent India immediately embarked upon a quite different course.

Other writers, such as Roland Berger, trace the idea of collective well-being through self-reliance back to Mao Tse-tung's use in 1945 of the expression *tzu li keng sheng*. Literally meaning 'rebirth through one's own forces', this refers to the forging of history through the social and cultural creativity of the people.[5] The same Maoist perspective would

---

2. This does not reduce the interest of Cuban social policy in the early years after the Revolution. Unfortunately, the same praise cannot be addressed to Sékou Touré.

3. See Björn Hettne and Gordon Tamm, 'The Development Strategy of Gandhian Economics', *Journal of the Indian Anthropological Society*, 6 (1), April 1976, pp. 51–66; and Detlef Kantowsky, 'Gandhi – Coming Back from West to East?', *IFDA Dossier*, 39, January–February 1984, pp. 3–14.

4. As Gandhi put it: 'After much thinking I have arrived at a definition of Swadeshi that perhaps best illustrates my meaning. Swadeshi is that spirit in us which restricts us to the use and service of our immediate surroundings to the exclusion of the more remote.' Quoted in Hettne and Tamm, pp. 60–61.

5. See Johan Galtung, 'Self-Reliance: Concepts, Practice and Rationale', in *Self-Reliance...*, p. 19.

include Kim Il Sung's *juche* principle and Albanian experiences under Enver Hoxha – neither pleasant to recall.

We do not need such exotic origins, however, to discover the practice of autonomy enabling a given social group to survive through its own resources. As Galtung quite rightly points out, it is as old as humanity and defeats any attempt to name a founding father.[6] As far back as we can go, most societies have had to manage for themselves, with the (usually minimal) help of what their neighbours could provide. Europe is no exception to this rule: it had to rely for a long time on its own resources to assure, with considerable difficulty, the subsistence of a majority of the population. And when merchants began to play an important role, they grew rich not by trading in what most people lacked, but by offering luxury goods (spices, gold or silk) that allowed the well-to-do to stand out from the common herd.

This is really the basic paradox of the 'theory' of self-reliance: it tries to formalize, coherently and exhaustively, the mode of life that has prevailed on earth since the dawn of humanity, but at the same time presents this as a discovery bringing an indubitably new element to the debate on 'development'! Here we see a fine example of the modern compulsion to take what goes back into the mists of time and to dress it up as if it had never been seen or heard of before. This simple observation allows us to gauge the extent of the ideological hegemony of the 'development' paradigm, one based upon growth, accumulation, competitive advantage, the fruits of international trade and opportunities taken. In order to gain acceptance, autonomy must justify itself in a language defined by the ruling ideology: it must take a position on the supposed benefits of international trade, defend the notion of social and economic equality, think afresh about the question of ecological costs that is ignored in fashionable theories, and so on. This simply shows that *the history of 'development' merges with the history of the progressive destruction of self-reliance.*

UJAMAA AND THE TANZANIAN EXPERIENCE

Having successively been a German colony and a British-administered trust territory, Tanganyika became independent on 9 December 1961. Following a *coup d'état*, the islands of Zanzibar and Pemba joined it in 1964 to form Tanzania. The new country had to face an especially

---

6. Ibid.

large number of difficulties, both internally and externally. Most of its income came from exports of raw materials (cotton, coffee, sisal, meat, tobacco, tea and, to a lesser extent, tungsten, lead, copper and mica). And it was caught up in various regional conflicts: the unilateral declaration of independence by Southern Rhodesia in 1965, the liberation war conducted by FRELIMO in Mozambique, and, of course, the constant problem of apartheid South Africa.

This situation made Tanzania highly dependent upon external finance that was never easy to obtain (the first Plan, of 1960–65, relied on it to the tune of 78 per cent, most of it coming from Britain). In addition, the terms of trade were worsening as a result of poor sisal sales, waged employment was declining and the population level markedly increasing. In 1964, a mutiny in the army forced the government to call in British troops – an action which highlighted the fragility of independence at a time when President Nyerere was trying to demonstrate his non-alignment by giving hospitality to a number of African liberation movements (ANC, FRELIMO, SWAPO, MPLA, ZAPU and ZANU). In the same year, following the union with Zanzibar, a quarrel broke out with Bonn over Tanzania's links with the German Democratic Republic.[7] The crisis with Britain flared up again in 1965, when Tanzania protested against British policy on Rhodesia's UDI by breaking off diplomatic relations with the country from which it derived 44 per cent of its foreign aid.[8]

In the first half of the sixties, then, Tanzania had repeatedly to assert its political independence *vis-à-vis* the Western powers on which it largely relied in economic matters. The financing of 'development' was proving problematic, despite the support given by the Scandinavian countries, the Netherlands, Canada and then China.[9] Inside the country, the British had kept a hold on the export sector, the banks and even part of the state administration, while the rapid enrichment of some functionaries and traders was stirring up social tensions.

---

7. Zanzibar had for some time had special relations with the GDR, whereas Tanganyika had received significant aid (especially military assistance) from the Federal Republic. After union, each part tried to retain its previous German links, but the so-called Hallstein Doctrine did not allow Bonn to recognize a country that had official ties with the GDR.

8. For a detailed history of Tanzania's external relations, see Okwudiba Nnoli, *Self-Reliance and Foreign Policy in Tanzania: The Dynamics of the Diplomacy of a New State, 1961 to 1971*, New York/London/Lagos: NOK Publishers, 1978.

9. Chinese aid was mainly for the construction of the Tanzam railway; the agreement was signed in 1968 and work began in 1970.

To complete this hasty picture, it should be recalled that Tanzania had two trump cards. First, there was its relative social homogeneity: more than 80 per cent of the population lived in the countryside, none of the 120 'ethnic' groups could claim to dominate the others,[10] and Swahili constituted a common language of communication. Second, President Julius Nyerere, who had led the country to independence, was widely respected and nicknamed the *mwalimu* ('the teacher').[11]

These were the circumstances in which the Arusha Declaration was adopted by TANU on 5 February 1967.[12] Here it should be enough to outline its main points.

1. Basic rights should be guaranteed to all. But the State should ensure that the exercise of individual freedoms does not lead to the growth of inequality and exploitation.

2. Dignity of the individual should result in the country's independence. By way of *concentric circles*, this should assist in the liberation of Africa and the achievement of African unity. Africa should work within the framework of the United Nations for world peace and security.

3. The socialist option presupposes a state 'in which all people are workers' and 'no person exploits another'. To this end, the peasants and workers should own and control the means of production, and TANU members should accept these socialist principles.[13]

4. The country is committed to a war on poverty. 'But it is obvious that in the past we have chosen the wrong weapon for our struggle, because we chose money as our weapon. We are trying to overcome our economic weakness by using the weapons of the economically strong – weapons which in fact we do not possess.'[14] *It*

---

10. The traders of Asian origin and (after 1964) the Arab population of Zanzibar obviously complicated the ethnic–social situation, but this did not pose insurmountable problems.

11. Born in 1916, Nyerere did his teacher training first at Makerere College in Uganda, then at the University of Edinburgh. He returned to Tanzania in 1953, founded the TANU and led the country peacefully to independence. As a committed Christian, Nyerere always tried to combat attitudes that were liable to generate hatred and violence.

12. Two other texts by Nyerere may usefully be read in conjunction with the Arusha Declaration: the 'Introduction' (1968) to the collection *Freedom and Socialism*; and the memorandum 'Principles and Development' (1966) reprinted in the same volume.

13. After the Arusha Declaration was adopted, the banks, industries, services and export sectors were immediately nationalized.

14. 'Arusha Declaration', in Nyerere, *Freedom and Socialism*, p. 235.

is therefore a complete illusion to think that money will solve the problems, for the simple reason that it is not available: it comes from taxes, and these cannot be increased.

5. Another obvious source of finance, about which there has been 'a fantastic amount of talk', is foreign aid in the form of gifts, loans and private investment. But 'it is stupid to imagine that we shall rid ourselves of our poverty through foreign financial assistance rather than our own financial resources.... Firstly, we shall not get the money. It is true that there are countries which can, and which would like, to help us. But there is no country in the world which is prepared to give us gifts or loans, or establish industries, to the extent that we would be able to achieve all our development targets.'[15]

6. *Foreign aid is a danger to independence.* 'Even if it were possible for us to get enough money for our needs from external sources, is this what we really want? Independence means self-reliance.... Gifts which increase, or act as a catalyst to, our own efforts are valuable. But gifts which could have the effect of weakening or distorting our own efforts should not be accepted until we have asked ourselves a number of questions.'[16] It is not a question of opposing foreign investment, which is welcome but cannot be relied upon to the point of putting the country's independence in hock.

7. This being so, it would be wrong to attach too much importance to industrialization, at least in the early stages of 'development'. For it would require financial, technological and human resources that Tanzania does not possess.

8. Whether the State's resources come from taxation or from abroad, they should be allocated first and foremost to the peasantry rather than the towns – especially as foreign loans are financed through agricultural exports. It is not right that peasants should bear the costs of urban development and that the countryside should be exploited by the towns.

9. Although possible revenue from export crops should not be passed up, the stress should be on subsistence agriculture and *food self-sufficiency*.

10. 'Hard work is the root of development.'[17] It is not normal that employees should work only 45 hours a week, as in the rich countries, and that 'women who live in the villages work harder

15. Ibid., pp. 238–9.
16. Ibid., pp. 239–40.
17. Ibid., p. 244.

than anybody else…. The energies of the millions of men in the villages and thousands of women in the towns which are at present wasted in gossip, dancing and drinking, are a great treasure which could contribute more towards the development of our country than anything we could get from rich nations.'[18]

11. *Hard work* plus intelligence have already enabled the peasantry to carry out many 'development' projects, and this is how things should continue. 'It would be more appropriate for us to spend time in the villages showing the people how to bring about development through their own efforts rather than going on so many long and expensive journeys abroad in search of development money.'[19]

12. 'In order to maintain our independence and our people's freedom, we ought to be self-reliant in every possible way and avoid depending upon other countries for assistance. If every country is self-reliant the ten-house cell will be self-reliant; if all the cells are self-reliant the whole ward will be self-reliant; and if the wards are self-reliant the District will be self-reliant. If the Districts are self-reliant, then the Region is self-reliant, and if the Regions are self-reliant, then the whole nation is self-reliant and this is our aim.'[20]

With its pedagogic style abounding in examples and proverbs, the Arusha Declaration was immediately understandable for those to whom it was addressed. The other side of the coin – in the eyes of Western commentators, and especially Marxologists – was the theoretical imprecision of the 'African socialism' that Nyerere advocated under the name of *ujamaa* (even if the actual word was not used in the Declaration).[21] It was socialism in that it envisaged collective ownership of the means of production, but it did not lay stress upon central control of the economy, industrialization or class analysis.[22] One might say that it was

18. Ibid., p. 245.
19. Ibid., p. 246.
20. Ibid., p. 248.
21. *Ujamaa*, usually translated as 'familyhood', has connotations of 'family sense' or 'shared family values', where 'value' has both a material and a spiritual meaning. 'The word "ujamaa" was chosen for special reasons. First, it is an African word and thus emphasizes the African-ness of the policies we intend to follow. Second, its literal meaning is "family-hood", so that it brings to the mind of our people the idea of mutual involvement in the family as we know it' ('Introduction' to *Freedom and Socialism*, p. 2).
22. It is to Nyerere's credit that he rejects the Marxist evolutionary view of capitalism as a necessary stage prior to the establishment of socialism. More generally, he warns against considering the works of Marx and Lenin as 'holy writ', for 'we are in danger of being bemused by this new theology, and therefore of trying to solve our problems according to what the priests of Marxism say is what Marx said or meant.' Ibid., p.15.

a kind of 'humanist socialism'[23] which rejected Western individualism in favour of a social ethic characteristic of the traditional African family. It was also socialism almost by opposition, because in Nyerere's view Africans were incapable of becoming true capitalists.[24]

However things stand with its concepts, the Arusha Declaration was crystal-clear in its purpose. At its heart were a small number of principles that were quite original in the context of the 'development' debates of the time.

(a) The principle of *self-reliance* (or independence) was the logical conclusion of the work of the dependency school. If it is true that the insertion of the national economy into the international system results in dependence, then it is necessary – as Baran and Sweezy, and especially Samir Amin, argued – to operate a strategy of 'delinking' from the system. Internal freedom and an autonomous foreign policy both rest upon a rejection of the economic domination working itself out in international relations.

(b) *Self-reliance does not mean autarky*. Aid and private investment are not ruled out, but they must stimulate the people's own efforts and not encourage them to be lazy. Nor is it forbidden to draw on expatriates for certain tasks that Tanzanians are for the moment unable to perform. But whatever the amount of aid, it will never be enough to achieve improved living conditions for the whole population.

(c) The aim is to practise a kind of 'economic judo'. There is no point in trying to fight someone stronger with the same weapons that he uses.[25] Hence the rejection of money as the key in promoting *ujamaa*. The main pillar of self-reliance is thus self-confidence: it requires a 'psycho-political change' in the way people relate to the economy.

(d) It is necessary to rely not on money but on people and their work, to orientate the society 'towards the development of man instead

---

23. 'First, and most central of all, is that under socialism Man is the purpose of all social activity … nothing is more central to a socialist society than an acceptance that Man is its justification for existence.' Ibid., p. 4.

24. 'Indeed, whenever we try to help Africans to become capitalist shopkeepers, capitalist farmers, industrialists, etc., we find that most of them fail because they cannot adopt the capitalist practices which are essential to commercial success.… Capitalism demands certain attributes among its practitioners which the majority of our people have never been forced to acquire.' Ibid., p. 18.

25. This principle recalls, on a different level, Gandhi's political tactics in India. It may have seemed utterly utopian to drive the British out through non-violent opposition, but their military superiority made it impossible for the Indians to fight on any other terrain. If the enemy could not be crushed, he had to be completely nonplussed.

of material wealth'.[26] Concretely, this means clear steps to prevent the exploitation of one part of the population by another (workers/ capitalists, townspeople/countrypeople), and to promote (relative) equality of conditions.

(e) African socialism cannot be achieved by copying foreign models, whether capitalist or socialist. This is true of both the economic and the political system. To think that the specific problems of Tanzanian society have been answered by others, and that copying is all that is now required, is to lose confidence in African values and to turn up one's nose at the people's aspirations and traditions.

The Arusha Declaration was, to be sure, a *normative discourse*, a declaration of intentions, a list of prescriptions. It was obviously going to be difficult to implement, for it implied changes in attitudes and behaviour inherited from the colonial period and exacerbated by the temptations of easy personal enrichment of leading 'cadres'.[27] That said, some courage was needed to chart a 'development path' so different from the one favoured by the international establishment: to downplay the role of international trade and industrialization, to advocate a re-turn to the land, and to claim originality for a lifestyle in keeping with traditional values. All this was necessary to ensure that what gleamed in people's eyes was not 'the age of mass consumption' but a form of *willing austerity* based upon discipline at work and equality of distribu-tion.

Nyerere's exemplary clarity of vision seems to have failed him in the proclamation of a series of measures – not present in the Arusha Dec-laration but ostensibly applying it[28] – which launched the village regroupment scheme in the autumn of 1967. This policy started out from two considerations. On the one hand, the scattered habitat char-acteristic of Tanzania prevented the peasantry from making rational use of the available infrastructure (schools, clinics, shops, irrigation, etc.), and did not allow them to come together easily to make local democ-racy work. On the other hand, the ever greater importance of cash crops had given rise to individualist behaviour and growing social in-equality, even in the rural world.

To confront this situation, Nyerere took over an old idea proposed by the colonial authorities in the 1940s, which he had already tried to have adopted in 1962 as the Village Settlement Scheme. Now he urged

26. Ibid., p. 32.
27. See ibid., pp. 30–31.
28. 'After the Arusha Declaration', in ibid., pp. 385 ff.

all Tanzanians to group together in 'ujamaa villages' in the name of three traditional values: respect for other people, common property, and the obligation for everyone to work.[29] The first task was to persuade people to group together of their own free will, and the final aim was to create community farms (in which small private plots could still exist). Nyerere was well aware of the difficulties, as not everyone might be disposed to work selflessly for the general interest.[30] But he still thought that this was the only way of creating a socialist nation.

In 1967 there were only twenty or so ujamaa villages. By 1973 some two million people were living together in them. But the President, unhappy with the slow pace, now made the resettlement compulsory as part of Operation Planned Villages. By 1975 they encompassed 9 million people,[31] and by 1977 a total of 7,684 villages housed more than 13 million people.[32] For Nyerere this was 'a tremendous achievement': 'It means that something like 70 per cent of our people moved their homes in the space of about three years!' It is true that it is no easy job to shift peasants around, but what were the results? Nyerere pointed to not insignificant improvements in health, education and equality of circumstances. But on the other hand, he honestly admitted setbacks in agricultural output and people's lack of enthusiasm in operating modern technology. One may also question the wisdom of these authoritarian measures on the part of a man who justified his actions by appealing to tradition. How could he have thought that the people most attached to the land where their ancestors lay buried would spontaneously choose to leave it for co-operatives directed by state personnel, and to modernize their agricultural practices? The most rational course is not always the most reasonable. It was therefore doubtful that 'heavy' tactics would be capable of mobilizing the people and gaining their support.[33] The will to create a 'new man', if it is imposed from

29. 'Socialism and Rural Development', in ibid., pp. 337–8.
30. 'Yet socialist communities cannot be established by compulsion. ...; the task of leadership and of government is not to try and force this kind of development, but to explain, encourage, and participate.' Ibid., p. 356.
31. Officially they were no longer known as 'ujamaa villages' but as 'development villages'.
32. Julius Nyerere, The Arusha Declaration: Ten Years After, Dar Es Salaam: Government Printer, 1977, pp. 41–2.
33. Nyerere rejects the charge that he wanted to use force, but he admits that 'there were widely publicized cases of maladministration, and even of mistreatment of people. Some few leaders did act without thinking, and without any consultation with the people who had to move.... But it is absurd to pretend that these cases were typical of villagization. They did occur; and they were bad examples of leadership

the top down, most often leads to dangerous manipulation. This is why it seems doubtful that the people could 'determine the development of their own place, and within the framework of our national policies draw up their own rules for living and working together'.[34]

There can be no question here of exhaustively analysing the successes and failures of the Tanzanian experiment in 'self-reliance'. In a way, the balance sheet was already drawn up by Nyerere himself: 'Ten years after the Arusha Declaration Tanzania is certainly neither socialist nor self-reliant. The nature of exploitation has changed, but it has not been altogether eliminated.... Tanzania is still a dependent nation, not an independent one. We have not reached our goal; it is not even in sight.'[35] Of course, external factors such as drought, crop failure or rising oil prices were among the causes of failure. But there were also internal reasons why it proved impossible to transform society. No doubt Nyerere had too idealized, or even romantic, a vision of the persistence of traditional values, and so he misjudged the change in attitudes among leaders who were little inclined to embrace a collectivism that blocked their own social ascent and personal enrichment. The ethic of 'love for one's neighbour' that the President advocated could not be generalized. And finally, it was difficult at one and the same time to base actions upon tradition and to modernize production by changing technology and adopting new crop strains linked to chemical fertilizers and pesticides.

Beyond the Tanzanian case proper, the strategy of self-reliance faced a more general problem in the shape of 'foreign aid'. Nyerere never ruled this out, of course, and only tried to set various conditions such as that it should increase self-reliance. In fact, there was a form of double bind, already present in Truman's Point Four, which made it necessary to 'help others to help themselves' – a paradoxical situation where what was done contradicted the declared goal. Even if self-reliance does not presuppose autarky, it cannot accept a form of external dependence, however good the intentions behind it. And in the end, it was the sympathy evoked by the Tanzanian experience which helped to bring about its downfall. At the time of the Arusha Declaration, the 'development professionals' most willing to see their certainties challenged thought of Tanzania as the laboratory for an original idea that should be given generous backing. So it was that by 1977

---

failure.... Yet it remains true that 11 million people could not have been moved by force in Tanzania; we do not have the physical capacity for such forced movement, any more than we have the desire for it.' Ibid., p. 42.

34. Ibid., p. 18.
35. Ibid., p. 2.

Tanzania's 'development' was being funded by international 'aid' to the tune of 60 per cent.[36] The least one can say is that the Arusha Declaration's counsel of prudence had not been respected, and that the result was a new form of *domination through giving*.

THE PRINCIPLES OF SELF-RELIANCE[37]

The essence of social autonomy, and its originality in comparison with the dominant model, will become clear from the following points.

What self-reliance is not

Self-reliance is not an abstract model but a historical process of struggle against a structure that is rejected.

Self-reliance cannot be introduced from above.

Self-reliance should not be confused with industrial processing of raw materials at the site of their extraction, which may be a condition for self-reliance but is also compatible with extension of the capitalist market.

Self-reliance is not just a matter of first producing the goods needed by the most destitute layers. For such a policy can also be applied within a bureaucratic–managerial perspective.

Self-reliance is not the same as self-sufficiency or economic autarky, although food self-sufficiency is one of its objectives.

The bases of self-reliance

Self-reliance prioritizes production within the country of goods useful to the population as a whole, instead of relying on international trade to import consumer goods (or weapons) that are of profit only to a minority.

Democratic control of production is a basic condition for self-reliance.

Self-reliance prioritizes the use of locally available factors of production, and does not consider international trade as a substitute for research.

Self-reliance stimulates creativity and confidence in one's own values.

Self-reliance adapts the people's way of life to the locally existing factors and environment, with positive ecological and cultural results.

---

36. Ibid., p. 50.
37. This section summarizes and adapts the main points contained in Galtung's 'Self-Reliance...'.

Self-reliance involves various forms of 'development' and rejects the imitation of imported models.

Self-reliance reduces the alienation stemming from lack of control over the economic process, and promotes horizontal solidarity.

Self-reliance permits a better ecological balance: it prevents one group from plundering or exhausting the resources of another group, and prohibits the export of polluting waste from the area where it is produced.

Self-reliance forces people to invent things for themselves instead of imitating what is done elsewhere; it involves a permanent learning process.

Self-reliance favours solidarity with others on the same level, both inside the country and internationally; it means that trade flows are able to bypass the main centres (including those within the country).

Self-reliance permits resistance to the dependence bound up with international trade and price fluctuations; it therefore aims to achieve self-sufficiency in strategic resources, particularly food. Self-reliance raises a country's defence capacity by enabling it to resist external pressure, and makes a military attack on population centres more difficult by decentralizing the economy.

Self-reliance puts an end to the centre/periphery opposition: the periphery is transformed into a multitude of 'centres' that depend on no one.

Possible adverse effects of self-reliance

Self-reliance reduces trade-related inequalities, but it can do nothing against those associated with the fact that some countries have resources which do not exist elsewhere. It should therefore go hand in hand with mechanisms of global redistribution.

Self-reliance may bolster exploitation at local or regional level if the democratic system does not function properly and a minority has control over the economy.

Self-reliance risks accentuating the division of the world between a 'developed' centre and an 'underdeveloped' periphery. Although self-reliance does initially involve delinking from the international market, it should tend towards new forms of association on an egalitarian basis.

Self-reliance risks lessening mobility between the various units. The aim is not to tie people to their area of birth, but to promote exchange between people in similar positions in different places.

Self-reliance risks creating a split between those able and those unable to practise it. On the other hand, regional and local forms of self-reliance should be practised within large (commercially independent) countries, while small countries may associate with their neighbours to practise regional self-reliance.

POSSIBLE FUTURES FOR SELF-RELIANCE

In order to gain acceptance for the new policy of self-reliance, the Arusha Declaration proclaimed: 'we are at war'. It was a metaphorical formula (indicating war on poverty), but it still expressed a truth. For it can be seen that self-reliance is mainly practised when the political, or military, situation makes it necessary to do so. Although it cannot be established by government decree – as the Tanzanian case clearly shows – *it becomes necessary when survival requires it.* Here the clearest example is that of the liberation movements which, having already liberated a part of the country (e.g. Guinea-Bissau or Mozambique), had no choice but to count on their own resources for the continuation of the struggle. It was exactly as if isolation – voluntary or forced – compelled the population to make a virtue out of necessity,[38] with the result that practices of self-reliance later disappeared together with the war economy.

Does this mean that a policy of self-reliance is limited to exceptional situations, and that it is doomed in a world of globalization? The question is badly formulated, because it suggests that there really is a globalization of markets. It is true that international trade is increasing – and the new World Trade Organization plans to increase it still further – but the networks that are being woven are far from uniform. A growing number of regions are being excluded from trade circuits, and the people living in them are being forced to fend for themselves. Is this is an aberrant form of self-reliance? No doubt it is, if one thinks of the 'active disinterest'[39] with which various parts of the centre keep their peripheries merely ticking over with humanitarian aid, when they

---

38. A compulsion to rely on one's own resources, as a result of international ostracism or military conflict, has always led to policies involving *some* aspects of self-reliance. Examples would be not only the Stalinist doctrine of 'socialism in one country', *juche* in North Korea, 'revolutionary war' in China, entrenchment in Albania, or *fokonolona* ideology in Madagascar, but also the effects of the (partial!) trade boycott of South Africa, or even measures taken in Switzerland during the Second World War. Clearly, then, there are major differences between self-reliance and forced autarky, the latter being perfectly compatible with exploitation.

39. The expression is borrowed from Jean-Christophe Rufin, *L'Empire et les nouveaux barbares*, Paris: J.-C. Lattès, 1991.

do not abandon them altogether to their own devices. In these conditions of 'generalized apartheid', it is to be feared that autonomy will end up as a tropical variant of 'development' reserved for the forgotten ones of history; a minority – in both North and South – will be gorged with consumer goods, while a majority, kept well out of sight, will survive on a pittance and be congratulated for its complete self-reliance.

In a more optimistic variant of this scenario, however, the countless victims of 'development' and those disenchanted with modernization no longer expect anything from the models they have been offered for the last half-century. They may be thought of as marginalized by the system, but they define themselves more as *voluntary turncoats* helping to reconstruct their society outside the dominant prescriptions and 'development programmes' of the governments to which they are legally subjected. Such people exist everywhere, but in a way they are so 'banalized' as to be scarcely noticeable.[40] They do not necessarily declaim against the State in which they live, but are more likely to hold themselves 'apart', adjusting economic laws to their own values, using trickery in dealings with the regime, and exploiting weaknesses in the dominant system. Eventually they settle into a form of existence different from the one they pursued while they still hoped to improve their lot through 'development'.

We are not talking here of some romantic celebration of 'joyful poverty', or of the 'noble savage' as testimony to a 'lost innocence' all the more attractive for not being shared. The point is simply that 'development', far from becoming general, changes as it comes into contact with societies that divert and neutralize it. Whereas the dominant strategy proposes a single path of 'development', what is now happening is a *diversification of 'developments'*. The theoretical sequence

---

40. For Mexico, see Gustavo Esteva, 'Regenerating People's Space', *Alternatives*, XII, 1987, pp. 125–52; for Asia, Ashis Nandy, 'Shamans, Savages and the Wilderness: On the Audibility of Dissent and the Future of Civilisations', *Alternatives*, XIV, 1989, pp. 263–77, and Majid Rahnema, 'Swadhyaya, The Unknown, the Peaceful, the Silent Yet Singing Revolution of India', *IFDA Dossier*, 75–76, January–April 1990, pp. 19–34; for Africa, Emmanuel Ndione, *Le don et le recours. Ressorts de l'économie urbaine*, Dakar: ENDA, 1992. For a general account, see Gilbert Rist, Majid Rahnema and Gustavo Esteva, *Le Nord perdu. Repères pour l'après-développement*, Lausanne: Éditions d'En Bas, 1992; Serge Latouche, *La Planète des naufragés. Essai sur l'après-développement et peuples autochtones*, Paris: La Découverte, 1991, and 'La fiction et la feinte: développement et peuples autochtones', *Ethnies* (review of *Survival International*), 13, Spring 1991.

of modernization is replaced with a multiplicity of new practices that spring forth at the crossroads of history and cultures.

Self-reliance strategies have often been criticized on the grounds that they cannot offer a real alternative to the dominant conception of 'development'. After all, did not Julius Nyerere, the nicest to know of their champions, himself admit to defeat? And what of Enver Hoxha, Mao Tse-tung, Didier Ratsiraka, Kim Il Sung or Fidel Castro, to name but a few of the incense-bearers of forced autonomy? The thought of how they insulted their peoples is surely cause for indignation. Yet it would be dangerous to draw hasty conclusions from these wretched examples. A policy of self-reliance is said not to 'work'. Maybe. But does the Rostow model have anything more to show for itself? Are Zaïreans better off than Tanzanians? Do people have an easier time of it in Sierra Leone or Liberia than in Madagascar or Cuba?

It is wrong to blame an original approach for not having yielded the results it expected – especially as disappointment is undoubtedly the most widely shared experience in the field of 'development'. For looked at more closely, the failure can be attributed not only to conjunctural causes but also to structural ones. The former have already been mentioned. In the case of Tanzania, they have to do with the impatience – plus a degree of force – with which the reforms were pushed through, as well as the lack of political mobilization, the ad-ministrative corruption, the excessive recourse to foreign aid, the bad climatic conditions, the sudden increase in energy prices, and so on. All this has been written about before, and there is no point in going over it again. A careful analysis should also be made of the (varying) reasons why other countries sank into the mire when they attempted something like a policy of autonomy. But more questions also need to be asked. What real chance of success is there for a policy of autonomy in a single country? Since the system is based upon international divi-sion of labour and expanding trade, is it really possible to extricate oneself from it and to conduct a totally different policy in isolation? The answer is probably negative. But the situation would be quite dif-ferent if self-reliance could become as widespread as the market system. The social autonomy strategy would not be limited to the countries of the South, but would become a system in which each country tried to reduce social inequalities and to use its own resources to acquire the means of existence. The aim would be to reduce the importance of international trade instead of promoting it further; to concentrate in-vestment on the exploitation of local resources, instead of playing on short-term productivity differentials in accordance with the casino economics that govern the financial markets; and to place the environment under the control of those who depend upon it, instead of mortgaging it to distant owners and abusers.

A utopia, no doubt. Besides, are not ideal cities always totalitarian – from Plato through Thomas More to George Orwell? Do they not always arouse legitimate distrust? There is no need to worry, though: the theoretical limits of self-reliance coincide with its geographical limits – and in a period of worldwide trade and market globalization, this means that the chances of self-reliance are next to nil. But nothing guarantees that things will always be so. The dominant system is said to be turning the world into a single village as it ties the most different people together ever more tightly. New means of communication create the illusion that people can 'get closer to each other' without moving from where they are. It is also true that disturbing problems such as environmental pollution are now planetary in scope. But this contraction of the world excludes people as much as – if not more than – it integrates them. Between those who have everything to gain from market expansion and those who have nothing more to lose, the scales are far from evenly balanced. The worst is not necessarily the most likely, and nothing indicates that salvation will have to come from 'new barbarians'.[41] But the gulf between the two parts of the world does not only allow the rich to consume in private among themselves; it also forces those left out to band together on a basis necessarily different from that which prevails today. Because self-reliance is linked to war economy or shortages, it could be imposed on people no longer able even to dream of enjoying the prosperity promised by the market. It remains to be seen whether the dominant system will be able to survive if a majority opts out of it.

41. See the three scenarios suggested by Rufin at the end of *L'Empire et les nouveaux barbares*.

CHAPTER 9

THE TRIUMPH OF THIRD-WORLDISM

The 1970s will go down in history as the decade when the South's power seemed to be growing. It was a time of hope and enthusiasm about the role that had finally been recognized for it within the international order. Even if the objectives of 'development' were far from accomplished, it was possible to think that a massive redistribution of wealth and power was bringing them within arm's reach. The industrial countries would have to compromise politically and share more in the realm of the economy.

There were numerous signs feeding this optimism. First, the seventies came in the wake of two major events: the Chinese Cultural Revolution in 1967, and the movement of 'May '68'. The resulting effervescence was at once challenging consumer society, the legitimacy of hierarchies, and the established distinctions between manual and non-manual labour. A blind eye was turned to the brutalities of the Chinese regime, and the people's communes were hailed in their vitality as a reconciliation of theory and practice that was abolishing the petty-bourgeois mentality and putting into practice a new model of 'development'.[1] In this intellectual climate, the dependency theorists had the wind in their sails. In the industrial countries, too, a growing number of people organized in support of Third World demands and built their discourse

---

1. It is hard today to imagine the influence of the 'Chinese model' on 'development' studies following the Cultural Revolution. Two works with significant titles may be mentioned here: Johan Galtung and Fumiko Nishimura, *Von China lernen?*, Opladen: Westdeutscher Verlag, 1978; and Sartaj Aziz, *Rural Development: Learning from China*, London: Macmillan, 1978.

around one simple principle: it is necessary to act upon the causes of 'underdevelopment', not just mitigate its effects; or, in other words, 'it is not a question of giving more but of taking less'. Debate tended to focus on the transnational companies, whose exorbitant profits testified to the exploitation they practised in the countries of the South. It was a serious business, and the United Nations set up a working group to examine the role of these new economic empires.[2] At a political level, the struggle against imperialism was symbolized by the Vietnam War, which showed day in day out that a 'barefoot army' could defy the greatest power in the world if it had the necessary popular support, imagination and creativity. Support groups for the victims of US-backed regimes mobilized to denounce the South African apartheid system, Portuguese colonialism and White rule in Rhodesia, or the military dictatorships in Latin America (especially Chile, Brazil and Argentina). Of course, the very existence of these focal points for grievances indicated the continuing vigour of the capitalist system. But facing it there was now an organized solidarity movement, which supported actual liberation struggles and opponents of repressive regimes.

The critique of industrial society was not, however, only a matter of intellectual agitation or militant commitment. In 1972, the United Nations itself held a major conference in Stockholm on the 'human environment', which for the first time drew world attention to dangers such as pollution, exhaustion of natural resources, desertification, and so on.[3] In the same year, an MIT research team defined the 'limits to growth' and showed how natural resources – above all, non-renewable ones – were gradually running out as a result of economic and industrial growth.[4] The birth of the ecological movement coincided with a period of gloom and creeping doubt in the industrial countries. The slowdown in growth and rising unemployment had become harder to combat since the United States decided on 15 August 1971 to tackle its chronic trade deficit by floating the dollar downwards.[5] Moreover, the transnational companies had found a way of splitting up the production process to take advantage of low wages in the periphery (especially in

---

2. Resolution 1721 (L.III) of the Economic and Social Council, 28 July 1972.
3. The conference took place from 5 to 16 June 1972 and issued a *Declaration on the Human Environment* (A/CONF.48/14/Rev.1) – not, as in Rio twenty years later, on the environment and 'development'.
4. *The Limits to Growth: Report to the Club of Rome*, London: Pan Books, 1972.
5. As many countries held currency reserves in dollars, this unilateral decision by President Nixon meant that some of them became considerably poorer as a result.

customs-free zones),[6] while in the North productivity gains associated with automation were anyway reducing employment. Prosperity did not seem to be directly threatened, but there were all manner of reasons to wonder whether it would continue.

It was in this conjuncture that the October War broke out in 1973. Although the Egyptians had the initiative in attacking first, they were beaten by the Israelis and could recapture only a tiny part of the Sinai Peninsula that they had lost in 1967. This new episode in the Middle East conflict had major consequences. Within two months the OPEC countries had quadrupled the price of oil, underlining the vulnerability of the Western (and especially European) economies, which largely depended upon Arab countries in this key strategic field.[7] *For the first time, the countries of the South – albeit the richest among them – were acting together in a way that could seriously disturb the economy in the North.*[8] Alarm bells began to ring in the industrialized countries.[9]

Meanwhile, in the guerrilla warfare of Guinea-Bissau, General Spinola was becoming aware that victory was impossible against Amilcar Cabral's PAIGC. In April 1974, the Carnation Revolution put an end to the forty-year-old dictatorship in Portugal and opened the way to the independence of Angola, Mozambique and Guinea-Bissau – an event which, happy enough in itself, is of interest to us here as an example of the North's changing under pressure from the South. Finally, in April 1975, North Vietnamese troops victoriously entered Saigon. The world's number-one military power had given in, and a little country had shown that guerrilla warfare could get the better of a large army boasting quite exceptional means.

---

6. See Volker Fröbel, Jürgen Heinrichs and Otto Kreye, *Die neue internationale Arbeitsteilung. Strukturelle Arbeitslosigkeit in den Industrieländern und die Industrialisierung der Entwicklungsländer*, Reinbek: Rowohlt, 1977.

7. On 16 October 1973, the price of a barrel of oil leapt from $3.02 to $5.12, and this was accompanied by threats to cut output by 5 per cent a month and an embargo that especially hit the United States and the Netherlands. In December 1973 the price went up to $11.6. For the Arab countries, of course, the aim was to punish the Western countries for their support of Israel. But the first increase barely made up for the loss of income resulting from the *de facto* devaluation of the dollar.

8. Of course, these measures also affected other countries in the South, especially the poorer ones. And although they were generally less dependent upon oil imports, the coup of 1973 played a major role in splitting the Third World among countries with ever wider income disparities.

9. The industrial countries failed to use the crisis, however, to rethink their energy policy and to gain public acceptance of curbs on consumption. In fact, as the crisis concerned only the *price* of oil, and the petrodollars (80 billion in 1974) were recycled in Western banks, the shock was soon absorbed with the help of inflation.

In many respects, then, the first half of the seventies seemed to mark the end of Western hegemony over the South. The roles were far from having been reversed, of course, and Latin America remained within the orbit of the United States. But it was difficult not to see the series of events as laying the foundations for a new equilibrium. Was the Third World not showing that it could break the chains of dependency in which it had so far been kept? Did the industrial countries not have to accept that their mode of 'development' was intimately bound up with certain strategic goods and manpower provided by the South? Was it not necessary to lay down new rules that would reflect these fundamental changes?

THE NEW INTERNATIONAL ECONOMIC ORDER

In this confrontational climate, the Third World countries had organized to press their case more forcefully. The Non-aligned Movement that came out of Bandung had formally established itself at Belgrade in 1961. UNCTAD had come into being in 1964 and was the favoured platform of the Group of 77. In 1967 this Group had adopted the Algiers Charter, which summed up all the grievances of the countries of the South against the industrial countries.[10] In 1970 the United Nations General Assembly had proclaimed the Second Development Decade,[11] this time, moreover, proposing a 'strategy' to indicate that development should be conceived in a global and integrated manner.[12] The same year, in Lusaka, another conference had adopted the principle of 'collective self-reliance'; and at Algiers in September 1973, a conference of heads of state and government of the non-aligned countries had concluded by calling upon the UN Secretary-General (through the offices of President Boumedienne) to convene a special session of the General Assembly to study 'problems relating to raw materials and development'. This session, which took place between 9 April and 2 May 1974, issued a Declaration on the Establishment of a New International Economic Order (NIEO), together

---

10. The Algiers Charter was adopted on 3 November 1967, at a preparatory meeting for the second UNCTAD conference (New Delhi, 1968).

11. Resolution 2626/XXV, 24 October 1970.

12. This was also the conclusion of a report commissioned by the World Bank from a commission headed by Lester B. Pearson: *Partners in Development*, New York: Praeger, 1969.

with a Programme of Action[13] – complemented on 12 December by the Charter of Economic Rights and Duties of States.[14]

The idea of recasting the rules of the international economy was thus prior to – though also politically sharpened by – the oil price rises of 1973. Four people played a key role in devising and sponsoring the texts of the NIEO: the Algerian President Houari Boumedienne, the Shah of Iran, the Mexican President Luís Echeverría Álvarez, and the Venezuelan Manuel Pérez Guerrero. This combination may be interpreted in different ways: the three heads of state 'represent' the three continents of the Third World (Africa, Asia, Latin America), while Pérez Guerrero provides the backing of the UN agency that gives the largest place to the countries of the South; or the socialist Boumedienne forms a pair with the modernizer Mohammed Reza Pahlavi, while the head of Mexico's Institutional Revolutionary Party is there to represent 'Third Worldist' sensitivities.[15] Another important point is that all four, whatever their geographical origin or political inclinations, came from oil-producing countries. Was it this which underpinned their consensus of views? It does indeed seem to have been far from extraneous to the content of the NIEO.

---

13. The resolutions in question – 3201 (S-VI) and 3202 (S-VI) – were both adopted unanimously on 1 May 1974.

14. Resolution 3281 (XXIX), carried by 120 votes to 6, with 10 abstentions. Strictly speaking, the NIEO refers only to the two resolutions of 1 May 1974, but it is often also associated with the Charter of Economic Rights and Duties of States. More generally still, it is used to cover a series of resolutions adopted by the General Assembly, specialized agencies or special conferences of the United Nations, which refer not only to 'development' but to a variety of related themes: Human Environment (Stockholm 1972), Population (Bucharest 1974), Industrial Development and Co-operation (Lima 1975), Women, Development and Peace (Mexico City 1975), Habitat (Vancouver 1976), and so on. All these texts are contained in: Alfred George Moss and Harry N.M. Winton, eds, *A New International Economic Order: Selected Documents, 1945–1975*, New York: UNITAR Document Service, 3 vols (n.d.). See also Gilbert Rist, *Towards a 'New' United Nations Development Strategy? Some Major United Nations Resolutions in Perspective*, Nyon: International Foundation for Development Alternatives, 1977 (mimeo).

15. President Echeverría was close to the 'Third World Forum', which dated back to the 1972 Stockholm Conference and brought together a considerable number of intellectuals (some holding important official posts), with a core of no more than fifty. The list included: Ismail Sabri Abdalla, Samir Amin, Gamani Corea, Celso Furtado, Godfrey Gunatilleke, Mahbub ul-Haq, Amilcar O. Herrera, Mosharref Hussain, Enrique V. Iglesias, Fawzy Mansour, Ngo Manh Lan, Enrique Oteiza, Manuel Pérez Guerrero, Justinian F. Rweyemamu and Juan Somavia. Most of these people later worked with the Dag Hammarskjöld Foundation and the International Foundation for Another Development. It would be a fascinating task to trace the history of this network, which was the dominant current in 'development' well into the 1980s.

New Order or Revival of Old Themes?

It is impossible to reproduce here in full the two basic resolutions of the NIEO.[16] There follow just a few extracts from the first, and then a synthetic presentation of their contents.

'*We, the Members of the United Nations,*

Having convened a special session of the General Assembly to study for the first time the problems of raw materials and development, devoted to the consideration of the most important economic problems facing the world community,

Bearing in mind the spirit, purposes and principles of the Charter of the United Nations to promote the economic development and social progress of all peoples,

Solemnly proclaim our united determination to work urgently for THE ESTABLISHMENT OF A NEW INTERNATIONAL ECONOMIC ORDER based on equity, sovereign equality, interdependence, common interest and cooperation among all States, irrespective of their economic and social systems which shall correct inequalities and redress existing injustices, make it possible to eliminate the widening gap between the developed and the developing countries and ensure steadily accelerating economic and social development and peace and justice for present and future generations, and, to that end, declare:

1. ... The benefits of technological progress are not shared equitably by all members of the international community. The developing countries, which constitute 70 per cent of the world's population, account for only 30 per cent of the world's income. It has proved impossible to achieve an even and balanced development of the international community under the existing international economic order. The gap between the developed and the developing countries continues to widen in a system which was established at a time when most of the developing countries did not even exist as independent States and which perpetuates inequality.

---

16. There is a considerable body of literature on the NIEO. See, among others: Daniel Colard, *Vers l'établissement d'un nouvel ordre économique international*, Paris: La Documentation française, 1977; Robert W. Cox, 'Ideologies and the New International Economic Order', *International Organization*, 33 (2), Spring 1979, pp. 257–302; Johan Galtung, *Poor Countries vs. Rich: Poor People vs. Rich: Whom Will NIEO Benefit?*, University of Oslo, 1977; Roy Preiswerk, 'Is the New International Economic Order Really New?', *The Caribbean Yearbook of International Relations*, Trinidad and Tobago, 1977, pp. 147–59; Daniel Holly, 'Les Nations unies et le nouvel ordre économique mondial', *Études internationales* (Quebec), VII (3), September 1977, pp. 500–15; Herb Addo, ed., *Transforming the World Economy? Nine Critical Essays on the New International Economic Order*, London: Hodder & Stoughton, 1984; Gilbert Rist, 'The Not-so-New International Order', *Development* (SID), XX (3–4), 1978, pp. 48–52.

2. The present international economic order is in direct conflict with current developments in international political and economic relations.... The developing world has become a powerful factor that makes its influence felt in all fields of international activity. These irreversible changes in the relationship of forces in the world necessitate the active, full and equal participation of the developing countries in the formulation and application of all decisions that concern the international community.

3. All these changes have thrust into prominence the reality of interdependence of all the members of the world community. Current events have brought into sharp focus the realization that the interests of the developed countries and those of the developing countries can no longer be isolated from each other, that there is a close interdependence between the prosperity of the developed countries and the growth and development of the developing countries, and that the prosperity of the international community as a whole depends upon the prosperity of its constituent parts. International cooperation for development is the shared goal and common duty of all countries. Thus the political, economic and social well-being of present and future generations depends more than ever on cooperation between all the members of the international community on the basis of sovereign equality and the removal of the disequilibrium that exists between them.'[17]

The text is so rich that a close exegesis would be in order to lay bare the nature of UN rhetoric. Here, though, we shall keep to the essentials.

(a) The preamble seeks to suggest a 'messianic' novelty through its use of the expression 'for the first time' – which, in fact, recalls President Truman's Point Four analysed above. In keeping with the religious structure of declarations on 'development', it first describes the present situation in dramatic terms ('inequalities', 'widening gap'), then contrasts it to a future of peace, justice, equity, co-operation and social well-being, and finally sets out the measures that need to be taken to achieve these objectives.

(b) The characterization of this as a new beginning rested, however, upon a falsehood. For it was evidently not 'the first time' that the United Nations had concerned itself with raw materials and 'development'. Had that been true, there would never have been such a thing as UNCTAD!

(c) Juxtaposition of the NIEO's founding principles served to mask the contradiction that existed between them – for actually it is in the name of equity that the sovereign equality of States should sometimes be questioned.

---

17. Resolution 3201 (S-VI).

(d) 'Interdependence' found a place in this UN discourse, but it was associated with 'common interests' and 'cooperation' as its presuppositions. In reality, however, there was no proof that sovereign States formed a 'world community' driven by common interests. The epoch was characterized by nascent globalization of the economy, under the impact of new technologies and transnational corporations.

(e) In the name of the sovereign equality of States, it is decided from the outset not to discuss the 'economic and social system' of the countries involved.[18] *Peoples are the great actors missing from the NIEO.*[19] Moreover, contrary to what the dependency school showed, it is as if changes in the international order had no effect upon internal social conditions.

(f) It is assumed that sovereign equality is not in contradiction with the reduction of international inequalities and 'existing injustices'.

(g) The several references to elimination of the 'widening gap' implies an evolutionary view of history in which the poor 'catch up' with the rich. It always considers poverty, and not wealth, to be the scandal – which is why development must be 'accelerated' to secure peace and justice.[20]

(h) The criticism of 'the present international economic order' is certainly radical: its evils are attributed both to the fact that it originated before the countries of the South became independent, and to the fact that it contradicts the 'irreversible' tendency of international relations. The new actors therefore demand a change in the rules that will give them a chance of winning – that is, allow them to dominate in their

---

18. The text goes on to affirm 'the right of every country to adopt the economic and social system that it deems the most appropriate for its own development and not to be subjected to discrimination of any kind as a result' (3201 (S-VI) 4.d). This might be understood as a kind of openness to multiple 'styles of development', but the real point is to foreclose any criticism from the outside.

19. Of course, the NIEO sometimes mentions 'peoples' or 'improvement of the well-being of all peoples' or of 'present and future generations', but this remains a marginal concern. It should be noted, however, that the *Charter of Economic Rights and Duties of States* insists: 'Every State has the sovereign and inalienable right to choose its economic system as well as its political, social and cultural systems in accordance with the will of its people, without outside interference, coercion or threat in any form whatsoever' (Article One).

20. The talk of 'steadily accelerating development' omits to mention the conditions and actors that will be responsible for it. The same evolutionism can be found in the proposal to adapt technology to the peripheral countries 'in the light of their special development requirements' (3202 (S-VI) III.d), as well as in the use of the concept of 'retardation' (3202 (S-VI) Introduction 1).

turn. On the international arena, however, it is not the UN General Assembly but the real relations of strength which define the rules. What is the point of making up laws if the process is 'irreversible'?

(i) The text always presupposes the reality of the 'world community', using it to define interdependence in a way completely opposed to that of the dependency school (for which international trade itself created inequalities). The 'close interrelationship' that the resolution asserts between prosperity of North and South is at odds with everything that had been said (in radical variants of dependency theory) about 'the development of underdevelopment' or (in more nuanced ones) about 'dependent development'.

(j) The appeal for 'cooperation on the basis of sovereign equality and the removal of the disequilibrium' between member states involves a contradiction in terms, for it is precisely sovereign equality that is the basis of national interests, and thus of the disequilibrium in question.

These few points show the ambivalence of the NIEO resolution. For if the States of the South (and the national bourgeoisies controlling them) criticize the international order, it is because it does not allow them to get rich as quickly as they would like. On the pretext of creating a new order, they claim a new share-out of the benefits of growth, without changing much in how it is achieved, and without giving much thought to the procedures and institutions of arbitration that might be necessary to make the 'new order' credible.

It is true that the tone is firm enough: the present system makes 'harmonious development impossible', and it is necessary to prevent the 'interference' of transnational companies 'in the internal affairs of the countries where they operate, and their collaboration with racist regimes and colonial administrations';[21] the role of 'producers' associations' is encouraged;[22] and the will of developing countries to practise 'collective self-reliance' is reaffirmed.[23] For political effect, use is also

---

21. 3202 (S-VI) V.a. This paragraph bears mainly upon the responsibilities of the transnationals in the overthrow of President Allende in Chile in September 1973, and their operations in Southern Africa.

22. 3201 (S-VI) 4.t and 3202 (S-VI) I.1.c. Obviously the authors were thinking of OPEC, which had sent shock waves through the economies of the North. But all the time, the text is at pains to link support for producers' associations to the expansion of international trade.

23. 3202 (S-VI) I.1.b; VII.1.e and 2. This was the first time the expression 'collective self-reliance' – which had entered the vocabulary of the non-aligned countries at the Lusaka Conference in 1970 – appeared in a UN document. It should be made clear, however, that it refers here (i.e. in the section on 'cooperation between developing countries') to a form of 'regional, subregional and interregional cooperation'. And in

made of old demands (dating back to Bandung!): the right to nationalization,[24] improved terms of trade through 'just and equitable' pric-
ing,[25] and 'more effective' participation by the countries of the South
in the decisions of the World Bank and the IMF.[26] The idea, then, is
that justice and equity demand special weighting in favour of the South
in international negotiations, in such a way that the abolition of inequalities is combined with sovereign equality of States.

Otherwise, the NIEO does no more than reinforce the existing order
of things; it proposes virtually nothing over and above the promotion
of 'development' envisaged in mainstream economics. *Three closely linked
concepts are at the root of the NIEO: economic growth,*[27] *expansion of world
trade,*[28] *and increased 'aid' by the industrial countries.*[29] All the concrete
proposals are intended to satisfy this threefold 'requirement'. But they
are not free from contradiction: one paragraph talks of helping the
countries of the South 'to achieve self-sustaining economic development',[30] while another wishes 'to ensure that developing countries can
import the necessary quantity of food without undue strain on their
foreign exchange resources'[31] – when one might think that food self-
sufficiency is the basis of 'self-sustaining economic development'! On
the one hand, hopes are expressed for the 'promotion of foreign investment, both public and private';[32] on the other hand, ways are sought of
regulating the activity of transnational companies. The development of

---

this context, the innovation is only terminological; the content had already been
defined at Bandung. For example, the *Charter of Economic Rights and Duties of States*
clearly affirmed: 'States have the *right* … to participate in subregional, regional and
interregional cooperation in the pursuit of their economic and social development.
All States engaged in such cooperation have the duty to ensure that the policies of
those groupings … are outward-looking' (Article 12; emphasis added).

24. 3201 (S-VI) 4.e. The right to nationalization had already been recognized by
the UN in 1960 (Resolution 1514/XV).

25. 3201 (S-VI) 4.j and 3202 (S-VI) I.1. The notion of 'just and equitable prices'
is particularly hazy: the dominant perspective defines it as that which is formed when
the supply of something encounters effective demand. The *Charter of the Economic
Rights and Duties of States* (Article 28) proposed 'adjusting' (that is, indexing) the
export prices of developing countries to their import prices.

26. 3202 (S-VI) II.2.c; II.1.d; IX.5.

27. 3201 (S-VI) 3; 3202 (S-VI) 1.3.b; X.b.

28. 3201 (S-VI) 4.j; 3202 (S-VI) I.1.b; I.3.a.v; I.3.a.xi; I.4.e.

29. 3201 (S-VI) 4.i; 4.k; 4.t; 3202 (S-VI) II.1.h; II.2.a; III.a; III.d; VII.2; IX.6;
X.f; X.1–3.

30. 3202 (S-VI) X.1.

31. 3202 (S-VI) I.2.f.

32. 3202 (S-VI) II.2.e.

'suitable indigenous technology' is recommended, but so is the transfer of 'modern technology'.[33]

When it was proclaimed, the NIEO was widely seen as expressing the 'revolt of the Third World'. In reality, however, *its aim was to realize a long-standing dream of world capitalism: that is, to ensure continuing growth of the system as a whole by better integrating the peripheral countries.*[34] For as soon as the existence of common interests is assumed,[35] everything that contributes to expansion of the market must be deemed positive; the priority is then to produce and export more[36] and, to that end, to lower tariff and non-tariff barriers. The *Charter of Economic Rights and Duties of States* goes further still: market expansion is not only a good thing to be profited from, but an actual duty: 'It is the duty of States to contribute to the development of international trade of goods.'[37] Whereas the dependency school defined the international arena as a space where domination effects are exerted – which encouraged ideas of withdrawal or delinking – the NIEO viewed international trade as the engine of growth, and therefore advocated a completely outward-oriented model.

Far from closing the gap between centre and periphery (as it proposed to do), the NIEO actually widened it. For it defined the centre as the ultimate source of 'development': through public 'assistance', of course, but also through private investment, further funding of international financial institutions, modern science and technology, the best remuneration for basic products, access to the markets of industrial countries, renegotiation of debt, and so on. The countries of the North were asked to make concessions on all these points, but this also meant that the key to the South's 'development' lay in the North. *Instead of combating dependence, the NIEO confirmed it.*

The Pretence and Reality of Power

As Immanuel Wallerstein has pointed out, 'in premodern systems, whenever there was real change it was justified by arguing that no change

---

33. 3202 (S-VI) IV.b and c.

34. Roy Preiswerk (p. 159) has calculated that in Resolution 3201 (S-VI) 16 'associative' or 'integrative' concepts (community, co-operation, equality, justice, equity, participation, harmony, etc.) appear a total of 79 times, while 10 'dissociative' or 'conflictual' concepts (sovereignty, gap, self-determination, integrity, etc.) appear only 19 times.

35. 3201 (S-VI) 3; 3202 (S-VI) I.1.c.

36. A stress on production for export – especially in agriculture – inevitably downgrades production for internal consumption and increases food dependency.

37. Arts 6, 12, 14, etc.

had occurred. In the modern world, whenever real change does not occur, it is justified by asserting that change has in fact taken place.'[38] Such is indeed the case with the NIEO. Despite its rhetorical list of demands, it proposes nothing new – or anyway, nothing that sheds fresh light on how to improve living conditions for the peoples of the South.

In many respects, the NIEO marks a retreat from what was already known. The gains of dependency theory and (to some extent) of self-reliance are ignored. As an international organization, of course, the United Nations could hardly attach itself to a particular school of thought (except the dominant one), nor take as a universal example the 'unrepresentative' experiences of a few countries. But there was one question – the environment – on which the UN had already declared itself but which figured very little in the various resolutions of 1974. The main one of these simply mentions that States have a right to control their own natural resources so as to exploit them better, and goes on to criticize waste.[39] As for the Plan of Action, its similarly managerial perspective stresses the 'ecological advantages' of natural as opposed to synthetic products, and limits itself to deploring 'desertification, salinization and damage by locusts'.[40] This is a far cry from the declarations of Stockholm, which warned of the dangers of industrialization and growth, and called for international norms to combat pollution.[41] Thus, the authors of the NIEO had either learnt nothing or forgotten everything from the debates of the early seventies on 'development' policies.

This appalling lack of theoretical imagination was due to the fact that, for the Southern heads of state and self-styled champions of the NIEO, the real issues at stake lay elsewhere. Their aim was not to work out a strategy to benefit the peoples of the South, but to ensure that the national bourgeoisies had a bigger share of the booty of world economic growth. Looked at in this way, all the measures proposed under the NIEO seem perfectly consistent.

---

38. 'An Historical Perspective on the Emergence of the New International Order: Economic, Political, Cultural Aspects', in *Transforming the World Economy?*, pp. 21–2.

39. 3201 (S-VI) 4.q.

40. 3202 (S-VI) I.1.f and I.2.c and d. The *Charter of Economic Duties and Rights of States*, as well as adopting the notion of a 'common heritage of mankind' (Art. 29), devotes Article 30 to the 'protection, preservation and enhancement of the environment'.

41. *Declaration on the Human Environment and Plan of Action* (A/CONF.48/14/ Rev.1; June 1972); see also Preamble 4, Rec. 39d, 92a, 109, etc. For example, 'Problems of pollution could be ameliorated by a reduction in the current levels of production and in the rate of growth' (Rec. 106a).

(a) The goal of more vigorous growth is obviously the simplest way of claiming a larger part at the time of the share-out.

(b) Greater international aid, increased exports of raw materials at a higher price, use of modern technology for industrialization, new loans from international institutions, better exploitation of natural resources, regulation of the activity of transnational companies – all these objectives have the common feature that they permit central control within the peripheral country in question, so that the ministries, central banks, customs departments and state enterprises can divide – or divert – the proceeds to their own account. In countries where tax collection yields only derisory sums, the ruling minority enriches itself mainly by appropriating external revenue through the machinery of state.[42]

(c) The system has an explicit lock in the shape of respect for national sovereignty and recognition of each country's right to decide its own economic and social system. To put it plainly, the surplus deriving from foreign operations can always be combined with exploitation of the local population.[43]

(d) Naturally, the NIEO implies a number of 'sacrifices' for the industrial countries, which would have to content themselves with a smaller share of global profits. They too, then, have an interest in doing everything to stimulate growth, so that at least in absolute terms their proceeds are as high as before. There is also some similarity here with the calculations of an employer faced with a wage claim: one might as well make a few concessions and so avoid a strike or a social revolt that could damage the work equipment; instead of killing the goose that lays the golden egg, maybe one should feed it better. Having learnt their lesson with the 'oil crisis', the industrial countries stood to gain if they granted the demands of Southern governments and thus secured their own supplies of raw materials. At the same time, by slightly

---

42. The NIEO 'is dependent on – indeed is the institutionalization of – the expansion of world trade as the vehicle for a new international division of labour in which the Third World bourgeoisies negotiate the terms of their dependence to participate more actively and profit more handsomely at the expense of the increased exploitation and the heightened super-exploitation of their agricultural, industrial and service, including government, workers.' André Gunder Frank, 'Rhetoric and Reality of the New International Economic Order', in *Transforming the World Economy?*, p. 199. See also Galtung, *Poor Countries vs. Rich...*, pp. 8 f.

43. Of course, one can always imagine different scenarios in which an 'enlightened' government carries out genuine redistribution (other than through trickle-down effects). But they are not exactly common, and besides, the scope for redistribution depends upon the existence of such means as control of producer prices, indexation of wages, decision-making power of local organizations, and so on.

increasing the size of the affluent minority, the 'vanguard of development', they could foster the illusion that the inhabitants of the South in general might one day 'catch up' with the living standards of the North.

We may conclude that *implementation of the NIEO would have been more dangerous than beneficial to the peoples of the South*. It is therefore in a way fortunate that it was stillborn, everything having begun and ended on the same day, 1 May 1974. There were four main reasons for this.

First, what was then called the 'Third World' broke up in the mid-seventies. At the very moment when it was vigorously expressing its collective demands, it ceased to exist as an entity with a common destiny: now there were ultra-rich countries living off the oil rent, 'least developed countries' (LDCs) sunk in extreme poverty,[44] and between the two, the 'newly industrializing countries' (NICs). The 'common interest' between these groups – an interest anyway based more on their colonial past than on a collective project for the future – had totally disappeared and could no longer sustain any kind of mobilization. This fragmentation evidently played into the hands of the industrial countries, which had every interest in separate negotiations rather than having to face the collective strength of a united bloc.

Second, the crisis in the industrial countries meant that they could not be as 'generous' as the NIEO had anticipated. At most there was a relocation of industry – linked to the systemic profitability crisis – which helped to strengthen the NICs, or to provide some new jobs in the LDC free zones.

Third, and more fundamental, the Western banks found themselves having to recycle the huge mass of petrodollars resulting from OPEC decisions. The loan facilities then offered to the countries of the South were taken up on a large scale, so that the NIEO demands were soon overshadowed by the problems of the coming decade: financial crises, debt and economic restructuring.

Fourth, it must be recognized that, over and above these conjunctural phenomena, the NIEO rested entirely upon a form of question-begging that meant it could never be implemented. The system dreamt up by

---

44. The term 'least developed country' once again smacks of the dominant evolutionism. The Planning and Development Committee (Tinbergen Committee) of the ECOSOC defined the LDCs in the early seventies as countries with a per capita GNP of less than a hundred 1968-dollars, an industry accounting for less than 10 per cent of GNP, and a literacy rate under 15 per cent in 1960 for the population aged under fifteen at that time.

the General Assembly involved, *mutatis mutandis*, applying to the international economic system a series of redistributive mechanisms tried and tested in the social-democratic countries. For this to have actually functioned, it would have had to have been not an international but a genuinely global (or supranational) system, with coercive powers to organize markets, to distribute profits and to make wealth more equal. It was a utopian vision – because the various states, in competition with one another to gather the spoils of growth, pursued nothing other than their own national interest. The 'new order', then, merely adjusted the rules of the old order to benefit actors who had appeared quite recently on the international arena. The guiding themes of enrichment and profit remained the same.

The NIEO appears in this light as the last avatar of the dominant economics. For it attached greatest weight to increases in production, while the new situation arising from the petrodollar reserves showed the crucial importance of financial flows for the economic system. It was a question not just of the relative importance given to various phenomena but of a major contradiction. For States can take the steps they think necessary to control output volumes and the amount of money (cash and notes) circulating on their territory, just as they can organize commodity trading at an international level, but they have no hold over the non-commodity money that banks can create at will by means of credit. Within the international setting in which they operate, States therefore seek arrangements to divide out the forms of wealth they can aspire to control, but the crux of the situation escapes them, as it is now financial flows which determine the real opportunities for profit.[45] In the sphere of bankers, hunter-gatherer methods do not get you very far.

AN ORIGINAL VOICE: THE 1975 DAG HAMMARSKJÖLD FOUNDATION REPORT ON ANOTHER DEVELOPMENT

The contradictions of the NIEO were directly linked to those of the international organization itself. Incantatory talk of the 'international community' and 'mutual interests' could not disguise the antagonisms

---

45. See François Rachline, *De zéro à epsilon. L'économie de la capture*, Paris: Hachette, 1994. Rachline shows convincingly that the neglect of money goes back a long way, and was already a feature of classical economic theory. Nevertheless, it has assumed new proportions since 1974.

between member states. This banal observation might lead one to suppose that a change in the institutional framework would make it possible to draw up more coherent and innovative proposals, to define other means of achieving the goal that everyone said they wanted to reach: the elimination of poverty.

Such is the background to the report generally known by the title under which it was published: *What Now*.[46] On the initiative of the Hammarskjöld Foundation and UNEP, more than a hundred people from all parts of the world who favoured a critical approach to 'development' gathered in small groups at Uppsala, The Hague and Algiers, or individually drafted working papers. The head of the project, Marc Nerfin, was then asked to sum up their deliberations in a report, and with the help of Ahmed Ben Salah, Ignacy Sachs and Juan Somavía he brought the whole operation to a successful conclusion just five months after it had begun.[47]

The report broke new ground in a number of the propositions that it put forward. First, 'development' is not simply an economic process, but a complex whole that has to arise endogenously, from deep down inside each society. It springs from the culture in question, and cannot be reduced to imitation of developed societies. *There is thus no universal formula for 'development'*. Second, it must be geared to satisfying the essential needs of the poorest sections of the population, who should rely mainly upon their own forces.[48] Third, the present situation is bound up with structures of exploitation which, though originating in the North, are relayed in the South by ruling classes that are at once 'accomplices and rivals' of privileged layers in the industrial countries. International aid should therefore be directed above all to states which undertake to reduce internal inequalities, and withheld from those which do not respect human rights. Fourth, 'development' should take

---

46. *What Now: The 1975 Dag Hammarskjöld Report, prepared on the occasion of the Seventh Special Session of the United Nations General Assembly, 1975*, published as a special issue of the Hammarskjöld Foundation journal, *Development Dialogue*, 1975.

47. The composition of the working groups is particularly instructive. Apart from those mentioned above (in note 15), the list included: F.H. Cardoso, R. Stavenhagen, J. Pronk, S. Ramphal, M. Rahnema, M. Strong, L. Yaker, J. Chonchol, J. Galtung, J. Ki-Zerbo, P.-M. Henry, R. Maheu, P. Bungener, B. Chidzero, L. Emmerij, D. Ghai, A. Peccei, Ph. de Seynes and M. Zammit-Cutajar. Some of these people were among the thirty-two authors of the Cocoyoc Declaration issued after a joint UNCTAD–UNEP conference held at Cocoyoc, near Mexico City between 8 and 12 October 1974, and published in *Development Dialogue*, 2, 1974, pp. 88–96.

48. The 'basic needs' strategy, which was officially recognized by the International Labour Office in 1976, will be presented in greater detail in the final part of this chapter.

account of the ecological limits associated with social and technological systems. Hence the countries of the North should change their life-styles, restructuring their economies and orienting them towards greater justice in international trade relations. Finally, the United Nations system needs to be profoundly modified to take account of the profound political changes that have taken place since the Second World War. Its functioning should be made smoother and less centralized so as to serve new forms of international co-operation; additional resources might come from a tax on income from the common heritage of mankind (especially the ocean depths) and from a reallocation of military expenditure.

Even this summary presentation clearly shows what distinguishes the Hammarskjöld Report from the NIEO. Both try to make the most of the new political situation following the emergence of OPEC and the American defeat in Vietnam. But their conclusions are sharply divergent, and it is not without reason that the Hammarskjöld Report looks to-wards 'another development' based upon needs satisfaction, self-reliance, harmony with nature and structural change. These elements are not necessarily new in themselves, but now they are unequivocally com-bined and relocated within a political context. At a distance from the world of official UN debates, it became possible to take an interest not only in international (economic) relations but also in the internal policy of States, and not to be afraid of exposing their inconsistencies.

The other novelty in the Hammarskjöld Report was that it con-sidered 'development' as a global phenomenon concerning not only the Third World but also the industrial countries. To illustrate what 'another development' might look like, it took two countries as exam-ples. As one might expect, Tanzania was selected for the South because the '*ujamaa* strategy' was the closest to the theses developed in the Report – although the weak points of the experience were by no means glossed over. More interesting, however, was the scenario for what 'another Sweden' might look like. Weighing the arguments both of those who consider economic growth to be indispensable and of those who reject it, the Report finally opted for controls on the content of growth according to its expected long-term consequences, especially for the environment. Its bold, almost sacrilegious conclusion – that 'the primacy of economics is over'[49] – would never be repeated in any international declaration. It led to four proposals to combat the ex-cesses of consumer society: the setting of an upper limit on meat and

---

49. *What Now*, p. 48.

oil consumption; more economic use of buildings; extension of the life of consumer goods; and replacement of privately owned cars with public transport and rented vehicles. These were presented not at all as austerity measures, but simply as ways of both improving the quality of life and fostering more equitable relations with the countries of the South.

The Report followed up these concrete examples by questioning the theoretical foundations of the international system: the existence of common interests, the sovereign equality of States, the natural character of economic 'laws', the efficiency of market allocation of resources. This is why it recommended for Third World countries both a strengthening of 'collective self-reliance' (which repeated, in a much deeper way, one of the planks of the NIEO) and selective participation in the international system − as the only guarantee of national independence and a distinctive style of 'development'.

What Now. The title of the Report was perfectly justified. Clear and precise in every connection, its proposals were capable of being implemented both within individual countries and at an international level − to the extent that there was political agreement. This crucial condition was not unknown to those who contributed to the Report, as many of them were (or had been) either government ministers or international civil servants. But their experiences actually seem to have led them to stress the gulf between economic theories and 'development' practice, even if this meant abandoning the diplomatic caution needed for their work to win broad approval. This interpretation explains why the Report had such little official impact, but also why it is of such great interest. No doubt it was necessary to choose between a lucid vision of the contradictions of the international order − one which spelt out their consequences and the radical cures that had to be applied − and an ideal portrait of an order which, though new, was like the old in failing to question the internal policy of States. The second option would have meant paraphrasing the NIEO. So it obviously seemed better to offer an original text from which not only NGOs but everyone unhappy with the injustices of 'development' could draw inspiration.

IN THE WAKE OF THE NIEO: FURTHER PROPOSALS

Carried away by the rhetorical success of the NIEO, the States of the South tried to widen the field of its possible application. A key document in this respect was the Lima Declaration on Industrial

Development and Cooperation,[50] which anticipated that the share of
the periphery in world industrial output would rise to 25 per cent by
the year 2000, but did not consider what type of industrialization was
desirable, what would be its effects on the environment, or what were
the mechanisms of dependent industrialization. Another initiative, this
time within the framework of UNESCO, was the New World Information and Communication Order.[51] This claimed to be fighting the
'cultural imperialism' of the richest countries, but it tended to envisage
a framework of state control over information, rather in the spirit of
the NIEO provisions. Nor did it achieve very much – except to open
up a major crisis within UNESCO in 1985, when the United States
and Britain walked out of the organization in protest at what they saw
as attacks on the freedom of speech. The damage to UNESCO was
particularly great, of course, in that these two countries were also large
contributors of funds.

In general, the Western countries were concerned much more with
the OPEC price rises and the climate of economic recession than with
the rhetoric of demands. In order to hold discussions outside the framework of the Southern-dominated United Nations, President Giscard
d'Estaing convened in Paris, between February 1976 and June 1977, a
Conference on International Economic Co-operation. The self-styled
socialist countries were not invited to this 'North–South Dialogue',[52] so
eight industrial countries and nineteen Southern countries were supposed to represent all the others in discussing the key issues of energy,
raw materials and trade, development and monetary–financial problems.
After eighteen months of difficult 'dialogue', the only agreement was
to create a special fund for the poorest countries and to continue
negotiating within the UN system. The Western countries got nothing
of substance on the questions that mattered to them most: oil supplies
and the security of investments.

Finally, mention should be made of two reports of the time that
tried to put forward a social-democratic vision of a 'new order'. The

---

50. The Declaration was published by the UN Industrial Development Organization (UNIDO) on 26 March 1975 (ID/CONF.3/31).

51. In fact the NWICO kept UNESCO busy between 1974 and 1984, without
ever being formally adopted. Hopes of an agreement appeared in 1978, but the only
major document to come out of it was the 'McBride Report': *Many Voices, One
World*, London: Kogan Page, 1980.

52. It was now that the supposedly neutral, geographical term 'South' began to
take over from 'Third World', with its political connotations going back to Sieyès.
The change was not free of misunderstandings, however, particularly as it tended to
suggest the existence of homogeneous blocs.

first of these was the 'RIO Report', *Reshaping the International Order*, which was presented to the Club of Rome by Jan Tinbergen.[53] Its main proposal was to continue along the path of liberalizing capital movements and trade, as mapped out by mainstream economic thinking, but to aim at reducing the gap between richest and poorest from the 13:1 estimated at the time to 3:1 by the end of the century. The Report drew largely on ideas prevalent in the 'development' milieux of Scandinavia and the Netherlands, and took account of the new priority given to the satisfaction of 'basic needs'. While recognizing the existence of dependency effects, it refused to consider delinking from the international economic system as a practical proposition for any country; instead, it offered a dualist perspective in which the poorest regions would gain by self-reliance, while the richest would be left to modernize according to the dominant conception. The Report's combination of 'globalism' and 'idealism' was both its strength and its weakness: its strength, because (in keeping with Club of Rome traditions) it did not gloss over either environmental or demographic problems; its weakness, because it was led into such ideas as a 'supranational' tax on transnational corporations, or a 'decentralized planetary sovereignty' which, under a UN umbrella and with the help of big companies and trade unions, would plan the world economy in a manner more equitable towards the disadvantaged – relying on a central world bank, a 'world food authority', and so on. Obviously, it took a good deal of naivety to come up with such bureaucratic innovations completely remote from the existing relationships of forces in the world.[54]

The other report – which in a way brought the decade to a close – was prepared by an independent commission of the United Nations chaired by Willy Brandt, and entitled *North–South: A Programme for Survival*.[55] It pioneered a new way of tackling problems that had been suggested by World Bank President, Robert McNamara: the UN Secretary-General appointed an independent commission under a widely

53. *Reshaping the International Order: A Report to the Club of Rome*, Jan Tinbergen, co-ordinator, Antony J. Dolman, editor, Jan van Ettinger, director, New York: E.P. Dutton & Co., 1976.

54. 'In the final analysis, our world is ruled by ideas – rational and ethical – and not by vested interests.' Ibid., p. 107.

55. *North–South: A Programme for Survival – Report of the Independent Commission on International Development Issues*, London: Pan Books, 1980. The Report was reviewed in a special number of *Third World Quarterly*, II (4), October 1980, the most memorable articles being André Gunder Frank's 'North South and East West: Keynesian Paradoxes in the Brandt Report' (pp. 669–80), and Dudley Seers's 'North–South: Muddling Morality and Mutuality' (pp. 669–80).

respected figure (Willy Brandt had been a Nobel Prizewinner in 1971 as well as West German Chancellor); the members of the commission then had a series of meetings in various parts of the world and interviewed numerous public figures on the spot;[56] finally, a secretariat collected the results and drafted a report, which was prefaced by the Chairman and delivered to the UN Secretary-General. The costs were covered by voluntary contributions from governments and by private funding.

The opportunity therefore existed to put forward new proposals on the basis both of 'development' experience (including its failures) and of the huge literature already available. But it must be said that the results were disappointing. While it recognized certain defects in the system – the spread of unemployment in the North and poverty in the South, the abuse of power by privileged minorities, and the lack of a political will to change the situation – the Report merely advocated a kind of 'worldwide Keynesianism' to shift resources on a massive scale, and thereby stimulate growth in the interests of all. On the one hand, it said that 'change is inevitable'; on the other, that change had to be based on solidarity and human rights. Its moralism was complemented with 'blackmailing' talk of catastrophe ('mankind has the moral obligation to survive'[57]), but at the same time it was argued that 'the rich cannot prosper without progress by the poor'.[58] To be sure, 'the world must aim to abolish hunger and malnutrition by the end of the century through the elimination of absolute poverty',[59] but the well-being of all was supposed to depend on the expansion of world trade.[60] Hopes were naturally expressed that there would be a 'common passion for peace',[61]

---

56. Members of the Third World Forum played only a minor role in the Brandt Report; only the Tanzanian Justinian Rweyemamu belonged to the secretariat set up in Geneva; and the commission itself was mainly composed of former ministers and diplomats (Eduardo Frei, Edward Heath, Olof Palme, Edgard Pisani, Jan Pronk, Shridath Ramphal, Layachi Yaker, *et al.*). Was it really a good idea for the 'North' to be represented by Social-Democratic ex-ministers who, when in power, had not tried to implement the measures they were now suddenly recommending? The long list of public figures interviewed by the commission included Luís Echeverría, Enrique Iglesias, Raúl Prebisch, Mahbub ul-Haq and Gamani Corea. Clearly the commission concentrated everywhere on contacts with the establishment, but it is strange that the World Bank – whose President had originally thought of the commission – was hardly consulted at all.

57. Ibid., p. 13.

58. Ibid., p. 270.

59. Ibid., p. 271.

60. Ibid., p. 276.

61. Pope Paul VI, met by Willy Brandt in 1979 in one of his numerous consultations, opined: 'Development is the new name for peace.'

military spending was deemed an insult to those in dire need that could be relieved through budgetary reallocation, and environmental questions were held to be of fundamental importance. But this hardly explained why there were supposed to be 'common interests' in the areas of 'energy, commodities and trade, food and agriculture',[62] or why it was so essential to increase the size of the economic 'cake' through growth and investment (if – as it was said almost in the same breath – economic growth would not automatically benefit 'broad masses of poor people'[63]).

This long catalogue of problems, dealt with in a discontinuous and superficial manner, was followed by a proposal à la RIO Report for some international taxes on trade or arms; a call was also made for the satisfaction of basic needs, and stress was laid on the importance of cultural identity. Like Truman's Point Four, the North–South Report stated that 'the task is to free mankind from dependence and oppression, from hunger and distress',[64] but the measures it proposed fell a long way short of the objective. There were at least two reasons why this was so. First, while the Report firmly admonished the countries of the North to step up their contributions to 'development', it did not adopt the same challenging tone in relation to the governments of the South. Yet it seems evident that the grinding poverty of huge numbers of people has internal causes that would be left untouched by a massive transfer of resources from North to South – indeed, the dictatorships responsible for the conditions of the poor would be further strengthened as a result. Second, from the point of view of the South, the Brandt Report actually represents a retreat from the NIEO, because it ignores the potential of such things as producers' associations or 'self-reliant development' in favour of increased aid to boost industrial exports from South to North.

Much more could be said about this huge report, which – perhaps to avoid the charges of utopianism levelled at the 'RIO' document – constantly hedged between correct observations, dubious assumptions, high-minded sentiments, and 'hard truths' likely to reassure the international establishment. It would be wrong, however, to blame Willy Brandt and his fellow-members of the commission; for their labours simply revealed the spirit of the age and the disappointments of 'Third-Worldism'. By the end of the 1970s it was already broadly established that most of the myriad 'development' projects had not fulfilled the

62. Ibid., p. 20.
63. Ibid., p. 24.
64. Ibid., p. 29.

hopes placed in them, that an ever greater part of the population in the South was sliding into 'absolute poverty', and that in its own interests the North was refusing to accept any radical change of international structures. With no way out in sight, what else was there to do but appeal to morality, Human Rights, solidarity and generosity, to the noble values on which the industrial countries prided themselves – even if North–South relations were evolving in the opposite direction? The Brandt Report had only a fleeting impact on international discussions of 'development', but it did mark the end of an era when hopes of tackling the causes of 'underdevelopment' had been high, and the beginning of a new era when, in the name of the same values, it was decided to make do with more and more palliative (or 'humanitarian') measures.

THE 'BASIC NEEDS' APPROACH

Political Counter-Fire

The so-called 'basic needs' approach, though partaking of the 'Third-Worldist' effervescence of the 1970s, occupied a place of its own. Its theoretical foundations were shaky, to say the least, and its concrete effects quite limited. But it experienced a certain vogue, both in the big international institutions and in non-governmental organizations, and it provides a textbook example of how *the ideological field of 'development' is structured outside any transformative influence on the living conditions of the most exploited layers.*

The concept made its first appearance at the annual speech of the President of the World Bank to its Governors, given in 1972 by Robert McNamara.[65] On this occasion, the President chose to reconcile the 'growth imperative' with social justice by sketching a dramatic picture of the conditions of people in the South, who were unable to take their destiny into their own hands because they could not satisfy their 'most essential needs'.[66] To deal with this appalling situation, it was

---

65. Robert S. McNamara, 'Address to the Board of Governors: Washington, D.C., September 25, 1972', in *The McNamara Years at the World Bank: Major Policy Addresses of Robert S. McNamara 1968–1981*, Baltimore, MD: Johns Hopkins University Press, 1981.

66. A few revealing expressions may be mentioned here: 'a developing world darkened by illiteracy' (ibid., p. 210); 'they who – despite their country's gross economic growth – remain entrapped in conditions of deprivation which fall below any rational definition of human decency' (p. 217); 'their lives are not developing' (p. 218); 'the poor farmer who has seldom seen an airplane, and never an airport' (p. 218); and so on.

necessary not only to increase public 'development' assistance by a considerable amount, but also to ensure that it actually reached the poorest layers – and to do this not by relying upon trickle-down effects but by committing large institutional resources. McNamara concluded with an almost martial exhortation to the governments of 'developing' countries to 'give greater priority to establishing growth targets in terms of essential human needs: in terms of nutrition, housing, health, literacy, and employment'.[67]

The idea seems so simple that one wonders why it took so long to see the light of day. As 40 per cent of people in the South live in 'absolute poverty',[68] does it not make sense to attend to the most urgent things first by enabling them to gain (or regain) decent conditions of existence? In order to live, everyone obviously needs to eat, to have a roof over their head, to clothe themselves, to have surroundings conducive to health, and to receive some education so that they can 'earn their living'. Should 'development' priorities not reflect these invariable basic needs of 'human nature'? Of course, the President of the World Bank was no humanist: even if 'the fundamental case for development assistance is the moral one',[69] *the ultimate goal was to raise the productivity of the poorest so that they could be brought into the economic system.* But it was an original approach, critical of the big economic conglomerates and hard on those who get rich at the expense of the poor. Without a doubt, it signalled a turn in the operations of the World Bank, which suddenly became more anxious to intervene at the grass roots, without ceasing to fund large-scale projects.

The policy change on the Bank's part had no immediate resonance: everyone's attention at the time was focused on the NIEO, which seemed to offer more radical, or more political, solutions to the problems of 'development'. Paradoxically, however, this gave a boost to the basic needs approach. For the theoretical opposition between macro-

---

67. Ibid., p. 228. McNamara no doubt recalled that he had been not only President of Ford Motor Company but also Defense Secretary between 1961 and 1968. Hence his talk of an 'enlightened struggle against poverty', of 'strategy', of 'an assault on the problem of poverty', and so on. Since then, McNamara has recognized that his military strategy in Vietnam was misguided. (*In Retrospect: the Tragedy and the Lessons of Vietnam*, New York: Times Books of Random House, 1995.) One day, perhaps, he will make the same admission concerning his 'development' strategy.

68. It was again Robert McNamara who, in his 'Address to the Board of Governors: Nairobi, Kenya, September 24, 1973', proposed a distinction between relative poverty and absolute poverty, defining the latter as 'a condition of life so limited as to prevent realization of the potential of the genes with which one is born' (in ibid., p. 239).

69. Ibid., p. 240.

economic perspective and concern for the poor concealed another agenda which – to put it bluntly – was one of *outside interference*. According to the provisions of the NIEO, interference in another country's affairs was excluded in the name of the sovereign equality of States; problems were to be resolved through international negotiation rather than the various influences that could be brought to bear by means of public 'development' assistance. However, the big suppliers of 'development' finance found this position difficult to accept. The beauty of the basic needs approach was that it offered new arguments (based on solidarity with the poor) that could justify intervention in the countries of the South, if necessary bypassing what local governments thought of the matter.

This was the context in which the ILO relaunched the debate in 1976 at the World Conference on Employment. The Declaration issued on this occasion stated:

> Basic needs, as understood in this Programme of Action, include two elements. First, they include certain minimum requirements of a family for private consumption, adequate food, shelter and clothing, as well as certain household equipment and furniture. Second, they include essential services provided by and for the community at large, such as safe drinking water, sanitation, public transport and health, education and cultural facilities.[70]

Thus, while the UN was still buzzing with the South's demands contained in the NIEO, here was a UN institution formally taking up the cudgels in support of a quite different approach. This isolated initiative is probably to be explained by the ILO's worsening relations with the United States in the seventies; in 1975, Washington had even given notice of its intention to quit an organization that had had the audacity to condemn Israel.[71] Everything had to be done, then, to avoid losing such an important provider of funds. This interpretation – as well as the incompatibility of the basic needs approach with the NIEO – is confirmed by the fact that the mention of the NIEO in the Declaration of Principles (§4), and then in the Plan of Action (§23), met with the liveliest opposition on the part of the United States and some other

---

70. 'Tripartite World Conference on Employment, Income Distribution and Social Progress and the International Division of Labour: Declaration of Principles and Programme of Action', *International Labour Office Official Bulletin*, LX (1977), p. 84.

71. The United States had suspended its contributions to the ILO in 1970, then resumed normal relations in 1972. However, the growing politicization of its debates (condemnation of Israel, inviting the PLO as an observer) led Washington to give notice of withdrawal in 1975; this took effect in 1977 and came to an end in 1980. See Victor-Yves Ghebali, *L'Organisation internationale du travail*, Geneva: Georg, 1987.

Western powers. That said, the basic needs idea was not entirely new: it had, as we have noted, already been introduced by the World Bank; and both the 1975 Hammarskjöld Report and the Cocoyoc Declaration (drafted in 1974 by a galaxy of intellectuals, many of them members of the Third World Forum) had taken it up with approval and stressed that 'development' should respect 'inner limits' (satisfaction of basic needs) as well as 'outer limits' (environmental constraints).[72]

This triple patronage (World Bank, ILO, Third World Forum) meant not only that the basic needs approach had a considerable audience, but also that the NGOs were (at least temporarily) at peace with the 'development' establishment, and in particular the World Bank.[73] All were united against the 'national bourgeoisies', which were seen either as making off with the fruits of 'development', or as refusing to comply with the funders' injunctions. Although their perceptions were thus fundamentally divergent, each partner in this strange alliance managed to acquire by association some of the credit given to the other: 'moral respectability' in the case of the NGOs, 'political legitimacy' in that of the international agencies. The whole episode shows that 'development' theories have more to do with ideological competition among the various actors (operating in a restricted field defined by the power that each can exercise over governments or public opinion) than with any real relevance to the problems facing the victims of 'development'. It is understandable, then, that collusion between antagonistic interests may sometimes result in apparently shared perspectives, expressed in new and equally surprising sets of phrases.[74]

Misleading Evidence

We must now consider what value should be given to the basic needs approach. It rests very largely upon the evident fact that people must eat to live. As the Club Méditerranée publicity used to say, holiday villages let you satisfy four needs: playing, drinking, eating and sleeping. The rhyming popular wisdom of Parisian graffiti is more realistic:

---

72. On the Cocoyoc Declaration and the Third World Forum, see notes 15 and 47 above.

73. In Switzerland, following a long parliamentary debate, the Development Cooperation and Humanitarian Aid Act of 1976 stated that the federal government 'should make a priority of supporting the efforts of developing countries, the most disadvantaged regions and population groups' (Art. 5, § 2). This stipulation, made under pressure from NGOs, was not unconnected to the 'basic needs' approach.

74. For example: adjustment with a human face, clean war, sustainable development, humanitarian interference, and so on.

'*métro – boulot – dodo*'.[75] But a combination of the two lists brings us close to the ones put forward by Robert McNamara or the ILO. They are not all quite so simple, though. Johan Galtung, for example, distinguishes between four types of 'needs': security, welfare, freedom and identity. This approach also has support from a number of psycho-sociologists: A. Maslow, for instance, tries to show through his 'needs pyramid' that certain basic requirements of existence have to be fulfilled before other, 'higher' ones can be met. As the Ancients used to say, *primum vivere, deinde philosophari*: you've got to live before you can philosophize. And Bronislaw Malinowski has no hesitation in basing culture on 'human nature': that is, on 'the fact that all men have to eat, they have to breathe, to sleep, to procreate, and to eliminate waste matter from their organisms wherever they live and whatever type of civilization they produce'.[76]

On the basis of these hard-to-deny truths, intense 'empirical-theoretical' activity got under way in the second half of the seventies to define more precisely what was meant by 'basic needs' and, above all, what means should be employed to satisfy them.[77] The ILO published a number of studies that clearly showed the limits of the exercise. The FAO, we learn from one of these, defines its 'reference man' as

> between 20 and 39 years of age[;] he weighs 65kg. He is healthy ... and physically fit for active work. On each working day he is employed for eight hours in an occupation that usually involves moderate activity. When not at work, he spends eight hours in bed, four to six hours sitting or moving around in only very little activity, and two hours in walking, in active recreation, or in household duties.[78]

---

75. That is: 'underground – work – sleep'.

76. Bronislaw Malinowski, *A Scientific Theory of Culture*, Chapel Hill: University of North Carolina Press, 1944, p. 75.

77. It is impossible here to review the huge body of literature on this question. Let us just signal a work that mainly brings together contributions by authors favourable to the basic needs approach: Katrin Lederer (in collaboration with Johan Galtung and David Antal), *Human Needs: A Contribution to the Current Debate*, published by the Berlin Science Center, Cambridge, MA and Königstein: Oelgeschlager, Gunn & Hain, Anton Hain, 1980. It includes pieces by Carlos Mallmann, President of the Bariloche Foundation in Argentina, who has developed a model of his own, as well as a contribution by Galtung, an abridged version of which is republished together with a number of critical texts in *Il faut manger pour vivre. Controverses sur les besoins fondamentaux et le développement*, Cahier de l'IUED (11), Paris: PUF/Geneva: IUED, 1980. Among the numerous studies published by the ILO, special mention should be made of D.P. Ghai, A.R. Khan, E.L.H. Lee and T. Alfthan, eds, *The Basic-Needs Approach to Development: Some Issues Regarding Concepts and Methodology*, Geneva: International Labour Office, 1977. And finally, for a 'popular' version of this approach, see *Ten Basic Human Needs and Their Satisfaction*, Sri Lanka, Moratuwa, Sarvodaya Community Education Series (26), 1978.

All this to demonstrate that the 'typical man' has to consume 3,000 calories and 17 grams of protein per day. But is this really an accurate identikit picture of a Third World peasant? Another example: it is estimated that an adult woman in Bangladesh needs 12.5 square yards of cloth a year to clothe herself decently,[79] and that a family of six needs two rooms of 150 square feet each.[80] Such bureaucratic naivety never ceases to astonish. *Yet it is indicative of the dead-end that is inescapable once spontaneously 'evident facts' are made the starting point of a chain of argument.* Without claiming in any way to wrap up this vast debate, let us conclude with a few brief remarks.

(a) To make 'need' the foundation of economics does not *ipso facto* establish it with certainty. The Robinson Crusoe scenarios that traditionally begin a course in economics, where an individual must choose among scarce resources to satisfy unlimited 'needs', overlook the fact that people are never alone but are always born within a society which, in a way, imposes its needs on them. The construction of universal or cross-cultural norms is therefore misconceived. 'Need' is only a 'proto-concept': that is – to quote Durkheim – one of 'the fallacious ideas that dominate the mind of the layman'.[81]

(b) The spontaneous idea that one must start with 'basic needs' and only later move on to 'higher' aspirations is contradicted by the evidence of anthropology. For

> in every society … the 'minimum necessary for life' is residually determined by the basic urgency of a surplus: of God's share, the share needed for sacrifice, the extravagant expenditure, the economic profit. It is this levy for luxury purposes which negatively determines the subsistence level, and not the other way around…. There have never been 'societies of shortage' or 'societies of abundance', because a society's expenditure – *whatever the objective volume of its resources* – is decided in accordance with a structural surplus and an equally structural deficit…. The survival threshold is always determined from above, never from below.[82]

---

78. Quoted in Michael Hopkins, *A Basic-Needs Approach to Development Planning*, World Employment Programme, Working Paper 3, Geneva: ILO, 1977, p. 10.

79. A.H. Khan, 'Basic-Needs Target: An Illustrative Exercise in Identification and Quantification', in Ghai *et al.*, eds, *The Basic-Needs Approach to Development*, p. 74.

80. Ibid., p. 86. According to the equally scientific calculations of the Bariloche Foundation, an African should have 7 square metres of housing, while a Latin American 'needs' 10 and an inhabitant of the industrial countries 20!

81. *The Rules of Sociological Method*, p. 32.

82. Jean Baudrillard, 'La genèse idéologique des besoins', in *Pour une critique de l'économie politique du signe*, Paris: Gallimard, 1972, pp. 84–5.

Before one can eat, a share must be set aside for the gods; before one can have somewhere to live, the temple must be built. Greek and Roman ruins, as well as cathedrals and mosques, testify to the care that must be devoted to things holy before one can think of oneself.[83]

(c) The 'basic needs' approach is totally inoperative in living societies; it can be useful only in relation to 'anti-societies' or 'non-societies'. From time immemorial, governors of prisons and boarding-schools, captains of long-range ships or generals of field armies have been at pains to calculate the precise subsistence rations of those in their charge. The same is true, alas, of people responsible for refugee camps, who have to plan the resources necessary for the survival of those in their care. But who will believe that this *managerial perspective* can be applied in the normal conditions of social existence, dominated by symbolic links between people?

(d) Just as 'development'/growth is based on a biological metaphor, *the basic needs approach rests upon a naturalistic conception of the social*. It is true, of course, that man is situated within nature. Like all animals, he needs access to proteins, calories, oxygen, sleep, and so on. But society cannot be reduced to a 'human zoo', in which the only needs not usually satisfied are the ones that are probably most treasured: space and freedom. Reference to a hypothetical 'human nature' is of little use in understanding how people actually live. Although certain conditions are necessary for survival, they are generally not enough to assure life within society. For unlike animals, which die as soon as their 'ecological niche' is taken away from them, men and women can live – thanks to human culture – in the middle of deserts as well as in the icy wastes of the North. It is not because they inhabit a hot country that people go around naked – far from it.

(e) The basic needs approach is perfectly consistent with mainstream economics (even if it stresses that growth alone is not enough in the absence of effective demand). Both assume that human history is determined by the struggle against scarcity, to satisfy 'needs' judged to be insatiable. Within such a perspective, only the (unlimited) growth of production can lead to the happiness of final satisfaction. But the race

---

83. It is significant that certain associations of African immigrants in France club together first to build a mosque – before a school or a clinic. Similar conclusions about the relative weight of the spiritual and the material might be reached in connection with funeral ceremonies, the *kula* ring, contemplative rearing, the respect shown to 'sacred cows', and so on.

or chase is, by hypothesis, endless – especially as in modern society, where social relations are mediated by things, what are called 'needs' are most often only a wish to be different, intensified by an individualist and egalitarian ideology.[84] This explains why, in a Western perspective, society appears always to have been dominated by shortage.

Supporters of the basic needs approach were far from discouraged by such criticisms, because what they were seeking was not so much epistemological coherence as political utility. In their view, 'development' projects were supposed to be directed to 'the grass roots', the poorest layers neglected by governments in which one could no longer trust. The 'small is beautiful' ideology was thus complemented by a new humanism. As UNESCO declared, 'development' was now to be centred on human beings and their basic needs. The ever-worsening conditions of life in the South meant that a morality of urgency took precedence over rigour of analysis; the time seemed to have come for action rather than reflection.

CONCLUSION

Something like a great turnaround took place in the course of the 1970s. The decade began in an almost revolutionary atmosphere marked by support for liberation movements, the growing influence of dependency theory, and hopes in Tanzania's original model of self-reliance. It reached a peak with the proclamation of the New International Economic Order, signalling the triumph of the 'Third World' over an old order marked down for disappearance. Then, suddenly, the victory seemed to pass over to the other side. The structural changes so well outlined in the Hammarskjöld Report, and so badly wanted by the countries of the South, ran up against the intransigence of the industrial North. A highly prestigious commission chaired by Willy Brandt concluded its work with a series of pious wishes. Whereas it had originally been intended to draw lessons from the past so as to tackle the causes of poverty, UNESCO simply proposed to make 'development' human-centred, the FAO struck a medal in honour of Mother Teresa (in 1975), and the ILO (which was supposed to defend workers'

---

84. See Georges-Hubert de Radkowski, *Les jeux du désir. De la technique à l'économie*, Paris: PUF, 1980.

interests) allied itself with a World Bank dominated by US capital to affirm that the road to 'development' went via the satisfaction of basic needs.

Turnaround and disenchantment. It is true that man had finally walked on the moon, but the world had hardly changed – or rather, it had hardened in its conservatism, and Ronald Reagan had been elected President of the United States. As for the intellectuals who had so far come up with the most original ideas, they gave their books titles such as *The End of Development*.[85] Everything was in place for what is often known as the 'lost decade' of the 1980s.

---

85. François Partant, *La fin du développement. Naissance d'une alternative?*, Paris: Maspero, 1982.

CHAPTER 10

THE ENVIRONMENT,
OR THE NEW NATURE OF
'DEVELOPMENT'

THE RETURN TO CLASSICAL ECONOMICS PLUS
A FEW HUMANITARIAN EXTRAS

The theory and practice of 'development' marked time during the 1980s. Policies of the North towards the South could be summed up in two words: *structural adjustment*. It is not our intention here to discuss the various measures that were imposed in the name of this new 'imperative', because it formed part of the dominant economic theory and did not present itself, as such, as a means to 'development'.[1] There must first be adjustment, it was said, and later there can be 'development' – certainly a revealing way of defining priorities. Here we shall confine ourselves to three remarks regarding the context, rather than the content, of the structural adjustment programmes.

First, structural adjustment was supposed to restore a number of equilibria that were thought necessary – especially at the IMF – for the harmony of the international system. How had the disturbances to equilibrium arisen? As regards national government finances, there were a number of possible culprits: the bloated administrative apparatuses designed to look after the regime's clientele rather than serve the public; the low productivity of nationalized corporations; tax evasion often

---

1. On the economic changes of the 1980s, see Georges Corm, *Le nouveau désordre économique mondial. Aux racines des échecs du développement*, Paris: La Découverte, 1993. For a critical account of structural adjustment, see Christian Comeliau, *Les Relations Nord–Sud*, Paris: La Découverte, 1991, pp. 55 f.

linked to activity in the 'informal' sector; or subsidization of basic foods to ward off popular discontent. Externally, a payments imbalance might be attributed at one and the same time to bad world prices for primary products (and therefore worsening terms of trade); a low level of foreign investment; excessive repatriation of profits; overpurchasing from abroad, especially of weapons; growing weight of debt service, especially in a period of rising interest rates; cutbacks in public 'development' assistance; high levels of smuggling; infrastructural development relying on costly imported goods, and so on. In practice, all these phenomena came down to the idea that government, companies and individuals were living beyond their means. It should also be stressed, however, that this situation came about because the industrial countries (especially the American commercial banks) fell over themselves to recycle the petrodollars in and after 1975. *This 'excess liquidity' led the financial institutions into a totally irresponsible credit policy.* Normally, before a banker agrees to a loan, he assesses the risk and demands all manner of guarantees that the borrower's use of it will yield profits at least as high as the anticipated interest.[2] In the second half of the 1970s, however, any sum was lent to just about anyone for any purpose, and as the industrial countries happily put up with inflation to lower the real cost of oil products, there was such a rise in interest rates that borrowers became unable to keep up payments.[3] This, roughly speaking, was the origin of the crisis of 1982, when Mexico's inability to meet its international obligations threw a number of US banks into crisis and resulted in the gradual spread of structural adjustment programmes.[4] The gravity of the problem was due to the cumulative character of the imbalance, for the recipient countries had to resort to fresh loans when they found themselves unable to repay or even to service existing debts on schedule. Mismanagement was no doubt also to blame, but this was widespread

---

2. A credit operation actually creates money in the expectation that it will eventually correspond to a set of goods and services. As a rule, a loan is thus a wager on future production – but it also runs the risk of fuelling speculation.

3. For the monetarist theory fashionable at the time, only high interest rates could discourage credit, and therefore inflation. This was music to the ears of the speculators, and increased the amount of unproductive income. A persistent level of high interest rates also puts the stress on the present at the expense of the future.

4. It was the NICs – Argentina, Brazil, Poland, etc. – which had the highest debt levels and paid the highest proportion of their export revenue in debt service. In 1982, Mexico's external debt had reached 80 billion dollars, while it was calculated that between 1979 and 1982 Mexican operators had placed more than 54 billion dollars abroad.

among all the protagonists; lack of rigour in the South corresponded to light-minded attitudes in the North.

'Monetary disorder' therefore meant that economies had to be 'adjusted' and trade balances 'corrected'. But the adjustment (through devaluation, for example) was demanded only of debtor countries – as if the surpluses of lenders were altogether more legitimate. Moreover, the United States constituted a huge exception to the rule that was doubly scandalous: first, because no one took offence, given that the dollar was the chief means of international payments which Washington could create at will; and second, because the Americans thought that in this case the responsibility for disequilibrium rested with those who profited from it – that is, with the Japanese and, to a lesser degree, the Europeans. In theory, international payments 'naturally' balance, with the deficits of some offsetting the surpluses of others, but things are very different in practice because a large number of transactions (from officially tolerated corruption, through mafia business, capital flight or drug deals, to corporate bribes to win contracts) are not entered in the books at all. *Hence, economists work with thoroughly unreliable figures, and their interpretations of them and the conclusions they draw vary sharply according to the country under consideration.*

Finally, it is clear that the budgetary austerity and market liberaliz-ation involved in adjustment policies often meant drastic cuts in the public service, in subsidies of all kinds, and in health and education benefits.[5] Well-being had to be adjusted downwards to the 'imperatives' of the market economy. To mitigate this new deterioration in living standards, someone thought up the term 'adjustment with a human face' – which was supposed to combine IMF-style austerity with the 'humanitarian' concerns of UNICEF. After the strange alliance between the World Bank and the NGOs around the concept of basic needs, here was a new way of making people believe in the harmless – even positive – character of a procedure with catastrophic effects. By a semantic trick, two opposites were joined together so that the value accorded to one was reflected upon the other, much more questionable term. A 'human face' was thus supposed to make adjustment acceptable.[6]

---

5. During the eighties, the various international institutions – especially the IMF and the World Bank – dismantled the States of the South with the same enthu-siasm that they had applied in strengthening them in the seventies.

6. See Giovanni Andrea Cornia, Richard Jolly and Frances Stewart, *Adjustment with a Human Face*, vol. 1, *Protecting the Vulnerable and Promoting Growth*, Oxford: Clarendon Press, 1987. The subtitle is particularly significant.

And with this new invention, the ideology of 'development' entered the realm of the oxymoron.[7]

Within the space of a few years, the international Keynesianism that tried in its way to organize trade was replaced by monetarism, wholesale deregulation and an international credit economy. Even if States sometimes had to bail out the most reckless banks in order to head off a major crisis, the 'laws of the market' now served as a universal doctrine, and 'development' issues were reduced to the humanitarian initiatives of UNICEF and the NGOs. For the pervading liberalism was not content to smash up voluntarist attempts at promoting greater equity; it also sounded the knell of 'Third-Worldism'.

Since the late 1960s, thinking about the Third World had largely been the preserve of intellectuals within the orbit of the political Left. In the case of France, this association had originated at the time of the Algerian War and continued in relationship to other anti-colonial and anti-imperialist struggles: support for Castroism in Cuba and Che Guevara more generally, solidarity with the African liberation movements, criticism of the US intervention in Vietnam, admiration for the Maoist Cultural Revolution, celebration of the victory of the Khmer Rouge, infatuation with the Sandinista revolution in Nicaragua, and finally a conviction that the Shah's forced departure in 1979 had been driven by a huge leap in Iranian cultural identity, expressed religiously in Khomeini's Shiism. This political militancy went together with a critique of Westernization as an ethnocidal project responsible for the failures of 'development' – hence the hopes placed in novel initiatives of 'autocentred development' and the defence of indigenous populations, especially in Latin America and Australia.

This set of convictions was quite widely shared in the world of NGOs and 'developers', but it received its first blow in 1983 with the publication of Pascal Bruckner's controversial *The Tears of the White Man*.[8] This essayist-novelist, who had already published two works together with the '*nouveau philosophe*' Alain Finkelkraut, did not have the best of credentials to be writing on 'development'. But although he attributed to 'Third-Worldism' a coherence it did not possess, he had a remarkable

---

7. An oxymoron is a rhetorical figure whereby contradictory terms are brought into conjunction, the classical example being the 'dark brightness' [*l'obscure clarté*] which the poet has fall from the stars. In literature, or in mystical texts, this makes it possible to say the unsayable by evoking the coincidence of opposites. In its ideological variant, however, the oxymoron constitutes a form of legitimizing camouflage.

8. *The Tears of the White Man: Compassion as Contempt* [1983], New York: The Free Press.

capacity to sum up its defects in a telling phrase. Briefly, Bruckner alleged that 'Third-Worldists', in holding the West responsible for all the ills of the South, closed their eyes to all the exactions committed in the name of anti-imperialism; they revelled in a form of anti-capitalist struggle by proxy, loudly demonstrating their support for all those who somehow or other helped to undermine 'development' based on competition and the market. Hence a kind of 'Don Juanism', or successive infatuation with revolutions whose main characteristic is repression rather than any advantages to those they are supposed to liberate. Hence – according to Bruckner – the bad conscience of those living in affluence while the other half of the world dies.[9] Hence the self-flagellation of the West, which proclaims as universal values that the 'noble savages' challenge elsewhere. Hence, too, that automatic solidarity (springing from both Christianity and Marxism) with anyone said to be oppressed by Western expansionism. Bruckner was wrong, of course, to ascribe to 'Third-Worldists' an influence over public opinion which they never had. He was also mistaken in thinking that they happily accept anti-Western dictatorships, or that they always imagine a directly causal link between the meat they guiltily consume and the wresting of grain from the poor. And he failed to appreciate the persistence, in the Third World, of forms of behaviour radically different from the individualist desire to accumulate by profiting from the 'laws' of competition. Nevertheless, was Bruckner not right to criticize 'Third-Worldists' for rejoicing at a regime in Saigon that they condemned in Prague, to ponder over the guilt-effects of media depictions of Third World poverty, to question a cultural relativism that justified the 'barbarism' of others while generating 'self-hatred', or to evoke the responsibility of Third World elites in exploiting the very peoples they claimed to be leading along the path of 'progress'?

The second challenge to 'Third-Worldism' came from the creation of *Médecins sans frontières* (MSF) by the Liberté sans Frontières (LSF) Foundation in 1985. This would have remained unnoticed if the Foundation's inaugural symposium (on 'development') had not deliberately excluded the NGOs – which for decades had devoted all their efforts to the improvement of Third World living standards – and if it had not soon become clear that the LSF's leading bodies included a

---

9. To borrow the title of the book by Susan George, one of the most important 'Third-Worldist' writers, *How the Other Half Dies: the Real Reasons for World Hunger*, London: Penguin, 1981.

number of figures from the political Right, even the far Right.[10] In
reality, the LSF's ideas left no room for ambiguity: they sought to do
away with a view of the Third World as eternal victim of Western
'pillage', a view which resulted in such disastrous pseudo-solutions as
'the new world economic and information order, the renunciation of
external debt, auto-centred development with no place for foreign trade,
or the introduction of so-called appropriate technology'.[11] The aim,
then, was to root 'development' in human rights and democracy (since
it was precisely the 'take-off' countries that did not apply the 'Third-
Worldists'' precepts), and to stop believing that the South's misfortunes
were caused by the North's selfish greed.

LSF was probably right (though not exactly original) in two of its
points: namely, that the term 'Third World' no longer corresponded to
anything, given the disparity of 'development styles' and commercial
interests in the South; and that South-East Asia was achieving remarkable growth rates by playing on free trade. Nevertheless, it was aston-
ishing that upholders of freedom and democracy should have taken to
celebrating the virtues of South Korea. And although it is true that
some countries then within the orbit of the USSR (Cuba, Angola,
Guinea, China, Vietnam, Iraq, etc.) did not excel in respect for human
rights, how could it have been forgotten that Pinochet, Somoza, the
Argentinian and Brazilian military, Mobutu, Bokassa, Suharto and others
had consolidated their hold on power through repression legitimated
by anti-communism with the support of Western governments? It may
be that, as LSF claimed, Third-Worldist 'myopia' led to 'resigned indul-
gence bordering on laxness towards the worst cases of oppression', and
'astigmatism' to 'perception of a distorted reality'.[12] But visual disorders
every bit as serious could be found among the self-styled champions of
human rights.

10. Under the heading 'Une bête à abattre: le "tiers-mondisme"', *Le Monde
diplomatique* published in May 1985 a dossier of some twenty-five pages on the debate
arising out of the Foundation's January symposium. Alain Gresh traced the links
between certain LSF members and two organizations well known for their anti-
communism: the CIEL, or Comité des intellectuels pour l'Europe des libertés (J.-F.
Revel, E. Le Roy Ladurie, I. Yannakis *et al.*), and L'Internationale de la résistance (F.
Furet, J. Broyelle, A. Besançon, *et al.*). In a subsequent issue of *Le Monde diplomatique*
(November 1985, p. 5), LSF tried to explain that these two movements also included
less clearly right-wing figures, and that a number of independent experts (G. Etienne,
J. Giri) were members of the LSF's leading bodies.

11. *Texte de présentation de la Fondation Liberté sans frontières, pour l'information sur
les droits de l'homme et le développement*, n.d. (actually January 1985), p. 5.

12. Ibid., pp. 11, 12.

More significant than these politicians' quarrels[13] was the fact that 'development' was now treated as just another part of general economics, escaping those who had made a profession of dealing with it – and had succeeded over the past thirty years in making 'development studies' a subject in its own right. For LSF, market 'laws' were universal in character, and any dispensation invented to favour the countries of the South (especially within the framework of the NIEO) merely confused the issue and limited what the play of competition might otherwise have achieved. Hence the evocation of a 'liberty without frontiers', its legitimacy beyond dispute and grounded upon human rights. From this point of view, *the objectives of LSF were in perfect harmony with those of structural adjustment.*

The other effect of LSF was to make 'development discourse' the property of doctors rather than of special experts in North and South (whether in the field or the academy, NGOs or international agencies). For it was Médecins sans frontières which launched the LSF Foundation, with – at that time – Dr Claude Malhuret as its president and Dr Rony Brauman as its manager.[14] To be sure, many MSF people distinguished themselves 'in the field' by their care for victims of war, famine or natural disaster, and by their undeniable expertise in dealing with such emergencies. But such qualities were quite different from those needed in long-term projects respecting local wishes and identities (which usually express themselves in a conflictual mode rather than in the harmonious form of explicit utterances). The good doctors who watch at the bedsides of the South do not trouble themselves with such exotic details: either the economy is in generally good shape and requires no more than a dose of market laws, or it is anaemic and needs humanitarian transfusions to get back on its feet. 'Humanitarian intervention',[15] and the matching 'adjustment with a human face', were the last avatars of the care for the poor upon which 'development' had always based itself.

Lastly, it should be recalled that the ultimate blow to 'Third-Worldism' was delivered by the fall of the Berlin Wall in 1989 and the

---

13. For the details, see Yves Lacoste, *Contre les anti tiers-mondistes et certains tiers-mondistes*, Paris: La Découverte, 1985.

14. Nor should it be forgotten that Médecins sans frontières was founded by Dr Bernard Kouchner, who – like Claude Malhuret – later became Minister of Health and Humanitarian Affairs. This new ministerial post did not replace the 'development co-operation' ministry, but it did signal a change of approach to relations with the countries of the South.

15. See Marie-Dominique Perrot, ed., *Dérives humanitaires. États d'urgence et droit d'ingérence*, Geneva: IUED/Paris: PUF, 1994.

subsequent break-up of the Soviet Union.[16] Now, it seemed, everything was a matter of *Realpolitik* rather than ideology. By trusting its political and economic future to the laws of the market, Russia conjured away a 'model' that had for so long been seen as an alternative to the dominant economics. No one, of course, regretted the aberrations of bureaucratic planning, or the irreversible damage to the environment resulting from triumphalist industrialization, or the 'internal colonialism' characteristic of the former Soviet empire. But like it or not, many had thought that beyond the absurdities – and the lack of respect for basic human rights – they could glimpse a different way of conceiving international relations, a possible (albeit politically calculated) source of support for attempts to break with the Western established order, and a way of setting prices other than through the mere play of supply and demand. Perfectly justified though the criticisms were, the Soviet regime had represented for many a conceivable (albeit desperate) resource against the Pax Americana.[17] But that, too, collapsed, and all these events together decisively (though not definitively) marked what seemed like the end of 'development'.

'SUSTAINABLE DEVELOPMENT' OR GROWTH EVERLASTING?

'Development' was too closely tied to the Western adventure to be simply engulfed by the dominant ideology amid public indifference. Besides, although the 'wasted decade' had not been wasted for everyone – especially the speculators – the problems facing the South had grown still worse. It therefore seemed necessary, and possible, for 'development' to 'bounce back' via the new Western fashion of ecology.

The revival began in the early 1980s, following a scenario very similar to that of the Brandt Report. In 1983 the General Assembly of the United Nations asked the Secretary-General to appoint a 'World Commission on Environment and Development', and he entrusted the chair of this to Mrs Gro Harlem Brundtland, a doctor who had for a time

---

16. There was also the Chinese 'four modernizations' policy shift of 1986, which set the objective of a 'socialist market economy' and marked the end of the Maoism that had fed the dreams not only of Sartre and countless 'sixty-eighters' but also of part of the 'development' establishment. (See Chapter 6, note 38 above.)

17. One thinks, for example, of the close links between the South African Communist Party and Nelson Mandela's ANC. Everyone knew of them, but at the time there hardly seemed any other (financial) means of securing victory for a cause that was by no means the same as that of Bolshevism.

been Minister of the Environment and was then Prime Minister of Norway. The Commission, as usual, drew upon the political personnel of various countries, some of whom had held high office within the United Nations system,[18] but it also contained fifteen or so people directly involved in environmental questions – including Maurice Strong (general secretary of the first Human Environment Conference in Stockholm in 1972, and subsequently organizer of the Rio Conference), as well as another Canadian, the OECD's environmental authority Jim MacNeill, who was appointed general secretary of the Commission. Unlike the Brandt Commission, then, which had consisted of 'political people', the Brundtland Commission was made up of environmental specialists supposedly familiar with the numerous works published during the previous twenty years,[19] plus former high functionaries of the UN supposed to have an overall view of 'development' questions and the problems development itself had created. Another difference was that whereas the Brandt Commission had mainly taken advice from political figures, the Brundtland Commission found the time, at public sessions in various parts of the world, to meet numerous representatives of militant ecological movements.[20]

Conditions were therefore optimal for a well-informed, original and stimulating report. Work on it was completed in March 1987, and it was published the following year under the title *Our Common Future*.[21]

---

18. Mansur Khalid from Sudan had been president of the Security Council, Bernard Chidzero from Zimbabwe had chaired the Development Committee of the World Bank and IMF and been deputy general secretary of UNCTAD, Mohammed Sahnoun from Algeria was a diplomat who would later be given the Somalian assignment, and Janez Stanovnik from Yugoslavia had been executive secretary of the Economic Commission for Europe. Only Shridath S. Ramphal, secretary-general of the Commonwealth and former Guyanese Minister of Foreign Affairs, had also served on the Brandt Commission, but among the 'special advisers' were the familiar names of Garmani Corea and Enrique Iglesias.

19. This was especially true of those active in 'eco-development' – a term suggested by Maurice Strong and Ignacy Sachs to indicate that 'development' should be based upon an *economic* theory renewed by *eco*logical considerations.

20. Extracts from these public hearings, at which anonymous committed citizens were able to have their say, are printed as boxes on the pages of the Report, and are one of its most interesting features – for they often made it possible to say what the Commission did not allow itself to express.

21. World Commission on Environment and Development, *Our Common Future*, with an introduction by Gro Harlem Brundtland, London: Fontana Books, 1988. Of the copious literature on the Report, we have space only to mention: Hans-Jürgen Harborth, *Dauerhafte Entwicklung (Sustainable Development), Zur Enstehung eines neuen ökologischen Konzepts*, Berlin: Wissenschaftszentrum Berlin für Sozialforschung (FS II 89–403), 1989; Hilkka Pietilä, 'Environment and Sustainable Development', *IFDA Dossier* (77), May–June 1990, pp. 61–70; Ted Trainer, 'A Rejection of the Brundtland

It has to be said that the Report gives an almost exhaustive list of threats to the planet's ecological equilibrium.[22] Deforestation, soil erosion, the greenhouse effect, the hole in the ozone layer, demography, food chain, water supplies, energy, urbanization, extinction of animal species, massive stockpiling of weapons, protection of the ocean and space – nothing was left out of the inventory that the Commission compiled on the basis of extensive information, and presented in the form of figures and tables. Governments could no longer ignore the many ecological dangers that could be, if not eliminated, then at least limited through binding legislation.

Now, whereas the theme of the Stockholm Conference had been the 'human environment', the Brundtland Commission had to consider the environment and 'development' together. This was a crucial difference, because it meant focusing on the ways in which both rich and poor societies damaged the environment (for different reasons). It also meant reconciling two opposite concepts: for on the one hand, it was precisely human activities – especially those stemming from the mode of industrial production synonymous with 'development' – which lay behind the deterioration of the environment; and on the other hand, it seemed inconceivable not to hasten the 'development' of peoples which did not yet have access to decent living conditions. How could respect for nature be married with a concern for justice?

To overcome this dilemma, the Commission proposed the following concept of 'sustainable development':[23]

Report', ibid., pp. 71–84; Olav Stokke, 'Sustainable Development: A Multi-Faceted Challenge', *The European Journal of Development Research* 3 (1), June 1991, pp. 8–31; and the article 'Environment' in Wolfgang Sachs, ed., *The Development Dictionary: A Guide to Knowledge as Power*, London: Zed Books, 1992, pp. 26–37.

22. The Commission remained quite discreet, however, on the problem of transport and the cumulative costs of motor vehicle use (pp. 198–9), and was unable to agree on nuclear energy (although the Chernobyl catastrophe had already occurred). Its conclusion on this issue is particularly vacuous: 'The generation of nuclear power is only justifiable if there are solid solutions to the presently unsolved problems to which it gives rise' (p. 189).

23. Already the North American Indians understood that, before undertaking something, one had to think of the effects on seven generations to come. 'Sustainable development' harks back to an old concern of Robert Malthus in *An Essay on the Principle of Population* (1798), as well as to the arguments developed in the 'Meadows Report': *The Limits to Growth* (1972). As to the term itself, it was already used at a United Nations seminar in 1979 and in a study jointly sponsored in 1980 by the IUCN (International Union for the Conservation of Nature and Natural Resources): *World Conservation Strategy: Living Resources Conservation for Sustainable Development.*

Humanity has the ability to make development sustainable – to ensure that it meets the needs of the present without compromising the ability of future generations to meet their own needs. The concept of sustainable development does imply limits – not absolute limits but limitations imposed by the present state of technology and social organization on environmental resources and by the ability of the biosphere to absorb the effects of human activities. But technology and social organization can be both managed and improved to make way for a new era of economic growth. The Commission believes that widespread poverty is no longer inevitable. Poverty is not only an evil in itself, but sustainable development requires meeting the basic needs of all and extending to all the opportunity to fulfil their aspirations for a better life. A world in which poverty is endemic will always be prone to ecological and other catastrophes.[24]

One might have thought that the Commission would pay special attention to defining the central term in the report; now was the time to create a new operational concept that would offer clear policy guidance. But the key passage we have just quoted is singularly lacking in content, managing to combine unwarranted assertions with points that run counter to the truth. Without claiming to offer a complete analysis, let us mention some of the essentials.

(a) The opening statement presupposes the existence of a collective subject ('humanity') endowed with reflection and volition – a subject, however, which cannot be clearly identified. 'Sustainable development' depends on everyone – that is, on no one. Use of the passive mood merely reinforces this impression, and makes it more difficult for the reader to challenge what is being said.

(b) *The opening statement involves a circular argument: it assumes as true what has to be demonstrated. Moreover, the very way of making the point makes it impossible to demonstrate.* The Report claims that 'the present' has 'needs' that have to be met without preventing future generations from meeting theirs. But how are these famous needs to be identified? Who will decide that one good or service rather than another belongs to the category of 'basic needs'?[25] And as it is impossible to define the

---

24. *Our Common Future*, p. 8.

25. Let us assume that there is a 'need' for drinking water. Is it enough to ensure that creeks are not polluted? Should communal water taps be installed everywhere, and if so, how many per thousand inhabitants? Is the wish to have a tap in one's kitchen a 'real need'? And if so, should one individual be allowed to use 500 litres a day (so long as he pays his bill), while others have to be content with a hundredth of that amount? There is no end to such questions, and it has to be admitted once and for all that they cannot be satisfactorily answered for the whole of 'humanity'.

current needs of humanity, how could one ever hope to know those of future generations?[26]

(c) Limits to 'development' are evoked, but their flexibility is underlined in the very next sentence. This is particularly confusing because although 'human activities' obviously do have 'effects' on the biosphere, the ones resulting from industry – which are shown to be the whole problem in a major section of the Report[27] – do not receive any mention at this point. (In the absence of any such specification, the 'effects' might be thought to refer simply to man's presence on earth for thousands of years.)

(d) The task, we are told, is 'to make way for a new era of economic growth'. Like most 'development' strategies, the Brundtland Report is not averse to messianic talk, but the 'new era' will also be marked by economic growth and so threatens to look much like the previous one. *People should be made to think that everything is changing, so that everything can remain the same as before* – as the main character in Lampedusa's *The Leopard* puts it.

(e) In the Commission's view, 'poverty is no longer inevitable'. Of course, the Commission is free to think what it likes, but instead of this negative assertion it should have considered the mechanisms through which widespread poverty has been socially constructed in the last few decades. No doubt this would have led it to denounce the mechanisms of exclusion operated by the economic growth it seeks to promote.

(f) 'Poverty is an evil in itself.' In a framework of moralistic dichotomy, this implies that 'development' is a good in itself. But a different reading – such as that of Nicholas Georgescu-Roegen – might have led to the opposite conclusion: that *from the point of view of environmental protection, sustainable development is the evil in itself.* For ordinary thinking, the scandal is always to be found on the side of the poor; they have to be consoled with 'aspirations for a better life'. But then the argument switches again to claim that 'a world in which poverty is endemic will always be prone to ecological and other catastrophes'.

---

26. The first question is: *how many* generations? Could those who lived at the turn of the century (Mrs Brundtland's grandparents, for example) anticipate the 'needs' for electricity, petrol (or leisure) of our contemporaries in the industrialized countries? For 'needs' vary according to technological and ecological changes, and these can seldom even be observed over a short period of time.

27. 'To bring developing countries' energy use up to industrialized country levels by the year 2025 would require increasing present global energy use by a factor of five. The planetary ecosystem could not stand this.' Ibid., p. 14.

As we can see, the Brundtland Report is not short on good intentions, but the positions it tries to argue are so vague that – despite a
number of valuable statistical contributions – it hardly offers a new way
of looking at the problem. For what is the point of denouncing the
fact that 'economics and ecology can interact destructively and trip into
disaster',[28] if it is only to reaffirm that 'what is needed now is a new
era of economic growth – growth that is forceful and at the same time
socially and environmentally sustainable'?[29] Of course, this growth will
be different from today's and less profligate with energy, but the Report has nothing to say about how to achieve it; most of the time, *it
merely expresses a hope that the necessary will become possible.* For example:
'Most of these sources [of energy] are currently problematic, but given
innovative development, they could supply the same amount of primary
energy the planet now consumes.'[30] Maybe – but the big question is
'how'? Or again: 'Urgent steps are needed to limit extreme rates of
population growth. Choices made now will influence the level at which
the population stabilizes next century within a range of 6 billion
people.'[31] Yes – but how? Or lastly: 'Given population growth rates, a
five- to tenfold increase in manufacturing output will be needed just
to raise developing world consumption of manufactured goods to industrialized world levels by the time population growth rates level off
next century.'[32] Does it make any sense to continue with this logic of
'catching up'?[33]

Some of these problems with the Report are probably due to a lack
of conceptual clarity. The old debate concerning the sustainability of
the environmental framework of human activity – a debate going back
to Malthus – revolved around the rate at which *living* species were
renewed. This was still the main preoccupation of the IUCN in 1980,
when it looked at 'living resources conservation strategies for sustainable development'.[34] As far as Western public opinion is concerned,

28. *Our Common Future*, p. 6.
29. Ibid., 'Introduction', p. xii.
30. Ibid., p. 15.
31. Ibid., p. 11.
32. Ibid., p. 15. The same phrase occurs on p. 213, but there the text continues:
'Such growth has serious implications for the future of the world's ecosystems and its
natural resource base.' No conclusion is drawn from this, however, and the next
sentence turns to something else.
33. But at the same time the Commission feels able to assert: 'The simple dupli-
cation in the developing world of industrial countries' energy use patterns is neither
feasible nor desirable.' Ibid., p. 59.
34. See above, note 23.

however, resource exhaustion first became an issue in 1972 with the publication of the Meadows Report, *The Limits to Growth*, and above all with the successive oil price shocks of the seventies. And in both these cases, the question at stake was the stocks of non-renewable mineral resources – which belongs to quite a different problematic. It is the misfortune of the Brundtland Report that it confuses these two perspectives. Somewhat schematically, we could say that 'development' (or here, the Industrial Revolution) makes it possible to increase production by using up reserves at a rate dependent not upon their necessary replacement time but on the state of existing technology. Coal and oil, for instance, can be extracted quickly or slowly, but the decision rests with the users. Fuel can be provided for as many engines as one wishes, and agricultural output can be considerably increased through the use of 'chemical' (that is, non-biological) fertilizer. The situation is quite different, however, for an economy that mainly uses living forest, plants or animals; it cannot increase output unless it respects the rhythm of their replacement, and storage difficulties mean that they cannot really be stockpiled. In ignoring this basic difference in growth potential between the two situations, the Brundtland Report fails to pose clearly the problem of 'sustainability'. For while the countries of the North can think in terms of almost unlimited growth (even if their use of reserves endangers the biosphere with its waste), the countries of the South cannot be sure of food self-sufficiency if their population growth exceeds the reproduction capacity of living resources, and if their attempts to 'develop' by copying the industrial countries force them to finance technology imports through loans on the capital market. As interest grows geometrically, such loans cannot be repaid on the basis of necessarily limited production that is tied to a different (arithmetic) rate of renewal. Hence the necessity – in the two cases of coal and oil – to overexploit the environment to cope with food problems and financial obligations. The theory of comparative advantage, which is used as a foundation for international trade, serves to consolidate the inequality of growth potential by referring to the international division of labour.[35] Thus, an undifferentiated treatment of renewable and non-renewable resources not only evades a fundamental problem, but also

---

35. These remarks are inspired by an unpublished paper by Rolf Steppacher, 'Probleme und Grenzen "nachhaltiger Entwicklung"' (April 1995, 7 pp.). See also his article, 'L'ingérence écologique et la globalisation de l'économie de marché', *Écologie contre nature. Développement et politiques d'ingérence*, (3), Geneva: IUED, Paris: PUF, pp. 99–114.

legitimates the dominant system. One might say that the latter explains the former.

In the end, the Commission's clearly asserted independence[36] did not stand in the way of diplomatic compromises. Between the lines one can read the disagreements out of which debates may again arise; one can even understand that it was impossible to condemn growth in itself, as that would have frozen inequalities on the pretext of safe-guarding the environment. Still, the Report's timidity is cause for some puzzlement, given that the whole point was to question the way of life of the rich in both North and South. Although it recognizes that 'painful choices have to be made',[37] the Commission hardly proposes anything that would encourage the industrial countries to make basic changes in their consumption pattern;[38] for them, too, it envisages annual growth of 3 to 4 per cent, so as to assure expansion of the world economy and an upturn in the 'developing' countries.[39] This is the old theory of international trade as the 'engine of growth', and of growth as the condition for a more equitable distribution of wealth.[40]

---

36. To quote Mrs Brundtland: 'As Commissioners, however, we were acting not in our national roles but as individuals…. It has been a truly wonderful team. The spirit of friendship and open communication, the meeting of minds and the process of learning and sharing have provided an experience of optimism, something of great value to all of us, and, I believe, to the report and its message.' *Our Common Future*, pp. xii, xiii.

37. Ibid., p. 9.

38. Basic needs arguments – assuming one subscribes to them – should really entail the illegitimacy of 'excess needs'. The minimum threshold should be matched by a maximum threshold beyond which any 'excess' attracts penalties. Yet in the Brundtland Report – which asserts the principle of 'producing more with less' – the people to blame are always in the South: 'The woman who cooks in an earthen pot over an open fire uses perhaps eight times more energy than an affluent neighbour with a gas stove and aluminium pans' (ibid., p. 196). Wolfgang Sachs points out that 'whereas in the 1970s the main threat to nature still appeared to be industrial man, in the 1980s environmentalists turned their eyes to the Third World and pointed to the vanishing forests, soils and animals there. With the shifting focus … the crisis of the environment is no longer perceived as the result of building affluence for the global middle class in North and South, but as a result of human presence on the globe in general.' 'Global Ecology and the Shadow of "Development"', in Wolfgang Sachs, ed., *Global Ecology: A New Arena of Political Conflict*, London: Zed Books, 1993, p. 11.

39. *Our Common Future*, p. 50. See also p. 89, where the argument is developed at some length.

40. In a box (pp. 50–51), the Report calculates both the growth rate and the time needed to reduce the 'poverty ratio' from 50 to 10 per cent. But its whole argument is based on redistribution not of existing wealth but of supplementary income – for 'redistributive policies can only operate on increases in income'. This classical conception of the trickle-down effect is contradicted by what has been known for a long time: that growth rarely favours the poor.

The main contradiction, then, in the Report of the Brundtland Commission is that *the growth policy supposed to reduce poverty and stabilize the ecosystem hardly differs at all from the policy which historically opened the gulf between rich and poor and placed the environment in danger* (because of the different rates of growth which can be achieved depending on the use of either non-renewable or renewable resources). Concrete suggestions are limited to a series of (often reasonable enough) hopes (for example, greater international assistance for environment-friendly projects, or more resources for organizations dealing with ecological issues), or to solemn appeals for more efficient management of the available resources.[41] Despite its claim that the problems must be tackled at root,[42] the Commission does little more than fire off recommendations to all and sundry: international agencies, governments, NGOs and individuals. All its members are doubtless concerned about the issues, and they repeat that action must be taken, but what they suggest are palliative measures (recycling and rationalization) rather than radical changes.

'Globalization' is now on everyone's lips, and one might think that this new way of imagining relations in the world would favour attention to environmental problems. Yet the opposite seems to be the case: market-induced 'globalization' is making ecological awareness an impossibility. Whereas an economy based upon local resources makes people immediately sensitive to any deterioration in their environment, and in most cases eager to preserve it,[43] the market makes it possible to take resources (oil, wood, water, etc.) from one region, to consume them in another region, and to dispose of the waste in yet another (either for payment or by dumping it in the biosphere). *Everything undertaken in the name of expanding international trade allows production to be dissociated from consumption and consumption from disposal* (that is, from conversion into visible or invisible waste). This spares the consumer-

---

41. Significantly, the cover of the French edition of the Report reproduces a photograph of the Earth taken from Apollo XI. This 'new view of the world' is evoked a number of times, for example: 'In the middle of the 20th century, we saw our planet from space for the first time.... Many such changes are accompanied by life-threatening hazards.' But the conclusion is derisory: 'This new reality, from which there is no escape, must be recognized – and managed' (p. 1).

42. See, for example, pp. 313 ff.

43. On the other hand, poverty also leads to deterioration of the environment (deforestation, excessive pasturage, etc.), because it is often expropriation of their environment (their best lands) which has led them into poverty. Nor should we forget the problems connected with the renewal rate of living resources.

polluter from realizing that he is involved in using up resources and accumulating waste, as the trade circuit obscures what is actually taking place. Transnational companies favour this dilution of responsibility, operating as they do in many different places at once and constantly splitting creation from destruction of resources. The 'polluter pays' principle does not do away with pollution, but implies that those with the means can reserve the right to pollute.

Furthermore, whereas one aim of environmentalists is to promote a diachronic view of resource use (by protecting the rights of future generations), market price responds only to effective demand expressed here and now, in complete abstraction from long-term effects. Thus, only legally binding measures can ensure respect for the environment – assuming that public opinion can force governments to adopt them! But more and more, the State is surrendering the control it used to exercise over certain markets – which obviously increases the risks to the environment.

Market economics takes no account of the fundamental distinction between renewable goods (which are part of the 'living' economy) and non-renewable finite resources. It also intensifies rivalry between national economies and excludes any concerted approach (by raw material producers, for example) in the name of principles supposedly favouring the collective interest. Indeed, the generalization of the market inevitably fans economic and military competition for access to (unevenly distributed) resources.

The mandate of the Brundtland Commission was to redefine the relationship between environment and 'development', and to propose 'a global programme for change'. At least three things were necessary for fulfilment of this task: (a) to understand how people and societies actually interrelate with their environment;[44] (b) to challenge the simplistic models that the dominant ideology claims to be the only ways of interpreting economic phenomena; and (c) to locate the concept of growth both culturally (as distinctively Western) and historically (as simultaneously involving mechanisms of enrichment and exclusion). Having failed to consider these three basic points, the Brundtland Report could only register the imbalances that threaten human survival but not work out any genuine solution.

---

44. This could have been based on the traditional knowledge acquired by non-Western (and non-anthropocentric) societies, as well as on the most up-to-date scientific research.

THE EARTH SUMMIT

The Brundtland Report ended by suggesting that the United Nations organize 'an international Conference ... to review progress and promote follow-up arrangements that will be needed over time to set benchmarks and to maintain human progress within the guidelines of human needs and natural laws'.[45] It was undoubtedly the last recommendation which was the best applied, for more than a hundred heads of State and thousands of delegates from all over the world (including representatives of a thousand NGOs) assembled in Rio de Janeiro between 3 and 14 June 1992 to take part in the 'Earth Summit', the United Nations Conference on Environment and Development (UNCED). Altogether, with some eight thousand journalists, a total of thirty thousand people were present.

Twenty years after the Stockholm Conference, Maurice Strong resumed duties to get this huge deliberative gathering off the ground, so that it could propose new measures to reconcile the environment with 'development'. Of course, it was an illusion to hope that such an event could pose problems more lucidly and incisively than the twenty-one members of the Brundtland Commission, but at least the media attention meant that the ecologists' concerns received a slightly wider hearing.[46] This was of no little importance – although we should not exaggerate the effect of such rituals in deepening people's knowledge. In any case, as Maurice Strong stressed in his opening speech, 'the Earth Summit is not an end in itself but a new beginning'.

The UNCED's work resulted in both documents (various legal statutes) and institutional measures. Alongside the 'official' UN event in Rio itself, moreover, there was a quite distinct 'unofficial' UNCED – also known as the 'Global Forum' – which brought together nearly twenty thousand people under the auspices of the NGOs.[47] The two conferences were obviously co-ordinated, and the NGOs also exten-

---

45. *Our Common Future*, p. 343.

46. We should recall that on 1 June 1992 sixty or so Nobel Prizewinners (plus Luc Ferry, Pascal Bruckner, Julia Kristeva, Alain Minc, Ilya Prigogine, Yves Lacoste and René Rémond) issued the Heidelberg Appeal to discredit the UNCED 'ecologists'. This appeal had been 'thought up' by one Michael Salomon, an employee of the drug company Sterting and Winthrop, which had no interest in the success of the UNCED (*Le Monde*, 19 June 1992).

47. For a detailed account, see Peter M. Haas, Marc A. Levy and Edward A. Parson, 'Appraising the Earth Summit: How Should We Judge UNCED's Success?', *Environment*, 34 (8), October 1992, pp. 5–15, 26–36. We have drawn liberally on this article in summing up the parallel UNCED conferences.

sively participated in the work of the official gathering. But interaction between them was quite restricted, as they took place 30 miles from each other.

Five documents emerged within the framework of the official UNCED.

1. The *Rio Declaration*, also called the 'Earth Charter', which proclaimed twenty-seven principles relating to the environment. Among these were the right of every country to operate its own policy on the use of its natural resources, the right to 'development', the necessity of reducing consumption patterns that conflict with 'sustainable development', the establishment of 'appropriate demographic policies', the principle of taking precautions,[48] and the 'polluter pays' principle. Despite the reservations of the United States, the text was approved by everyone.

2. The *Convention on Climate Change*, which dealt mainly with the greenhouse effect. This text had been drafted as long ago as 1988 by the *Intergovernmental Panel on Climate Change* (which also included scientists) and then by the *Intergovernmental Negotiating Committee* (which did not include scientists). As the United States refused to accept a clause aiming to reduce carbon dioxide emissions to their 1990 level by the year 2000, any reference to a precise timetable was omitted: the South's 'victory' was thus emptied of content. The text of the Convention was ready by 9 May, and was signed in Rio by 153 States. It provides for financial assistance so that the countries of the South can take the necessary measures, as well as for institutional follow-up machinery.

3. The *Convention on Biodiversity*. Negotiations on this convention had begun in 1988 under UNEP auspices in Nairobi. Its aim was to preserve biological diversity and to utilize it in a reasonable (or 'sustainable') manner, sharing equitably the profits bound up with the exploitation of genetic capital. Debate centred on finances for the countries of the South, profit-sharing and rules governing genetic engineering. A total of 153 States signed the Convention in Rio, the United States not being one of them.

4. A *Declaration on the Forest*. The original draft for this had been prepared under FAO auspices, but given the disagreements between countries of the North and the South (especially Malaysia) on the type

---

48. This states that it is better to act at once, before the scientific community has reached unanimity on a subject, rather than wait for certainty and act too late.

of forest requiring protection, it was simply agreed to accept 17 non-binding principles that related to forests in general.

5. *Agenda 21* (that is, for the twenty-first century), which was written up as the 'bible of sustainable development' in eight hundred pages. Its numerous recommendations have no binding force, but each government undertook on its own behalf to implement a certain number of them. Each of the forty chapters of the document sets out objectives and priorities, identifies institutional questions, and assesses the cost of the measures proposed (a total of 600 billion dollars a year, with 125 billion of it payable by the industrial countries).[49] *Agenda 21* also set up a new United Nations Sustainable Development Commission, whose job it was to report to the ECOSOC on progress in applying the Agenda's recommendations. Its mandate was vaguely defined, however, and the frequency of the reports it was supposed to receive from governments was not specified.

The NGOs, for their part, produced a considerable amount of documentation both for the 'official' Conference and for the Global Forum they had organized. Within the framework of the Forum, they also negotiated a number of agreements on the most varied subjects. Among those agreed before the end of the Conference, the following are especially worthy of mention:

- The *Earth Charter*, an eight-point document parallel to the Rio Declaration.
- An NGO Co-operation and Institutional Building Cluster, which finalized agreements on technology, an NGO code of conduct, resource-sharing, communication and the media, and the peoples of the Americas.

---

49. The forty chapters are divided under four headings: economic and social dimensions (sustainable development in the South, poverty, change in consumption models, population dynamic, health, sustainable human habitat, environment, development and decision-making processes); conservation and management of development resources (atmosphere, soil planning and management, deforestation, desertification, development of mountainous regions, agriculture and rural development, biological diversity, biotechnologies, oceans, water, toxic products, dangerous waste, solid waste and purification, radioactive waste); strengthening the role of major groups (women, children, young people, indigenous peoples, NGOs, trade unions, business milieux, scientists, farmers, etc.); means of implementation (financial resources, technology transfer, science, education and public opinion, institutional support, international institutional agreements, international legal instruments, information for decision-making).

- An Alternative Economic Issues Cluster, which drafted agreements on alternative economic models, transnational corporations, trade, debt, consumption and lifestyles.[50]
- A Major Environmental Issues Cluster, which produced agreements on the climate, forests, biodiversity, biotechnology, energy, the oceans, and toxic and nuclear waste.
- A Food Production Cluster, which drafted treaties on 'sustainable' agriculture, food safety, drinking water and fishing.
- A Cross-sectorial Issues Cluster, which proposed agreements on racism, militarization, women, population growth, young people, education on the environment, urbanization and indigenous peoples.

Another document produced within the Global Forum was *Changing Course*,[51] published by a Business Council on Sustainable Development made up of forty-eight industrialists. This listed forty individual cases, and showed that business could also make money by concerning itself with the environment. It was almost a caricature of the 'Rio spirit', dominated as it was by *technocratic solutions*.

Finally, outside the UNCED proper, the NGOs decided to create and finance a Costa Rica-based 'Planet Earth Council', made up of twenty-eight world-famous scientists under Maurice Strong. This independent group, with information from governments and NGOs at its disposal, could play an important role in stimulating debate on the environment – rather like that of Amnesty International in the area of human rights.

In negotiations such as those that took place at Rio, *a kind of displacement tactic is often used to make the partner think you agree on essentials while disapproving of a seemingly minor point*. On this occasion, the industrial countries had major reservations about the attempts of the South to obtain additional aid and to reaffirm its 'right to development'. How could 125 billion dollars a year be paid out for environmental protection, when the OECD's total public 'development' assistance did not exceed 60 billion?[52] Although the sum in question was still less than the 0.7 per cent of GNP considered necessary since the 1960s, a

---

50. The plan of action on consumption followed a hierarchy from 'revalue' at the top through 'restructure', 'redistribute', 'reduce' and 'reuse' to 'recycle' at the bottom.

51. Stephan Schmidheiny, *Changing Course: A Global Business Perspective on Development and the Environment*, Cambridge, MA: MIT Press, 1992.

52. Of course, when the international financial system is in danger, 50 billion dollars can be found in a couple of days – as was the case in the 'second Mexican crisis' of 1995. It all depends on the priorities.

'flexible' formula involving no precise commitment made the World Bank's Global Environment Facility (in collaboration with the UNDP and UNEP) responsible for making up the deficit – despite the objections of the countries of the South. It was a pragmatic way of entrusting 'sustainable development' to an institution which, being largely controlled by the countries of the North, could not be certain to raise the issue of their responsibilities for the environment.

REFLECTIONS ON DELIBERATE AMBIGUITY

The Brundtland Report and the Rio Conference may perhaps be summarized in two points that have the advantage of also characterizing the nineties.

First, these two major events aroused widespread interest in 'environmental problems' – that is, mainly problems for the environment caused by industrial society, not vice versa (as is too often made out to be the case). Now the finiteness of nature could no longer be ignored. The 'development battle', like any other, has its own distinctive slogans,[53] and 'sustainable development' has become part of the language of every 'developer'. No project is taken seriously any more (that is, given funding) unless it has an 'environment aspect'. This ought to be cause for rejoicing, so extensive and worrying is the damage done to the setting of life.

Now, *it is to its ambiguity that the term 'sustainable development' owes its success*. For ecologists, the interpretation is clear enough: sustainable development implies a production level that can be borne by the ecosystem, and can therefore be kept up over the long term; reproduction capacity determines production volume, and 'sustainability' means that the process can be maintained only under certain externally given conditions. To use a (cautious) analogy with the realm of the living, we might say that whereas cell growth is necessary to a child's development, an excessive proliferation of cells makes the continuation of life impossible. Or again – to draw on French popular wisdom – 'if you wish to travel far, spare your steed': the important thing is the journey rather than the speed, life on the planet rather than the pace of 'development'.

---

53. As Elias Canetti points out (*Crowds and Power* [1960], Harmondsworth: Penguin Books, 1973, p. 49), the word 'slogan' comes from two Celtic words: *sluagh* (host of the dead) and *gairm* (shout or cry). It is difficult to know whether 'the battle-cry of the dead' is uttered by those who lack 'development' or by those who are its victims.

The dominant interpretation is quite different. It sees 'sustainable development' as an invitation to keep up 'development' – that is, economic growth. With 'development' already universal and inescapable, it has to be made eternal. In other words, since 'development' is regarded as naturally positive, it must be stopped from becoming asthenic. Sustainable development, then, means that 'development' must advance at a more 'sustained' pace until it becomes irreversible – for what the countries of the South are suffering from is 'non-sustainable development', 'stop–go development' constantly unsettled by ephemeral political measures.[54] For conventional thinking, then, 'sustainability' is understood in the trivial sense of 'durability': it is not the survival of the ecosystem which sets the limits of 'development', but 'development' which determines the survival of societies. As 'development' is at once necessity and opportunity, the conclusion is perfectly obvious – so long as it lasts!

These two interpretations are at once legitimate and contradictory, since two antinomic signifieds correspond to the same signifier. The Brundtland Commission and the Rio Conference both avoided choosing: both oscillated between reminders of the environmental limits on 'development' and exhortations to advance boldly into a 'new era of economic growth'. *Hence their recourse to oxymoron, to the rhetorical figure that joins together two opposites such as 'structural adjustment with a human face' and 'humanitarian intervention'.* In a poetic or mystical text, expressions such as 'dark brightness', 'presence of the absent God' or 'learned ignorance' make us think by producing an excess of meaning without establishing a hierarchy between the signifieds. But the Brundtland Report is neither a poem nor the record of an inner dazzling; it does not try to speak the unutterable, or to make us feel the weight of the enormous nothing that is 'sustainable development'. It is a text which belongs to what Gunnar Myrdal once called 'diplomacy by terminology'.[55] Consequently, the political nature of the discourse thins down

---

54. This interpretation may be found in the article by Jean Massini in *Revue Tiers Monde* (XXXV, 137, January–March 1994), and above all in the one by Gérard Destanne de Bernis, which takes Algeria and Mexico as crisis-hit examples of 'non-sustainable development' unable to maintain their growth rates (ibid., p. 98). See also 'What Is Sustainable? Sustainable Development Is Development That Lasts', *World Development Report*, New York: Oxford University Press and World Bank, 1992, p. 34 (quoted in Wolfgang Sachs, 'Global Ecology', p. 8).

55. Gunnar Myrdal, *Asian Drama: An Inquiry into the Poverty of Nations*, Harmondsworth: Penguin Books, 1968, vol. 3, Appendix I, pp. 1839–42. Here the object of Myrdal's attack was not oxymorons but use of the antiphrasis 'developing countries' to mean 'underdeveloped'.

the surfeit of meaning that a real oxymoron would evoke, so that the expression becomes a 'pseudo' or 'second-order' oxymoron escaping the absurdity of contradiction only by subordinating one term to the other. From both a grammatical and a practical point of view, it is the noun which has the edge over the adjective; the latter's only function is to legitimate the former with a guarantee coming from outside.[56] For the contradiction is no longer at the level of words (as darkness is opposed to brightness) but at the level of practices that are now detestable (structural adjustment, interference), now admirable (human face, humanitarian). 'Sustainable development' is cast from the same mould. As 'development' bears the main responsibility for damage to the environment and threatens the desired 'sustainability' of the eco-system, the essentially positive quality that one expects from the environment is presented as if it were enough to offset the problems with 'development' and to justify the pursuit of growth. *The contradiction is there in the practices, not in the words.* Thus, the point of the Brundtland Report and the Rio Conference was not to sublate antagonistic phenomena within a Hegelian synthesis, but to make 'development' appear necessary by according it the supreme value recognized in the environment.[57] From this angle, 'sustainable development' looks like a cover-up operation: it allays the fears aroused by the effects of eco-nomic growth, so that any radical challenge can be averted. Even if the bait is alluring, there should be no illusion about what is going on. The thing that is meant to be sustained really is 'development', not the tolerance capacity of the ecosystem or of human societies.[58]

One last point remains to be considered. If 'sustainable develop-ment' is only a way of gaining acceptance for ever more questionable practices, would everything change as a result of heeding environmental constraints? The answer is not clear-cut, for it is impossible to bracket out the *power issues* that determine practices in the real world.

There can be no doubt, however, that some measures of moderation or conservation will be taken in the name of ecological concerns. The

---

56. The various ways of legitimating modern practices through values inscribed in ancient myths have been described at length in Marie-Dominique Perrot, Gilbert Rist and Fabrizio Sabelli, *La mythologie programmée*. See also Marie-Dominique Perrot's article in *Dérives humanitaires*, pp. 47–62.

57. Similarly, the 'dirty war' conducted by a US-dominated coalition against Iraq under UN auspices was described as a 'clean war'.

58. 'In fact, the UN Conference in Rio inaugurated environmentalism as the highest stage of developmentalism.' Sachs, 'Global Ecology', p. 5.

Rio Conference did not manage to impose mandatory regulation, but it did awaken a new sensitivity (kept alive by numerous pressure groups) which will certainly lead to concrete actions – even if these are only palliatives,[59] or if they allow more production with less pollution through a so-called 'efficiency revolution'. But it may also be feared that, in the predominantly managerial optic of the Brundtland Report, the environment will serve only to increase the inequalities brought about by 'development'.

(a) The 'developed/underdeveloped' dichotomy might give way to a 'polluted/underpolluted' one which, in the name of international equality, installs a new *international division of the environment*. Polluting industries or toxic wastes might then be transferred even more easily than today to regions relatively free of environmental nuisance[60] – even if a number of 'reservations' are set aside at the same time for the numerous vanishing species.[61]

(b) As we can see from the Rio texts, environmental protection will give rise to an international bureaucracy like the one produced by 'development' (with its experts, its training centres and its pilot projects). One could imagine a new kind of 'world bank' distributing the planet's genetic capital in proportion to the stakes of its shareholders.

(c) 'Public assistance for managing the environment' would make it possible to keep tight control over the policies of dominated countries, while 'environmental imperatives' might impose programmes of structural adjustment to the environment.

Other scenarios would doubtless be less cynical, but also less plausible. One might imagine that the countries of the North will abandon the growth dogma, and that the economic warfare between the United States, Europe and Japan will come to an end. One might dream of reducing unemployment through a reallocation of income and work-time, of imposing a tax on capital transfers so as to redistribute some of

59. One thinks here of the Montreal Protocol of 1987 on substances destroying the ozone layer – which will eventually prohibit the use of CFC gases. National sovereignty was doubtless limited in this case, but it should be borne in mind that CFCs take twenty years to reach the ozone layer.
60. This has already been proposed in the case of industry by M. Summer of the World Bank. (See Susan George and Fabrizio Sabelli, *Faith and Credit: The World Bank's Secular Empire*, Harmondsworth: Penguin, 1994.) On the subject of toxic waste disposal in new territories, Chapters 19 to 22 of *Agenda 21* do not prohibit such practices but merely call for better risk evaluation and the prevention of illegal storage.
61. See Sabelli, ed., *Écologie contre nature*.

the world's wealth, of establishing quotas for energy consumption, of banning or severely limiting individual transport, of rediscovering a different quality of life in voluntary frugality, of putting an end to frenetic productivism. One might stop making the means more efficient until the ends have been redefined…

It is always possible to dream, but no one wants to see an Orwellian world, even if the imminence of ecological catastrophe seemed to justify the imposition of a different way of living. For the moment, the South is forcefully asserting its 'right to development' and claiming to implement it before it thinks seriously (and at great cost) of protecting nature. This, too, is a way of imitating the dominant model. As for the North, it is resigning itself to economic growth, even if this undermines the environment and results in social exclusion. Contrary to what is often said, knowledge is not always linked to power. What is the point in ever more exhaustively listing the main dangers that stalk the human race? For the *longue durée* characteristic of 'ecological time' conflicts with the short-term rhythms of political life – not to mention the immediacy of market time.[62]

At the heart of this debate, then, is the modern social construct that is called 'development'. We can see veiled behind it the dominant economic assumptions that make the problem out to be the solution.

---

62. See Christian Comeliau, 'Développement du "développement durable" ou blocages conceptuels?', *Revue Tiers Monde*, XXV (137), January–March 1994, p. 70.

CHAPTER 11

A MIXTURE OF REALISM
AND FINE SENTIMENTS

The 1990s began on a note of hope. After the fall of the Berlin Wall in 1989 and the implosion of the USSR, it was possible to imagine that the 'development' of the South – at last rid of any political ulterior motives – would become a real priority, especially as the now-redundant military budgets could release huge sums for more constructive purposes. The South might, as the UNDP proposed, be able to cash in on the 'peace dividend'. It is true that the end of Sovietism looked like the final triumph of economic liberalism, and it was suspected that considerable funds would have to be earmarked for the 'development' of an Eastern Europe whose state of dilapidation had not been fully appreciated. But the 'forty years war' that had split the world in two was finally over. And since well-entrenched dictatorships had had to surrender, why should not more recent ones be toppled just as suddenly? In the South, the Argentinian and Brazilian military had already withdrawn (1983 and 1985), Pinochet had made room for others in power (1988), Stroessner had gone (1989), Sékou Touré had disappeared, Bokassa was in exile, Mandela was at liberty, Nujoma had been elected (1989), and Alpha Konaré had replaced Moussa Traoré.

There had been good news, then, even if it could not erase the memory of the impotent National Conferences in Zaïre and Togo, the massacre on Tienanmen Square, the clan warfare in Somalia, the horrific bloodbaths in Rwanda, Burundi and the former Yugoslavia, or the never-ending conflict in Angola – to mention just a few dramatic cases.

In this context, it seemed that 'development' might be able to gain a new lease of life, as two recent initiatives had already suggested.

THE SOUTH COMMISSION

So far, the dominant theories of 'development' had been produced either by people of the North (Truman, Rostow, Perroux, etc.) or from within the international organizations (UN General Assembly, ILO, UNCTAD, UNDP, World Bank, etc.). As for the South, its distinctive contributions had been the dependency school and the Tanzanian attempt to define and practise 'self-reliant development'.[1] Although all these intellectual efforts had scarcely improved the lot of the peoples of the South, it was possible to think that the responsibility for this should be spread around to take account of the international relationship of forces. Did the industrial countries not persist in defending their own interests at international negotiations, and give support to regimes that cared little for the well-being of their subjects? And what of the measures imposed by the IMF, or the manipulative practices of public assistance programmes and transnational corporations? If the governments of the South were free to apply policies based upon their own cultures and history, would the results not be different? If the intellectuals of the South had time to formulate proposals outside the mould of the international organizations, would they not be imaginative and creative, realistic and innovative?

This is why people were entitled to expect a lot from the Report of the South Commission.[2] The procedure was similar to the one operated in the Brandt and Brundtland Reports: appointment of commission members (in 1987), creation of a secretariat and expert groups,[3] working meetings in various continents,[4] and drafting of the report. After all, there are not too many ways of producing a collective document. The one big difference was that this time the initiative had come not from

---

1. It should be borne in mind, of course, that – with the (notorious) exceptions of the World Bank, IMF and GATT – the international organizations are largely dominated by the countries of the South, which play an active and important role in them. Thus, most of the wishes expressed at Bandung came true, and the initiative for the NIEO Declaration was taken by the non-aligned countries. That said, the international forums are places where the majority often has to make major concessions to obtain the necessary consensus.

2. *The Challenge to the South: The Report of the South Commission*, under the chairmanship of Julius Nyerere, Oxford: Oxford University Press, 1990.

3. The Secretariat, it should be noted, was installed in the same offices in Geneva that had been used by the Brandt and Brundtland Commissions. Its staff was different, however: only Branislav Gosovic took part in the work of both the Brundtland and the South Commission.

4. Unlike the Brundtland Commission, the South Commission did not hold any public hearings.

the Secretary-General of the United Nations but from the Prime Minister of Malaysia, Mahathir Mohamad, who had persuaded the former Tanzanian President Julius Nyerere to take charge of the work.

Everything then depended on the choice of the twenty-six commissioners. Some of them belonged to the 'South establishment' and had been involved in most of the big 'development' events since the Stockholm Conference of 1972: people like Ismaïl Sabri-Abdalla (chairman of the Third World Forum), Gamani Corea, Celso Furtado, Enrique Iglesias, Shridath Ramphal (who had already served on both the Brandt and Brundtland Commissions), and Layachi Yaker (a member of the Brandt Commission). The expert groups also contained a lot of familiar faces, inseparable from the experience of more than twenty years of reflecting on 'development'.[5] Right from the start, it was a closely knit team: they did not always have the same views,[6] but the 'hard core' had a long past in common that was the source of connivance and friendship. This can unquestionably help to make work on a project more effective. But the other side of the coin was that intellectuals from the South who were less well versed in diplomatic niceties had little opportunity to influence the content of the report.[7] Moreover, the Commission members and experts had intimate knowledge of all the basic texts – many of which they had helped to draft – and they seemed incapable of looking at them with sufficient distance to offer the original perspective expected from representatives of the South.

Some truths need saying, of course, and do not suffer from repetition: 'development implies growing self-reliance, both individual and collective [; ... it] has therefore to be an effort of, by, and for the people ... achieved through the participation of the people acting in

---

5. There were nine groups of experts, with a maximum of ten people in each. The names which crop up most often are those of Marc Nerfin (4 times), Surendra Patel (3), Michael Zammit-Cutajar, Mahdi Elmandjra, Abdellatif Benachenhou, Dharam Ghai and Pablo Bifani (2). Among the others are Chakravarthi Raghavan, Joseph Ki-Zerbo, Enrique Oteiza, Osvaldo Sunkel, Mahbub ul-Haq, Samir Amin and Manfred Max-Neef.

6. We need only mention the presence on the Commission of Cardinal Arns and of Abdus Salam, Nobel Prizewinner for Physics and director of the International Centre for Theoretical Physics in Trieste. Salam, for example, played a crucial role in the proposals concerning restrictive use of the most up-to-date technologies (pp. 253 ff.), with some modest references to what the NIEO called appropriate technologies (p. 109).

7. The critical sense of many people involved in the South Commission is not at all in question. But their long participation in international debates undoubtedly made them overcautious about what could and could not be written in a report of this kind.

their own interests as they see them';[8] 'not only the growth of the
national product but what is produced, how and at what social and
environmental cost ..., should be taken into account in the formulation
of policy';[9] 'as the countries of the South differ from one another, they
will have to take different routes to the common goal of development';[10] 'there is a deep awareness of the limitations of past development strategies and a growing conviction that the way out of the present
crisis does not lie in returning to those strategies';[11] 'modernization
should not be antithetical to the culture of a people';[12] the rule of law
and respect for minorities must prevail; 'development is a process of
profound structural transformation – it cannot be simply imported'.[13] It
is certainly not warnings about past mistakes and 'imitative development'
which are lacking anywhere in the Report,[14] but to declare the South's
specificity is not enough to make it a reality.

The fact is that *one would search the Report in vain for any outline of a
new path, or for some key ideas around which the text is structured.* Like all
such bodies, the South Commission attempted to make a survey of the
problems (growth, demography, industrialization and employment, international trade, 'international assistance', South–South co-operation, technology, respective roles of State and market, globalization, basic needs,
environment, democracy and popular participation, role of women,
culture, etc.), but it did not seem too bothered about consistency. For
example, what is the point of constantly stressing the need for self-
reliance and respect for indigenous cultures, if 'the demands of economic
growth are such that the South has to accelerate the pace of acquiring,
adapting and using the stock of technological knowledge built up in

---

8. *The Challenge to the South*, pp. 11, 13. Nyerere's chairmanship certainly encouraged the Commission to affirm the importance of self-reliance. But the Report
is far from consistent, and proposes many measures that are totally at variance with
this principle.

9. Ibid., p. 13. See also pp. 79, 80, and 272, where it is stressed that 'these
[development] patterns cannot simply be a replica of the past or a blind copy of the
consumerist models of the advanced industrial countries of the North'.

10. Ibid., p. 14. The Report also suggests that the countries of the South should
pursue 'relatively autonomous paths to development' (p. 16).

11. Ibid., p. 79.

12. Ibid., p. 80. Yet the section entitled 'Culture and Development' contains fewer
than three pages (pp. 131–3) and – like UNESCO or most 'conventional' texts on the
subject – it mixes up an anthropological definition of culture with considerations on
the culture industry and 'cultural products'.

13. Ibid., p. 274.

14. Nor, for that matter, the ritualistic observation that 'the world is at a moment
of historic challenge and opportunity' (p. 9).

the North',[15] or if there is a need for 'doubling the volume of concessional transfers of resources to developing countries by 1995'?[16]

It is hardly surprising, then, that the Report reaffirms a 'development imperative' that must be realized through 'rapid and sustained economic growth'.[17] Zero growth is incompatible with the improvement of living conditions in the South – that is well enough known. But why does the Report say in one breath that 'there is a need to continue the struggle for independence, political and economic, through self-reliant development and South–South cooperation',[18] and in another that 'developing countries need active assistance to catch up with the rest of the world, or at least to shorten the distance that now separates them from it'?[19] While the Report honestly admits that the failures of 'development' also involve mistakes on the part of governments in the South (especially the frequent deprivation of democratic rights), it offers no new way of bringing about a change of course. Thus, its 'six-point global programme of immediate action'[20] does no more than urge action 'to remove the overhang of the external debt', to protect 'the global environmental commons and [ensure] sustainable development', to double 'the volume of concessional transfers of resources' from North to South,[21] to evaluate 'the requirements of developing countries, the norms and indicators for [their] performance', to help sales of the South's products in the markets of the North, to stabilize the

---

15. Ibid., p. 109. Moreover, a subsection entitled 'Science and Technology' (both terms 'evidently' being singular!) puts forward a scientistic and highly optimistic vision, without mentioning, for example, the problems that hybrids produced in agronomic research centres pose for peasants in the South. A single sentence notes: 'New technologies, while offering immense possibilities, also present potential threats.' We think of those who are endangering the environment, but the Report is worried about something else: 'Purely commercial considerations can distort priorities for technical innovation and product development' (p. 256). Other chapters do, of course, mention damage to the environment.

16. Ibid., p. 269.

17. Ibid, pp. 12, 82 and *passim*. The expression 'qualitative growth' is not taken over from the Brundtland Report, but it is recognized that growth is not in itself a guarantee of 'people-centred development'. Otherwise, we find the usual theme that 'growth and development in the South' are 'a condition for sustained expansion of the world economy as a whole [and] for the preservation of the environment' (p. 214).

18. Ibid., p. 8.

19. Ibid., p. 253.

20. Ibid., pp. 268–70.

21. This would finally achieve the target of 0.7 per cent of the GNP of industrial countries which, since 1964, was supposed to be allocated for 'official development assistance'.

international prices of primary commodities, and to protect developing countries from excessive fluctuation in interest rates and exchange rates. All that had been said before, many times. *It had also long been known that lists of good intentions – even if they have international approval – carry no weight when pitted against the defence of national interests.* In fact, the Commission makes a major admission in the last chapter of the Report: 'We do not claim to have made an exhaustive study of all the formidable challenges the countries of the South might face in the period ahead. In particular, we have not dealt with international political issues'![22] But was that not precisely one of the main issues at stake?

The Report's definition of 'development' – always a difficult task, it is true – is a good illustration of its general tone. Once again, the exercise of definition becomes an important moment when it is a matter of clarifying the object of discourse and proposing a new vision. This is what the South Commission says:

> Development is a process which enables human beings to realize their potential, build self-confidence, and lead lives of dignity and fulfilment. It is a process which frees people from the fear of want and exploitation. It is a movement away from political, economic or social oppression. Through development, political independence acquires its true significance. And it is a process of growth, a movement essentially springing from within the society that is developing.... The base for a nation's development must be its own resources, both human and material, fully used to meet its own needs.... Development has therefore to be an effort of, by, and for the people. True development has to be people-centred.[23]

The goal is so noble that it is impossible to criticize it. But we should note that this is not a definition, because no such phenomenon can be observed anywhere in the world – not even, of course, in the 'developed' countries. It will be said, of course, that the definition is of the 'true development' to which everyone aspires. Maybe – for no one can be found who would refuse 'a life of dignity and fulfilment'. But then why does the Report merely propose to strengthen the measures which have brought about 'false development' ... and which the Commission says it wants to end? No doubt the answer is that the Commission believes in its wishful thinking and presents it as reality. Right at the outset, it states that 'the South of today [is] even less homogeneous than the South of yesterday' – which has anyway been common knowledge since the

---

22. Ibid., p. 271.
23. Ibid., pp. 10–11.

1970s. But then how can it be justified that a Report should speak on behalf of the South in general? The Commission does not let this disturb it, and continues: 'Yet in this diversity there is a basic unity. What the countries of the South have in common transcends their differences; it gives them a shared identity.'[24] What is this bond? It is 'their desire to escape from poverty and underdevelopment', and their will to reshape the international system. This is scant fare, and anyway it proves nothing at all. For 'development imperatives' set up a *sauve-qui-peut* mentality that every day destroys a little more of the South's ostensible unity. Similarly, the introduction to the Report denounces the fact that 'the widening disparities between South and North are attributable not merely to differences in economic progress, but also to an enlargement of the North's power *vis-à-vis* the rest of the world'.[25] It is therefore quite clear that the functioning of the international system leads to domination effects, and that the South risks being 'still more forgotten and margin-alized'. But then, as if nothing had been said, the old theory of mutual interests is reaffirmed – with the simple addition that the relationship 'must' be changed from subordination to partnership.[26] For 'the bases for a new international development consensus – a pact of global solidarity between South and North – are in place, and increasingly evident to any impartial observer'.[27] From which we learn to be suspicious of things evident…

One can accept that a report of this type opts for a *normative discourse*. Why should it not be said what 'ought' to be done? But it needs to be said clearly, and we need to be shown how the proposed solution differs from other solutions on offer, or from various policies in force. Instead, the Report revels in diplomatic fuzziness, with its characteristic intensifiers ('improve', 'increase', 'more', 'better', etc.) and modal auxiliaries. For example: 'The search for improved domestic policies has to be pursued and the mix of policies must depend on a country's particular circumstances.'[28] Or: 'Because of the inevitable time-lags in economic and social processes, there is need for early policy action if these opportunities are to be exploited and undesirable outcomes main-tained.'[29] Or again: 'There are many uncertainties about the future, and

---

24. Ibid., p. 1.
25. Ibid., p. 3.
26. Ibid., pp. 20, 211 f.
27. Ibid., p. 225.
28. Ibid., p. 15.
29. Ibid., p. 271.

the discontinuities with the past may be pronounced.'[30] Or finally: 'The South has additionally to recognize that in the search for new models of international relations, ideas have a critical role, especially ideas rooted in the shared needs and common aspirations of humanity.'[31] Because everything is at once true and false − or neither true nor false − how is it possible to resist drowsing off when utter banalities are added to straightforward twaddle?

No doubt this will seem a harsh judgement, but it matches the disappointment felt on reading the Report. What is said is often enough correct. Living conditions in the South only get worse. People's fate hinges on decisions taken without their knowledge, many of them in the North. Governments are incapable of controlling financial flows, and this increases their marginalization and impotence. Dependence has the edge on interdependence. All very true. Moreover, Julius Nyerere has the courage to say in his chairman's preface that 'responsibility for the development of the South lies in the South, and in the hands of the peoples of the South'.[32] But the Report then had to build on these premisses, to show how some peoples get round the constraints of 'development' in order to live (and not just survive), to explain why application of 'the laws of the market' leads to social exclusion, to question all the 'exigencies' of mainstream thinking which the practice of 'development' has respected for the past forty years. It is also possible that the key to the problem is already present in the title of the Report. Hunger, disease and want − to use President Truman's terms − are undoubtedly 'the challenge to the South'. And there is just as little doubt that the South must primarily face the challenge with its own resources. But why not say that this also concerns the North? It is not a question of sinking into sterile criticism, or of making others shoulder one's own responsibilities, or of begging for some extra aid. *But it is impossible to consider the poverty of the South without also seriously examining the wealth of the North.*

THE UNDP AND 'HUMAN DEVELOPMENT'

For many years, the international organizations had scarcely put forward any new ideas on 'development'. Since the great debates of the seventies on the New International Economic Order and 'basic needs', there had

---

30. Ibid.
31. Ibid., p. 287.
32. Ibid., p. vii.

been little other than 'structural adjustment with a human face' – a toned-down form of IMF prescriptions to maintain the internal and external balance of high-debt countries. It was therefore time to re-launch the debate, if only to make it look as if the 'wasted decade' had been spent in working out new formulas. The initiative came from the UNDP. Its Administrator, William H. Draper III, allocated the project to a well-known figure, the Pakistani Mahbub ul-Haq, who seemed ideally qualified. He had worked for a long time at the World Bank, but was also critical of it; he was a member of the Third World Forum; and he had contributed to the Hammarskjöld Foundation Report, as well as those of the Brandt and the South Commission. He had a group of consultants around him which comprised Paul Streeten (also a former World Bank consultant and for a short time director of the Institute for Development Studies in Sussex), Frances Stewart (who had helped to make the 'human face' of structural adjustment better known), Meghnad Desai (a member of one of the South Commission's expert groups), Gustav Ranis, Amartya K. Sen, Keith Griffin, Aziz Khan, Shlomo Angel, Pietro Garau and Mashesh Patel. It was this compact team, assisted by the UNDP Secretariat, which elaborated the concept of 'human development' in a series of annual reports.[33]

This new oxymoron came in for a lot of sarcasm. What use was 'development' unless it was 'human-centred'? Why had it taken so long to make this obvious point? Had development previously been 'in-human'? But the point, of course, was *to rehabilitate a largely discredited concept by giving it a spiritual boost that it would be in bad taste to refuse.* Fashion also had something to do with it, for the great collective or social projects (the word 'socialist' could no longer be used) had been replaced by a more individualist vision – humanist in the sense of human rights now loudly proclaimed as universal, or humanitarian in the sense used to describe the North's favoured mode of intervention in the countries of the South. 'Human' was therefore a timely epithet which gave the impression that something new was happening under the sun of 'development'.

The innovation was twofold. First, to escape the tyranny of GNP, a new 'human development indicator' (HDI) combined three variables for each country: income, life expectancy and level of education – to which the 1991 Report added human liberty. The aim of the operation

---

33. *Human Development Report*, Oxford: Oxford University Press, 1990 et seq. The editorial team, it should be noted, varies from year to year.

was clear: to break out of the economistic rut and to define the 'development performance' of the countries of the South in a different way.[34] One can only rejoice over this initiative. For once, an international body dared to speak of a number of cases of 'high levels of human development at modest income levels, and poor levels of human development at fairly high income levels'.[35] And for once – this was almost a revolution! – an international report referred to the classical authors, and based its argument on Kant, Quesnay, Adam Smith, Ricardo, Malthus, Marx and John Stuart Mill. Even Aristotle contributed a quotation: 'Wealth is evidently not the good we are seeking, for it is merely useful and for the sake of something else.'[36] Increases in income were therefore to be considered a means rather than an end. This reorientation was all the more striking in that the HDI took account not only of total income but also of how it was distributed.[37] The choice of variables can, as always, be disputed: it might have included per capita energy consumption, for example, by setting maximum and minimum values that would evidently have penalized the industrial countries. In this respect, the UNDP Report remains rather conventional, and shares the traditional Western values.[38] Nevertheless, its world table for 'development performance' breaks new ground by no longer confusing per capita income with overall

34. This exactly corresponded to one of the six points in the South Commission's 'global programme of immediate action' (p. 269). The participation of Meghnad Desai in the UNDP team and in the development indicators expert group of the South Commission doubtless explains this happy coincidence.

35. *Human Development Report 1990*, p. 10. Or again: 'The link between economic growth and human progress is not automatic' (p. 3).

36. Ibid., p. 9.

37. On the mode of calculation, see ibid., pp. 11 ff, and the refinements introduced in the reports for later years.

38. Although the HDI weights the income variable in a number of ways, the basis of calculation continues to depend on GNP. It has long been pointed out, however, that GNP adds up disparate values without taking into account whether they are positive or negative. For instance, the social and environmental costs of individual transport (medical and vehicle-repair expenses following accidents, the clearing of arable land for motorways, etc.) are simply added to the new value created in production (of motorcars in this case). Moreover, GNP embraces only market values and neglects everything taking place outside the money circuit. Ahmed Insel has calculated for France that the (monetary) value of non-market relations is equivalent to three-quarters of GDP ('La part du don, esquisse d'évaluation', in *Mouvement anti-utilitariste dans les sciences sociales, Ce que donner veut dire. Don et intérêt*, Paris: La Découverte, 1993, pp. 221–34.) If it were applied to the countries of the South, the same calculation would obviously give much higher figures, as well as explain how people can live on such apparently trifling sums.

excellence (even if the first twenty places are still occupied by OECD countries).[39]

The second innovation is of a *managerial* character. The 1991 Report offers a way of evaluating the allocation of funds (both national budgets and 'official development assistance') and of checking whether they really help to accomplish what are regarded as the priority tasks. The idea is to reconsider the basic needs strategy 'from the other end', as it were. Instead of (vainly) seeking to define 'needs', and then to quantify the various means needed to meet them, the Report sets out a number of 'social priorities' (basic education, primary health care, water supply) and assesses their relative weight in the following manner. First, total public expenditure is calculated as a percentage of GNP. The portion allocated to social spending (education, health, social security, water-supply infrastructure, etc.) is identified. And finally, the percentage of such spending used on social priorities is worked out. Chain multi-plication of these three ratios then defines the 'human development expenditure ratio', which in the best of cases will be between 5 and 10 per cent. If it is below 3 per cent, the public budget will need to be restructured: that is, it will be necessary to allocate less to the military, law and order, public enterprises or large-scale public works, and/or to rein in spending on major hospitals and universities, so that more is available for the social priority areas.[40]

The same method is applied to international 'assistance', so that the donor countries can better evaluate their action. Here, too, three ratios are multiplied in succession: the 'assistance ratio' ('official development assistance' as a percentage of GNP), the ratio of 'assistance' to the social sectors, and the ratio of 'assistance' to the priority social sectors. The result is the 'priority development aid ratio', which shows that the Netherlands, Denmark and Sweden allocate more of their official 'assistance' than the United States or Italy to priority sectors.

---

39. Thus, according to the 1990 Report (pp. 128–9), classification by HDI pushes the Sultanate of Oman down 56 places (by comparison with GNP classification), the Arab Emirates 50 places and Gabon 46 places, while Sri Lanka 'moves up' 45 places, China 44, Vietnam 40, Cambodia 38, and so on. Among the industrialized countries, the United States slips 17 places and Switzerland 2, while Spain, Australia and the Netherlands all 'gain' 10.

40. The statistics in the 1991 Report allow interesting comparisons to be made between countries that spend a large part of their income on priorities (Zimbabwe, Malaysia, Jordan, Costa Rica) and others that neglect them (Tanzania, Argentina, Pakistan). The 1991 Report also shows, for example, that 'Sri Lanka managed a life expectancy of 71 years and an adult literacy rate of 87% with a per capita income of $400. By contrast, Brazil has a life expectancy of only 65 years, and its adult literacy rate is 78% at a per capita income of $2020' (p. 2).

These new technical indicators are useful to the extent that they measure the real interest of national States or 'development assistance providers' in the improvement of living conditions for the poorest layers of the population. Moreover, they come at a time when all government budgets, in both North and South, are having to be recalculated downwards. In a way, then, they are a tool with which to implement the liberal slogan: 'doing better with less'. The UNDP prescriptions can be used to justify the privatization of loss-making public companies. But their method also makes it possible to judge 'development investment' by its efficiency, and no longer by its volume. How high is priority spending in comparison with the government budget? What proportion of 'development cooperation' money is used to finance basic infra-structure? And what (or who) profits from the still sizeable remainder? The various Human Development Reports have the merit of posing these questions and trying to give answers – even if, in the end, they reduce 'development' to what can be done through international co-operation, whereas the scale of the problems is far too great for that.

So what is 'human development'? The answer is the same in each report:

> Human development is a process of enlarging people's choices. In principle, these choices can be infinite and change over time. But at all levels of development, the three essential ones are for people to lead a long and healthy life, to acquire knowledge and to have access to resources needed for a decent standard of living. If these essential choices are not available, many other opportunities remain inaccessible.
>
> But human development does not end there. Additional choices, highly valued by many people, range from political, economic and social freedom to opportunities for being creative and productive, and enjoying personal self-respect and guaranteed human rights.... According to this conception of human development, income is clearly only one option that people would like to have, albeit an important one.... Development must, therefore, be more than just the expansion of income and wealth. Its focus must be people.[41]

Once again, the 'definition' is normative. The authors describe what they *hope* to see. In the abstract, 'enlarging people's choices' may appear to be regarded as a positive measure.[42] On reflection, the formula

---

41. *Human Development Report 1990*, p. 10.

42. In fact, 'development' does not necessarily help to make it easier for everyone to choose what they want. Industrial societies keep increasing the choice between different car models, but limit the choice of employment; they expand the range of goods offered to those with effective demand, but reduce people's access to clean air, unpolluted water, and products uncontaminated at any point in the food chain. 'Development' is also a process of loss, a *Verlustgeschichte*.

does not mean very much: the process is open (it leads to the 'expansion' of possibilities) and is in principle unlimited. It does not contradict the classical definition of economics as the art of choosing between scarce resources to satisfy unlimited 'needs', and it proposes only a reduction of scarcity so as to expand the range of possible choices. Nor is the text free of evolutionism, for it assumes the existence of 'stages of development'. Finally – although the Report maintains that 'people cannot be reduced to a single dimension as economic creatures'[43] – its objectives are still just as individualist: people should live well and long so as to produce in freedom. That is not such a bad thing in itself, of course. But – if we have to remain in the normative mode – what has happened to conviviality and personal relations, not to speak of what Bataille called the 'accursed share' [la part maudite]?

These are necessary criticisms, but against them must be set the Report's break with the sacred cow of economic growth[44] and its distinction between the accumulation of wealth and the 'good life'. Besides, the successive reports do suggest real tools for highlighting facts that have never before been systematically presented or subjected to such precise international comparison. This is why the UNDP, which lost some credit as a result of the World Bank's alliances with the ILO over 'basic needs' and with UNICEF over 'adjustment with a human face', has now gained fresh legitimacy in the 'development' field. It has also won the support of the NGOs, whose modest resources force them to keep 'close to the grass roots', but which have a major impact on public opinion in the industrialized countries.

Since the late seventies, the *Zeitgeist* has taken on board a 'new humanism' that marries generosity with individualist withdrawal, commitment to the poor with political intervention, concern for human want with praise of competition that allows the best to win. These uncertainties and ambiguities – of which oxymorons are only one manifestation – have come to dominate the economic and political arena. The defence of human rights justified war on Iraq and armed intervention in Somalia; while the terrible plight of the Rwandans

---

43. Ibid., p. iii.

44. Is it just an accident that the 1991 Report insistently declares that 'just as economic growth is necessary for human development, human development is critical to economic growth' (p. 2)? Or had the first Report in 1990 gone too far in its critique? Similarly, while the 1991 Report recognizes that 'markets alone cannot ensure good human development', it also stresses the need 'to open global opportunities – to increase the productivity and competitiveness of developing countries, especially the least developed' (pp. 4–5).

legitimated French military action and allowed President Mobutu to recover some measure of prestige. 'Ethnic cleansing' is proceeding smoothly in the former Yugoslavia, because the UN protects only 'humanitarian corridors'; President Aristide, the champion of human rights, has returned to Haiti, but his enemies were able to leave with honour. *'Human development' is part of this basic contradiction that makes it possible to denounce what one urges, and to practise what one regards as unacceptable.*[45] We have left behind the world of Pirandello, where everyone constructs their own truth; now it is necessary to put up with lying truths, to play tricks with evidence that is both true and false, to agree to wage war to protect human persons. As a result, 'development' appears as if suspended between the necessity and the impossibility (or uselessness) of its own realization. The talk about the 'world community' or 'global village' and the benefits of economic 'globalization' never ceases, but two-thirds of the planet is being increasingly separated off as the North patiently erects a wall to keep out the 'new barbarians'.[46] Apartheid has been abolished in South Africa, only to be reborn on a world scale. Does 'development' have a future in these conditions? Or should one hope, more simply, that there is a future after the end of the 'development era'?[47]

---

45. The 1992 Report is devoted to two themes: deepening inequalities in the world, and the opening of markets. But it recognizes that 'developing countries enter the market as unequal partners – and leave with unequal rewards' (p. 1).

46. In 1990 the income of the richest 20 per cent on earth was sixty times higher than that of the poorest. Given the skewed distribution of national income, the richest 20 per cent of the world's population get at least 150 times more than the poorest 20 per cent. *Human Development Report 1992*, p. 1. On the imagery of 'new barbarians', see Jean-Christophe Rufin, *L'Empire et les nouveaux barbares*, Paris: J.-C. Lattès, 1991.

47. See Gilbert Rist, Majid Rahnema and Gustavo Esteva, *Le Nord perdu. Repères pour l'après-développement*, Lausanne: Éditions d'En Bas, 1992.

CHAPTER 12

THE POSTMODERN ILLUSION: GLOBALIZATION AS SIMULACRUM OF 'DEVELOPMENT'

When a photographer wants to convey the atmosphere of a landscape, he must select certain features and adjust his lens to them. A similar 'focusing' is called for here – or the adoption of a selective 'viewpoint'. Among all the practices that claim to be about 'development', we should focus on those which seem most significant for the spirit of the age or – to use Foucault's expression – the contemporary *episteme*. Hence the necessarily provisional character of the exercise. For whereas, in hindsight, it is relatively easy to put the past into perspective (more optical metaphors!), it is much trickier to pin down the meaning of things happening today. Are they part of a groundswell that is shaping history, or just foam on a wave that will soon wash ashore? Amid the surfeit of information chasing and cancelling itself out, how are we to tell what belongs to the end of one cycle and what to the start of another? How can we resist the common feeling that we are at a turning point in history?

Prophecy has always been a major temptation in the social sciences. But those who claim to make scientific predictions through the use of mathematical formulae do not usually fare any better than clairvoyants or practisers of horoscopy; they have their successes, but only as a random occurrence. Often, what seems likely to last breaks down in a short space of time. Who could have thought, when visiting the Colonial Exhibition in Paris in 1931, that the French Empire was soon to disappear? Who could have predicted that Khomeini's mullahs would send the Shah of Iran packing? Or that the USSR would fall apart in a matter of months? Or that Mandela would be released by the head of the National Party in South Africa?

Are 'development' concerns on the wane, or will they be revived? Before examining some points that should help to provide an answer, let us note that the question itself is new. Doubt has crept right into the heart of a conviction sustaining the various economic and political doctrines that have mobilized people's hopes since the Second World War. The grand theories that promised a generalization of material well-being have lost their credibility – which is all the more remarkable, given that this loss does not seem due to mere denunciation of the particular interests which those theories served to justify. The core of the system is now affected, for the numerous attempts to control or plan social change are far from having lived up to the hopes that they aroused. This is a banal observation, and, naturally enough, repetition of it has led to a wider scepticism. If nothing works (or if success is all too rare), what is the point of continuing?

This final chapter will offer a general interpretation of the broad movement associated with 'development', attempting to grasp its historical role and to assess the present limits of its mobilizing capacity. Now that we have looked at the various stages in the evolution of the doctrine, we need to consider the elements of both continuity and discontinuity between them, as well as the consequences of the wave of liberalization (or globalization) for the 'economic' and 'altruistic' concerns that have always been the two axes of development discourse and practices.

Our starting point here will be the dual meaning that 'development' immediately assumes in any debate. Why do supporters of co-operation always counterpose 'real development' to 'development *tout court*'? Are they just stressing that the promise of happiness remains even if it has not yet been kept, and arguing that new methods on offer discredit the ones previously thought up? Or do the two meanings reflect two kinds of belief in 'development'?

This leads on to the hypothesis that the period from the end of the Second World War to the end of the Soviet empire was marked by two forms of 'development': the first kept up the stock belief that inspired the extension of market society and its colonial expression; while the second was more akin to religious messianism in its voluntarist enthusiasm to establish at once the ideal of a just and affluent society. *Two parallel mechanisms were thus supposed to hasten the coming of a new era: the Welfare State in the North, and 'development' strategies in the South.*

These messianic stirrings died down in the early nineties; the 'globalization' that took their place may be considered a new manifestation of the same belief (adapted to postmodern culture) in which the real and the virtual merge into one. *'Development' now withdraws behind its appearances, and persists only in the form of an 'as if', a trompe-l'oeil whose verisimilitude is enough to make us forget its lack of reality.* For the vanished object is so important that it must be preserved for the time being, if only in the form of a delusion.

ON THE USEFULNESS OF TALKING AT CROSS-PURPOSES

Whenever the subject of 'development' is debated, one can be sure that the greatest confusion will arise from the many contradictory images held by those taking part. This ambiguity of the concept – itself bound up with the interests confronting one another – means that it is possible to play on different registers by stressing either what ought to be or what is, either signs of what is hoped or the reality of what can be observed. Each can come to form a self-enclosed picture of the world, constructed according to particular cognitive interests. So in order to make clear what each involves, let us imagine a possible dialogue between a critic of ordinary thinking and an activist in the cause of 'development'.

'What critics define as "development" is no more than the spread of the market, but that is not what we supporters of co-operation understand by "real development"!' – 'But is it not in the name of "development" that the multinationals try to patent biodiversity and that people are mobilized as "human resources"? How can you overlook the fact that "development" exists first of all in what are called the "developed" countries?' – 'That may be so. But what we call "development" are first of all the actions, projects and programmes of organizations co-operating with partners in the South.' – 'Even if we take such a narrow definition, however, is the conclusion so different? Is not the aim still to increase productivity, profitability, rationality? Is not the point to integrate those who are "still" kept outside the market system?' – 'Of course, but that is not all there is to it. The main purpose of "development" is to promote human fulfilment and to allow the less well-off to take their fate in their own hands.' – 'That is a noble aim, but there are more defeats than successes, and what we see in the end is greater impoverishment, growing inequalities and a gradual spread of market relations.' – 'That is often true, alas, but "development" is a challenge that has to be constantly taken up. For is not "real development" a universal demand?' – 'That is what everyone claims. When you say that, you are at one with the champions of globalization, who are also convinced they are promoting "development"!' – 'Not at all. What we want is "real development"!' – 'But how do you distinguish between "real" and "false" if they both lead to the same result?' – 'We know what is real, because we believe in it.'

What, in the end, is being talked about in the critique of 'development'? Is it the belief in a moral duty to help the poor and work for everyone's happiness, which mobilizes the energies of numerous organizations? Or is it the economic practices reflecting the interests of various actors and producing the opposite of the claimed beliefs? Even if these two levels can be distinguished in theory, they are closely bound up with each other and make it possible to switch in a flash between solution and problem, antidote and poison, hope and reality. For some, 'development' is synonymous with the broad movement which has been carrying the market system along for the last two centuries; for others, it is the whole set of measures through which the world should be made a juster place despite the rationality of capitalism. The usefulness of this talking at cross-purposes is that it allows everyone 'good reasons' for continuing with their activity. For the same belief can have a number of different effects.

Before analysing the present situation, we should therefore examine the causes and consequences of the ambiguity fundamental to the concept of 'development'.

(a) *An unchallenged belief in the necessity of growth*. At the origin of the broad 'development' movement, we find a belief whose roots lie deep inside the Western imagination; political leaders, economic agents, public and private international organizations, as well as sections of the population in both North and South, were willy-nilly converted to it. According to this belief, the 'good life' can be assured for all through technological progress and ever-rising production of goods and services – from which everyone will eventually benefit. Such 'development', then, offers the promise of general abundance, conceived in biological imagery as something 'natural', positive, necessary and indisputable.

These structural components could doubtless be refined, but they are enough to characterize a picture that is held in common because it has won through everywhere. The belief does not, however, correspond to any historical reality: the world never has been and never will be true to this high-minded dream, although it does shape some of the relevant practices. *If modern societies all proclaim the necessity of 'development', this is because they have made it into a holy truth symbolizing their practices as a whole and conferring on them an obligatory force. If people are made to believe, it is so that they can be made to do something.*

Being eminently social, this belief is a *product of history* (in which old Western conceptions of the world are mixed up with realities of the last two centuries of exceptional growth), but it is also an instance that *produces history*. There was nothing in the past to suggest that one day every society would see its collective history as a constant effort to increase the quantity of goods and to make such growth the principle of government. Yet this is precisely the objective that is held in common; 'development', like any other belief, has become a historical agent. Together with frozen embryos, nuclear power stations, the hole in the ozone layer and many other monstrosities, 'development' has become one of what Bruno Latour calls the totally invented 'quasi-objects'[1] (which, in a way, are also 'quasi-subjects') at the interface of nature and society. It is no longer enough that these have a life of their own; they now shape policies, dictate behaviour, and sometimes demand sacrifices. 'Development' is certainly a social creation, but now it has the appearance of a 'natural' phenomenon with laws of its own that govern societies. Men and women are no longer the only ones who make history – for they have to take account of these strange new creatures which neither exist in nature nor have a personality, which are neither objects nor subjects but lie halfway between the two and combine the properties of both. This is why it is so difficult to get rid of them – assuming one wants to in the first place. 'Development' thus belongs to our universe and takes part in its transformation. Everywhere it wins acceptance for the growth imperative. How could the future be imagined without it? What conceivable policies could fail to call for it (even if the moral duty is fulfilled in the very act of proclamation rather than in any actual success)?[2]

After this admirable consensus, things start to become extraordinarily complicated! For many contradictory practices stem from the belief. Abundance does not emerge spontaneously, and economic growth is not 'natural' in any sense applicable in the realm of biology. Certain conditions therefore have to be established before it can appear – which comes down to applying the theories of economists who, since Adam Smith, have defined how best to bring about the 'progress of opulence'. For, considering the prodigious rise in the 'standard of living' in the West during the past two centuries,[3] is there not good reason to trust in those theories? Is not the market – which, since Mandeville, has been thought of as converting private vices into public benefits – capable of making the belief come true? And conversely, if many nations

---

1. *We Have Never Been Modern.*

2. See Fabrizio Sabelli, *Recherche anthropologique et développement*, Neuchâtel/Paris: Institut d'ethnologie, Maison des sciences de l'homme, 1993, p. 22.

3. For a critique of this concept, see Serge Latouche's article, 'Standard of Living', in Wolfgang Sachs, ed., *The Development Dictionary*, pp. 250–63.

are 'still' excluded from the benefits, is it not because they are unaware of the virtues of competition, of individual interest, market rationality, utilitarian morality, and the mutual advantages of trade?

A belief has thus spread within the body of society – even if it is not continually reaffirmed as such – which has inspired all the productivist practices current since the beginning of the Industrial Revolution. In either the liberal or the Marxist variant, it is the 'development of the productive forces' which is of primary importance. No doubt the final goal of general abundance is held to be still far off (and is ever receding, like the visible horizon). But the conviction remains that it lies within our grasp – albeit at the price of frenzied exploitation of nature, growing inequality and universal commodification. Such negative aspects are made easier to swallow by pointing out that – contrary to Marx's predictions – the impoverishment of the working class has not occurred, and that capitalism has survived its contradictions. Industrialization, burgeoning trade, new agricultural technology, profitability requirements, reinvestment of profits – all these are supposed to make it possible to create wealth or, in other words, to stimulate 'development'.

Most Christians come to accept the gap between their belief in a world ruled by love of one's neighbour and the harshness of everyday social relations, so that they are scarcely bothered by the fact that their own practices regularly contradict the values to which they say they adhere. Similarly, most political and economic leaders use 'development' as a pretext to convert natural and social relations into commodities, and to widen the gulf between rich and poor, without seeing anything contradictory in what they do.

(b) *The messianic decades*. No religion escapes attempts at reform or 'revival'. When the belief loses its originality and becomes routinized, or when compromises become too blatant, movements spring up to restore the 'true doctrine' against backsliding on the part of lukewarm believers. Hence the messianic creeds that promise a new order, a Kingdom of God on earth. Messianism, in the sociological sense of the term,[4] is a form of impatience with an unkept promise, a wish to take

---

4. See Henri Desroche's highly synthetic article (*Enyclopaedia universalis*, 15, 1989, pp. 7–10), which defines messianism as 'the common store of doctrines that promise perfect happiness on earth under the leadership of one person, nation or party, of collective movements within which various reforms – ecclesiastical or political, economic or social – are presented in the form of orders or norms identified with divine "missions" or even "emissions"'.

the belief literally and to make it come true *hic et nunc* by foreshortening history, by jumping ahead to a better world formerly promised for the afterlife or for a distant future. The new community does not challenge the old belief but reinterprets it as an immediate demand, thereby consigning to outer darkness those who have settled down to use it for their own advantage. The 'true believers' differ from others by their urge to create the new world straight away, instead of prolonging the wait. The end of the Second World War provided the opportunity for the 'reformation' that had become necessary after years of economic crisis and unspeakable horrors. The time seemed to have come to ensure that the dream of an ideal society took visible shape, through a social experiment in which the abundance promised to all would come into view.

To this end, the boldest or the most 'visionary' tried to establish a dual variant of the concrete utopia: the Welfare State or social democracy in the countries of the North, and 'development' programmes in the South.[5] In both cases, the idea was to encourage economic growth (seen as the 'hard core' of the system) through voluntarist steering that presupposed a strong State with powers of redistribution and planning. The similarities and differences between the two approaches cannot be exhaustively discussed in the present context, but it should be noted that the whole project brought to the fore the central problem of 'development economics' – that is, its attempted reconciliation or combination of the contradictory postulates of the Marxist and neoliberal models (both based on the necessity of growth).[6]

How else is one to explain that religious fervour which generated all the vocations and institutions, donations and debates considered in previous chapters? Think of all those documents (from President Truman's Point Four through Rostow, the NIEO and the Brundtland Report to the conclusions of the South Commission) which ritually heralded a new era rich in promises and eschatological hopes. Is it not

5. The parallelism is apparent in the Hammarskjöld Report (in *Development Dialogue* (1975)), which argues for 'another development' (that is, 'true development', as opposed to mere extension of the market) on the basis of the Swedish and Tanzanian experiences. An attempt to generalize the principles of social democracy may be found in the Brandt Report.

6. See Albert Hirschmann, 'The Rise and Decline of Development Economics', in *Essays in Trespassing: Economics to Politics and Beyond*, Cambridge: Cambridge University Press, 1981, pp. 1–25. For Hirschmann, 'development economics' (unlike Marxism) emphasizes mutual advantage and (unlike neoliberal economics) argues that economic theory needs to be made more specific when it is applied to 'developing countries'.

a special feature of religious reform movements to want to adapt reality
to dogma, to found the 'true Church' against the decadence and
fecklessness of existing institutions – in short, to bring heaven down to
earth? So it is that a secularized messianism – which began as a minority
phenomenon – took flight in the 1960s and won over numerous
followers. It is true that not everyone was free from ulterior motives.
But has that not always been the case? Have not the most 'spiritual'
movements often been the locus of a struggle for power?[7] This also
explains the endless counterposition of 'true development' to 'false
development', for it is in the nature of every messianism to want the
religious community to achieve paradise amid this vale of tears, whereas
others, however sincere, are content with a commitment that does not
question what they actually practise. The divisions concern not so much
the belief itself as the means and temporality of its realization.

This perspective helps us to understand how it is that a fundamen-
talist minority of 'true developers' assumes sole responsibility for the
completion of history, while excluding from the field mere believers in
'growth' or 'development'. For even if the latter share the same belief,
they appear as half-hearted individuals too much concerned with their
immediate advantage and happy to let the distant future achieve the
promised 'good life'.

If we consider 'development' as the mobilizing slogan of a social
movement that created messianic organizations and practices, then it
has in the end suffered the same fate as that of other messianisms.
Despite the vast resources placed at its disposal, despite its wide range
of methods and the persuasiveness of its believers, the enterprise has
been defeated first of all by its own overambition, but also by inevitable compromises with the mass of people seeking to use the various
initiatives for their own profit. This summing-up may seem reductionist
and 'over the top', or anyway too cut and dried. Yet it is a simple fact
that the enthusiasm of the early sixties has gradually crumbled away.
Nor can it be denied that projects intended to 'enable communities to
take their fate in their hands', or to assist 'the development of each and
all', have most often ended in failure and even hastened the transformation of social relations into marketable goods and the commodification of nature. Economic growth, the aim of everyone involved, has
indeed occurred – but far from bringing the 'good life', it has only

---

7. There is no other explanation for Engels's interest in Thomas Münzer and the
Anabaptists. Asian religions of 'renunciation' (Louis Dumont), on the other hand,
have not generally pursued the goal of power.

increased inequalities and marginalization. This is indeed the conclusion reached by Hirschmann:

> [T]he decline of development economics cannot be fully reversed: our subdiscipline has achieved its considerable lustre through the implicit idea that it could slay the dragon of backwardness virtually by itself or, at least, that its contribution to this task was central. We now know that this is not so.[8]

Hirschmann's brevity will hardly satisfy those who wish to find the historical reasons for the failure of such a noble and grandiose (and morally legitimate!) project. Let us here simply mention three facts which, in addition to the 'developers'' incapacity to come up with clear signs of the new world they advocated, have dashed the hopes of a worldwide spread of 'development' in accordance with the prevailing belief.

The first fact is the high levels of debt incurred by supposedly 'developing' countries since the beginning of the eighties. Granted, this was not the developers' fault but the result of a borrowing frenzy among the ruling classes of the South that was actively encouraged by the bankers of the North. Granted, falling prices for raw materials set up further pressure for international organizations to demand structural adjustment. In the end, however, the responsibilities count for little. It is enough to point out that the sudden compulsion to apply harsh market laws dispelled the promise of redistribution. A series of devaluations, combined with public-sector layoffs and a drive to recover the costs of public services, demonstrated the limits of the model. To put it another way, the failure of attempts to tame 'wildcat capitalism' meant an end to the pursuit of general affluence.

The second historical fact undermining 'development' (understood as a drive to generalize material comfort here and now) was the collapse of 'actual socialism' and the Soviet empire. The economic and social dilapidation of the state-directed societies finally convinced sceptics that it was impossible to promote 'development' through compulsory rules or voluntarist policies.[9]

Third, it became evident that the Welfare State led to financial and budgetary shortfalls once technological change did away with jobs. In countries where 'development' seemed to have succeeded best − in Scandinavia, for example − its continuation could no longer be assured.

---

8. Hirschmann, p. 23.
9. This conclusion actually went too far, because the proper functioning of the market also depends upon precise institutional conditions.

Hence the neoliberal movement associated with Reagan and Thatcher assumed massive proportions, and asserted itself everywhere as the new orthodoxy. The hunting down of deficits, which began in the countries of the South, soon spread to the North, where people impotently watched the gradual dismantling of the Welfare State, and the rise of unemployment and social exclusion as a result of corporate relocation and restructuring. Let us for the moment simply note that if Hirschmann is right in treating 'development economics' as a combination of Marxist and neoliberal postulates, then it effectively perished with the implosion of the USSR and the discrediting of the paradigm on which it had been based.

End of sequence. End of game. The lights that made the hope glow have gone out. The huge enterprise that began in both North and South at the end of the Second World War, with the aim of accelerating 'development', has come to a complete end. *It is time to recognize that the world cannot be changed with the help of concepts and strategies belonging to the dreams of yesteryear.* The messianic fervour that was supposed to bring worldwide plenty will no longer mobilize people's efforts. The times have changed, and the new actors have different priorities.

At the moment, however, two issues are still up in the air: namely, the future of the 'development' organizations having to face reconversion, and the consequences of the gradual absorption of 'development' by the globalization process.

ORGANIZATIONS ON REPRIEVE
OR IN MUTATION?

Although the hope that all the world's inhabitants will enjoy material affluence has now vanished, the organizations set up to take charge of the project cannot disappear overnight. Not only do all institutions seek to maintain and reproduce themselves, but 'development' (as an organizational phenomenon) has become a sector of economic activity in the same way as tourism, computing or consultancy, and too many interests are at stake for it to be simply wound up. It would be a huge task to calculate the number of all those who live from 'development administration' – World Bank and UNDP functionaries, but also the mass of field and office workers managing 'development programmes' for UNICEF, the FAO, WHO, UNESCO and the ILO, just to mention the main UN agencies. And then there are all those, in both North and South, who work for the government 'development' ministries: bureau-

crats and experts, VSO recruits, agricultural popularizers, sundry organizers, trainers, supervisors, agronomists, foresters, hydraulics experts,
planners, healthcare personnel, and so on. Who could ever add up the
number of full-timers and volunteers coming under the thousands of
NGOs, with their public relations staff, their accountants and project
leaders, their barefoot doctors and moped literacy workers, their cross-
country drivers, caretakers and 'village informants'? How many are the
brokers and consultants, the researchers employed by such major organizations as the CNRS, ORSTOM or INRA (just to speak of France),
the 'development institute' lecturers and the houses publishing what they
write, the conference organizers, the advisers hired for people leaving
on VSO or coming back? And what of all the jobs deriving from activities that could not exist without secretaries, telecommunications and
transport, office buildings, materials of all kinds, and airline companies?

The volume of 'official development assistance' from OECD countries
has decreased since 1993, despite a small increase in 1994 (with a global
sum of $59.152 billion). For 1995, it amounted to 'only' $58.894 billion.
This global tendency concerns both the absolute sums involved and
their average value in terms of GNP, which fell from 0.34 per cent in
1983–84 to 0.29 per cent in 1995. The economic slowdown and crisis
of public finances in the industrialized countries will probably accentuate
this trend.[10] Second, the 'assistance' in question is no longer allocated
only to the South; it is also going to the former 'socialist' countries –
which means a reduction in the share of the poorest countries. On the
other hand, private financial flows have been increasing very rapidly –
from $25.5 billion in 1991 to $92 billion in 1995. But of course, this
capital is being invested mainly in the 'emerging markets', not in
'marginal' areas, so that in 1995 twelve countries attracted three-quarters
of private flows and 80 per cent of direct investment.

Things being so, the 'development' agencies have two options open
to them. On the one hand, they can convert from the discourse of
'basic needs' satisfaction to celebrate the new orthodoxy of the market.[11]

---

10. Thus, the loans that France is committed to make to the UN's specialist
agencies under the rubric of 'development assistance' have recently been cut by 60
per cent. These austerity measures particularly affect UNICEF, UNDP, WHO, WFP
and UNHCR (*Le Monde*, 30 November 1995). Similarly, the United States, which
has already pulled out of UNESCO, has announced that it intends to quit UNIDO
at the end of 1996 (*Le Monde*, 6 December 1995).

11. In the case of the World Bank, it would hardly be such a 'conversion' because
Article 1 of its Statutes lists the encouragement of private investment and the growth
of international trade among its objectives; the 'messianic period' under Robert
McNamara was thus the exception.

The World Bank's *World Development Report 1994* is a perfect example of this nineties 'revolution in attitudes':[12] it advocates the privatization of infrastructure in the name of efficiency and profitability, whereas everyone had previously agreed that these tasks should be assumed by the State. Although the World Bank accepts that the State may, in some cases, subsidize the provider of a service, all the charges have to be calculated in such a way as to cover costs – with the result that such essential services as water or electricity are available only to users with the means to pay. As for the UNDP, it argues that 'free markets provide the most efficient mechanism yet devised for the exchange of goods and services', but its 'human development' doctrine seeks to make these markets 'people-friendly' and to complement them with 'social safety nets ... to look after the temporary victims of market forces and to bring them back into the markets'.[13] It is likely that this road will enable the agencies to survive through their giving international sanction to the market.

The other option, which mainly concerns NGOs, is to become part of the new niche of humanitarian aid. The field is huge enough – and is bound to grow larger still. For the collapse of empires or States is everywhere triggering new conflicts manipulated by identity discourse and various forms of 'ethnic cleansing' that are becoming almost banal: in the former Yugoslavia, in the Great Lakes region of Africa, the Caucasus, Sri Lanka, Kashmir and Kurdistan, to mention only the most extensive and dramatic instances. Furthermore, the triumph of market economics is deepening inequalities everywhere, both inside countries and internationally. Not only is an ever larger part of the population (including in the industrial countries) excluded from all participation in national life and consigned to extreme poverty, but whole countries have now been marginalized from the major flows of trade and infor-

---

12. Without exaggerating the importance of vocabulary, we might note that in the first twelve pages summarizing the Report, the 'old' terms are relatively little used. 'Development' (not counting 'developing countries' or 'developing world') appears 8 times, and 'the poor' or 'poverty' 12 times. 'Users', however, features 28 times, and 'competition' 24 times.

13. *Human Development Report 1993*, pp. 30 ff. The expression 'people-friendly markets' is yet another oxymoron, while the strategy of providing 'safety nets' for victims of the market so that they can be reintegrated into the market is, to say the least, paradoxical. Even if the UNDP also stresses the importance of infrastructure in health, education, roads, electricity and telecommunications, it leaves open the question of whether the State or the private sector should be responsible for the necessary investment. The whole tenor of the Report, however, is in favour of private initiative. 'Accompanying measures' are mainly designed to do away with 'arbitrary government controls and regulations'.

mation. This dramatic situation calls for urgent help, and it is impossible to refuse it even when there is no illusion about its real effectiveness or about the secondary effects it is likely to have.[14]

Why are these the two main paths open? Simply because they are 'in tune' with the globalization process that is now reorganizing space and values. Fire-raisers and fire-fighters have always had common interests. One side helps to destabilize States, which then become incapable of maintaining public order and carrying out their redistributive functions, so that the gates are flung wide open to violence and pauperization. The other side tries to soften the negative effects created in this way by stepping up so-called humanitarian efforts. For both, the world has become 'without borders':[15] each practises its own form of intervention − either by default (by stripping the State of its control powers) or by excess (by substituting itself for the State).[16]

GLOBALIZATION, OR BACK TO NORMAL

Once the messianic parenthesis had been closed − the one in which people had done their utmost to mould the world to a dream of shared plenty − it was normal enough that pragmatism should recover its rights. Was it not common sense to follow the precepts of nature? What was the point in pulling on a shoot to make it grow faster? On the contrary, that kind of intervention could only do harm. Growth or 'development' were not themselves questioned, but there seemed to be other ways of achieving them − especially through a return to the self-regulating market.

Suddenly, everything that used to seem just and necessary (in both North and South) became useless and dangerous − planning, of course, but also all the 'rigidities' that blocked initiative, stifled entrepreneurship and kept obsolete structures alive. Nationalized corporations were said to distort competition, taxes to penalize investors, collective agreements to undermine the freedom to hire labour, public services to ignore

---

14. See Marie-Dominique Perrot, ed., *Dérives humanitaires: États d'urgence et droit d'ingérence*, Nouveaux Cahiers de l'IUED, 1, Geneva: IUED/Paris: PUF, 1994.

15. Significantly, the World Bank's *World Development Report 1995* (New York: Oxford University Press, 1995) is entitled *Workers in an Integrating World* − or, in French, *Le monde du travail dans une économie sans frontières*.

16. The Gulf War and the US/UN expedition to Somalia were good examples of the merging of globalization and humanitarian intervention (even if territorial concerns and national interests also played an important role).

profitability, and national frontiers to constrict the field of the market. This new rhetoric of globalization focused on one main target, the State, supposedly guilty of regulation that allocated resources in an irrational manner, and was therefore inherently wasteful.

Beyond such discourse, there were indeed many signs of the declining autonomy of States (and hence of economics in the sense of *National-wirtschaft*).[17] First of all, the mere possibility for banks to create token money out of nothing[18] overthrew the regal power over the currency whose two sides symbolized the (seemingly indissoluble) link between State and market. Second, the fact that currencies (or even exchange and interest rates) had become exposed to speculative operations deprived the State of one of the 'fundamental levers' of economic policy. Control over exchange rates was undermined still further by the fact that much of the public debt (40 per cent in the case of France) was held by foreigners, with this 'xeno-currency' market lying in wait for changes in the 'rating' of debtors. Third, globalization enabled big transnational corporations to break loose from their nation-state of origin, by means of relocation or cross-frontier mergers and acquisitions.[19] Their capital was thus invested where profits were highest, which was usually where labour regulation was most feeble. To maintain their 'industrial fabric', governments had no other solution than to 'adapt' to the weakest norms of social protection. Globalization without borders erodes political power by forcing it to follow the market, and worsens the lot of workers-consumers by making their possibilities (or conditions) of employment dependent upon criteria of the 'virtual economy'.[20]

The consequences are well known. The dismemberment of social policies hitherto entrusted to the State has widened the gulf not only between rich countries and poor countries, but also between rich and poor within individual countries:

---

17. See the stimulating analyses in Bertrand Badie, *La Fin des territoires. Essai sur le désordre international et sur l'utilité sociale du respect*, Paris: Fayard, 1995. Badie clearly shows that the State has not been abolished but severely shaken and subjected to a kind of 'selective deterritorialization'. This is linked to the appearance of a geography of communications, finance and manpower networks, and to a new 'grammar of space'. In addition, ethnic movements have been destabilizing old States by demanding the creation of new nations.

18. See François Rachline, *De zéro à epsilon. L'économie de la capture*, Paris: Hachette, 1991.

19. See François Chesnais, *La Mondialisation du capital*, Paris: Syros, 1994, pp. 250 ff.

20. Henri Bourguinat, *La Tyrannie des marchés. Essai sur l'économie virtuelle*, Paris: Economica, 1995. In this creation of 'virtual', or nomadic, companies, the centre of gravity is nowhere at all – at once 'offshore' and 'out of soil'.

The division between developed and underdeveloped countries has grown deeper throughout all five continents. This has led to a still more radical break – between those who will be in the grip of real time for the main part of their economic activities within the virtual community of the *global town*, and those who will be worse off than ever in the real space of *local towns*, that great planetary suburb which will probably embrace the (thoroughly real) community of people without a job and without a habitat favouring harmonious and long-lasting socialization.[21]

Cries of alarm have even been making themselves heard.[22] So what has happened to the ideals of old? Has the world become completely cynical? Is there no more hope in shared abundance? For the supporters of globalization, however, nothing has really changed. Economic growth is at the heart of their concerns, so how can they be suspected of neglecting collective happiness? Indeed, far from wanting to keep the privileges of wealth for themselves, do they not invite the rest of the world to join them and to share their convictions? Why should the poor complain about that? Access to wealth is not being denied them. All they have to do is stop applying rules other than those of the market, free competition and free trade. It is well known, of course, that poor people still exist, and that their situation is a difficult one, but it is no longer necessary for them to be given special treatment. To escape their plight, they have only to accept the common law that exemplary traders are proposing to them, then they alone will achieve the miracles once promised by the 'developers'.[23] In this conception, 'development' is not a *sine qua non* for rightful participation in the wider international market; it is a consequence of that participation. It no longer has to be sought for its own sake; it is given 'into the bargain'. Finally, is not 'globalization' a synonym for 'universalization' or – to paraphrase Braudel – for the 'world-society' to which all belong?[24] The signs are already

21. Paul Virilio, *La Vitesse de libération*, Paris: Galilée, 1995.

22. In this respect, the relative courage of the UNRISD report (*States of Disarray: The Social Effects of Globalization*, London: UNRISD and Banson, 1995) is to be welcomed. Not only does it speak out against growing inequalities; it also shows that the ideal of the champions of liberalism is a simplified model corresponding to 'no place on earth' (pp. ix, 19). Similarly, the organizers of the 1996 Davos Forum clearly indicated the limits of globalization, but their reservations were quickly brushed aside by those attending.

23. Thus the *World Development Report 1995* boldly states: 'fears that increased international trade and investment and less state intervention will hurt employment are mainly without basis.... Market-based development ... is the best way to deliver growth and rising living standards for workers' (pp. 2–3).

peeping through: the East–West frontier has fallen, the WTO is organizing more and more exchanges without borders, the Internet is open to all because it belongs to no one, and CNN News travels the world in real time.[25] There seem to be many reasons, then, to redraw the map of the world and to celebrate a potential unity that has been partially recovered. Does not the future lie with information networks, with the sharing of new values?

Are there really two discourses, or is there, rather, an antinomy between discourse and practice? Would there be so much talk of exclusion if globalization had not simultaneously become the buzz word of economists? Is not 'globalization' an instance of *antiphrasis* – that is, of saying the opposite of the truth, in the manner of the sailors of Antiquity who used the name Euxeinos Pontos ('hospitable sea') for a Black Sea that they feared because of the 'savages' peopling its shores? These contradictions cannot be explained unless we further examine the new but continuing role of the belief in 'development'.

VIRTUAL REALITY AS A REFUGE FOR CONTINUING BELIEF

No society can do without dream or belief, unattainable utopia or reassuring verity. Globalization could never play this role, being experienced by most people as a brute fact that mainly involves duress and violence. Nor can there be much enthusiasm for the idea that 'adaptation' is indispensable, when it is not known to what. Globalization therefore relies upon the vast means of communication to persuade people that there is simply no alternative.[26] But it is still necessary to 'use up the leftovers', as it were, to assure social cohesion through the

---

24. Globalization fits into a universalist and individualist discursive system that does not bother about intermediate levels such as the State or symbolic roots. This neglect breathes fresh life into identity demands, which spawn conflicts based on a 'voluntary ghetto' conception of ethnic territory. Such conflicts are all the more understandable in that the cult of immediacy ('real time') stresses *now* at the expense of *here*, whereas everyone wants to live *hic et nunc*. It is not enough to be a citizen of the world; it is also necessary to be from *somewhere*. And globalization rests upon the spread of a 'particular universal', part and parcel of Western sociocentrism, which removes from history the possibility of collaboration between different societies proud of their own autonomy and respected by others.

25. Only international migration escapes the globalization process as States feel compelled to keep control of movements into their territory. See Badie, p. 183.

26. This TINA formula is current in the World Bank. See Susan George and Fabrizio Sabelli, *Faith and Credit: The World Bank's Secular Empire*.

belief that although globalization has apparently changed everything, the final goal is still the same whatever the sacrifices required. Here is the real paradox. *The belief has never been more remote from prevailing discourses and practices, yet it certainly seems to survive in the backdrop or horizon of history.* 'Development' has never been more than a pretext for expanding the realm of the commodity, but throughout the 'messianic' period this was obscured by a stream of promises and policies, declarations and measures, which kept up the illusion whereby people could be made to act in certain ways. Consequently, at the very moment when globalization is achieving hegemony (as both discourse and practices), it is practically impossible to dispense with the legitimacy stemming from 'development'. For 'development' has a *meaning*, based on an old tradition, whereas globalization has none.

Thus Durkheim's argument according to which every society needs shared beliefs that 'belong to the group and unify it' is still valid.[27] It is impossible to do without such indisputable truths that hold the body of society together. For as we have seen, the truth in question not only goes back a long way (in the West) and thus has the value of being unquestionable; it also corresponds to a legitimate aspiration. Nevertheless, it is no longer possible to believe that material plenty can be rapidly generalized, through forcing the pace of history.

Now, myths and beliefs are products of history. Each epoch works on them anew, modifying them to make the present inhabitable. The old Aristotelian conception of growth/'development' was constantly reworked until it applied to the accumulation of knowledge, and then to manifestations of unlimitable material abundance. It is this 'hard core' of the belief which has made it possible to justify the programme of modernity and all the 'development' strategies devised over nearly fifty years. But our epoch, too, tinkers with the foundations of belief, re-interprets ancient truths, modifies the mechanisms of belonging so that they fit the new networks of meaning which correspond to the present 'order of things'. It is a necessary adjustment, which alters the conditions of belief while permitting the act of belief to survive. In other words, *people go on believing, but they can no longer believe as before.*

What now interferes with and transforms the old forms of the belief is the *irresistible advance of virtual reality*,[28] whose successes are closely

---

27. Émile Durkheim, *The Elementary Structures of the Religious Life*, p. 41.
28. It should be stressed that we are talking of virtual *reality*. As Philippe Quéau has said, the virtual is not the opposite of the real but is simply alongside it. What we are witnessing, then, is a reduplication of existing phenomena.

bound up with the characteristic ambivalence, uncertainty and ambiguity of the epoch. Everywhere misunderstanding is a source of fascination, deception seduces with an air of truth, illusions come thick and fast. 'Isn't that a splendid marble statue?' 'Sure, only it's a hologram!' – 'How nice it would be to live in the new house before it is built!' 'No problem; the architect will make up a virtual one for you!' – 'What bliss to be physically close to your loved one across the seas!' 'A data device will do the job by offering you remote presence and remote contact!'[29] It may be objected that these are again utopias, or experimental projects, far removed from everyday life. It is true, of course, that Jules Verne was also dreaming when he imagined a rocket trip to the moon. More prosaically, how is one to distinguish between 'real' scenes and the synthetic images presented to us in the cinema and on television? Once upon a time our society used to build cathedrals. Nowadays it builds Disneylands, also known as *Magic Worlds*. Snow White and the Seven Dwarfs are no longer the product of our imagination, because we can actually talk to them; the Indians with feather headdress attacking the stagecoach are no longer a memory left behind in the writings of James Fenimore Cooper, because the attack takes place every day at fixed hours; Sleeping Beauty is not dead, because you can see her breathing in her castle bed as she unknowingly waits for Prince Charming to appear. And if the world were to become like a huge life-sized Disneyland, where would all the extras be found for an unfinished dream, an unfolding tale, a truth in search of reality? As Baudrillard has said,

> we prefer the virtual illusion even more – that of the neither true nor false, of the neither good nor evil, of a lack of distinction between the real and the referential, of an artificial reconstruction of the world where, at the cost of total disenchantment, we would enjoy total immunity.... The sad consequence of all this is that we no longer know what to do with the real world. We can no longer see any need whatever for this residue which has become an encumbrance.[30]

The ludic uses of virtual reality make it seem so familiar that the contamination of reality by simulacra no longer causes offence. This is why account must be taken of the way in which the imagination is being trans-

---

29. The consequences of 'cybersex' – which replaces amorous transports with 'cybernetic orgasms', making it a kind of 'technophilia' in which love games become a mere society game cancelling the existence of 'couples' – were anticipated with remarkable foresight in Paul Virilio's *La Vitesse de libération*.

30. Jean Baudrillard, *The Perfect Crime*, London: Verso, 1996, pp. 41, 42.

formed through imperceptible shifts and disjunctures. Not long ago in France, a lot of ink was spilt over the possibility of a 'real-look' passport, or *passeport vrai-faux*,[31] but this deliberate confusion is much more frequent, even if it is no longer noticed. The constant mingling of true and false, virtual and real in current economic practices is perhaps the best example of this contagion. For the 1,200 billion dollars that are traded daily on the financial markets are one of the main elements in the globalization now under way. They are also the source of the highest profits: first, because the sums in play are some sixty times greater than the total amount of international commercial transactions and direct investment, but above all because the disconnection (or 'derealization') of economics means that profit no longer has to depend upon production, as it did throughout the industrial era.[32] Marx's formula M–C–M′ clearly indicated that profit, or surplus-value, was linked to production (and the exploitation of surplus labour). In the new world of the globalized virtual economy, this detour is no longer necessary: there can be a straight route from M to M′. Previously, speculators based their hopes on the quality of the security they bought or sold, and paid close attention to the actual performance of companies quoted on the stock exchange. This is no longer the case today, as currencies, interest rates and options have themselves become the object of speculation. So how is one to distinguish between the real and the virtual, fictitious money and concrete profit, the underlying asset and the derivative product? Doubtless no one can. But the habit of no longer asking such naive questions has now caught on.

In the absence of certainties, it is enough to act *as if*. This is the new mould in which belief is cast: as if growth would save jobs, as if the liberalization and deregulation of markets were to everyone's benefit, as if States were sovereign, as if election promises were serious, as if ethnic differences were sufficient explanation for genocide, as if economic rationality were universal, as if today's ills carried the seed of tomorrow's happiness.

Thanks to the banalization of this indifference to reality, 'development' can go on creating illusions – no longer as the *a priori* justification for practices of globalization, but as their possible yet uncertain

---

31. See Michel de Fornel, 'Les paradoxes du vrai-faux', *Traverses (Le fantôme de la vérité)*, 8, Winter 1993, pp. 28–39. There are also bags in 'real-look' leather, as well as television interviews or news reports that 'look real'.

32. The wave of privatizations provide so many opportunities to place this foot-loose capital in profitable sectors, but these sources of profits (tied to real assets) are far from the only ones.

consequence at the end of history. 'This is exactly like the way we pray to put off the Last Judgement for ever: we pray that He should never come back, that He should stay up there. We pray that we should be able to go on praying.'[33] Doubt no longer paralyses action, then – on the contrary, it is action which restores consensus around the belief. All everyone has to do is act *as if*: as if 'development' were generalizable, as if the foreign debt could be repaid, as if it were possible for the poor countries to catch up with the rich, as if limitless growth could be kept up in the long run. As if the virtual could triumph over the real.

Because the virtual is now part of everyday reality, there is a risk that the radical change in the situation will be overlooked. *Whereas the idea was once to make people believe in order to make them act in certain ways, the point now is to do anything (but something, at least) to make people believe that one believes.*[34] As we have seen, 'development' is enclosed within a long history that has produced various myths either solemnly sanctified or surreptitiously imposed; it thus accompanies the society which brought it into being, and helps to provide a meaning for its practices. Everyone removes from it some little characteristic of truth, and adds a little bit of falsehood – 'mainly that marvellous falsehood which is the most pleasant'. Everyone knows it cannot be true, but all that is necessary is that it should seem plausible; that is enough 'for these fables to keep the quality of histories'.[35]

This has a strange consequence. 'Development' (as a programme for collective happiness) no longer exists except as virtual reality, as a synthetic image in the full-length film of globalization. *It is like a dead star whose light can still be seen, even though it went out for ever long ago.* Because 'development' has effectively disappeared from reality (including the reality of what are called 'developed' countries), it plays the role of a compensatory fiction, a simulacrum standing in for reality. It has

---

33. Rex Butler, 'Acheter le temps', *Traverses*, 33–34, January 1985, p. 144 [translated here from the French]. This formulation shows the precise difference between messianic impatience and the spreading of the promise over time. This also explains why the payment of international debts can be postponed indefinitely; the fiction of a due date (ever rolled forward) is enough to keep the pressure up on debtors.

34. There can be no other explanation for the countless plans to boost consumption levels, to encourage investment, to offer incentives for car purchase, to encourage suburban renewal, and so on, all of which are announced with great solemnity even if everyone knows that the effect would at best be only marginal. Today the struggle is waged against unemployment as it used to be against 'underdevelopment' – through decrees or declarations, as if the declamatory effect heralded a real effect.

35. Bernard Le Bovier de Fontenelle, 'De l'origine des fables', in *Oeuvres complètes*, ed. G.B. Depping, Geneva: Slatkine Reprints, 1968, II, pp. 389, 393.

abandoned the place of a myth organizing and legitimating various practices, to play the metaphorical role of a 'revenant' unhappy at being left unburied because no one could risk pronouncing a graveside elegy. This is why, for the time being, there is no other option than to go on believing in it as one does in other things, because one believes that others believe in it, but without knowing where the frontier between the real and the virtual lies. But is the reality principle actually still necessary? And is it not characteristic of illusion not to be tracked down as illusion?

BEYOND 'DEVELOPMENT'

It would seem that the world has never been as rich as it is today: output is rising in both North and South; trade is expanding thanks to liberalization measures; and production costs are coming down as a result of restructuring and 'downsizing'. These successes have a price attached, however, as we can see in the growth of unemployment, shantytowns, homelessness, population clearance, marginalization. The names change from place to place, but the reality looks pretty much the same, even if frustrations increase according to the closeness of unattainable wealth, and even if the pace of exclusion follows that of growth itself.

Economists might be expected to help show a way out of these contradictions.[36] But in fact, their theoretical inertia is a major reason why well-worn paths hold no surprises in store. The theoretical space is not completely empty, of course, as work in the fields of socio-economics,[37] institutional, contractual and ecological economics, is challenging whole swathes of the dominant paradigm, exposing the market's inadequacy for the making of coherent long-term choices, or insisting that economics should be included within a much broader system of society and nature. It is no mean achievement to define other criteria than GNP for the calculation of national wealth, to think up ways of marrying available resources and technological choices, to tackle the contradiction between microeconomics (which sets productivity

---

36. Economists are not the only ones, of course, but they do claim a commanding position not only in the 'development sciences' but in the social sciences as a whole.

37. One thinks, especially, of the work of Amitai Etzioni and his colleagues in the Society for the Advancement of Socio-Economics, founded at Harvard in 1989.

constraints) and macroeconomics (which advocates limitless growth), and
to identify other modes of regulation and production that take account
of collective choice, not just individual preference. In practice, however,
who takes any interest in applying these new ways of conceiving and
constructing economic reality? True, the World Bank sometimes makes
a show of concerning itself with institutional economics.[38] And recently
an internal UNDP document spoke highly of the concept of 'social
capital', as the set of relations assuring social regulation through respect
for the democratic and juridical norms passed on by numerous different
institutions and associations.[39] According to the author of the paper, this
new form of capital (corresponding to a form of shared civic culture that
makes it possible to anticipate how other members of society will behave)
is as important for 'development' as such traditional factors of production
as labour, finance capital and natural resources. Besides, an abundance of
the latter cannot make up for a deficit in social capital, which is usually
bound up with cultural and social deconstruction caused by modernizing
strategies. From now on, the aim must be to promote 'sustainable human
development' that favours the poor, nature, women, children and long-
term perspectives. 'The time has come', it concludes, 'to completely
rethink the theory and practice of development.' Such a view can only
be applauded, but no doubt it will remain at the level of incantation.

For what would a 'total revision' of economic theory mean? Of
course, new parameters such as social capital or the monetary valuation
of externalities are not without interest, and would help to modify
many economic calculations, just as the creation of the HDI (human
development indicator) led to a 'league table' of nations very different
from one based only upon GNP. But is that enough to bring about the
radical changes considered necessary? Obviously not. For the problems
are of a different order.

If there really were a commitment to 'completely rethinking economic theory', the first thing to recognize would be that it is currently
upside down. Its scientific pretensions derive from a dictated epistemological confusion between the descriptive and the normative, so that it
either tries to make reality conform to a simplified model,[40] or turns
the results of possible observation into the basis of general 'laws' which

38. See Robert Piciotto, *Putting Institutional Economics to Work: From Participation
to Governance*, Washington, DC: World Bank Discussion Papers (304), 1995.
39. Stefan de Vylder, *Sustainable Human Development and Macroeconomics: Strategic
Links and Implications*, a UNDP discussion paper, 1995, mimeo.
40. The construction of models is evidently a legitimate heuristic operation, but
there is a great temptation to act 'as if' the model described reality.

supposedly explain all social practices relating to the use of goods. It is as if, having seen one black swan or one white horse, one were to decree that all others *should* be the same. There is no doubt that, under the pressure of resource limitation, people sometimes make choices to achieve certain objectives rather than others. What is much less clear, however, is that this represents a paradigm for all possible situations. Economists, it is true, go beyond strict individualism by allowing for collective goods that could not be privately appropriated. But apart from the fact that their premisses are still those of methodological individualism, their way of thinking about these things is not adequate. For observation of how 'economic agents' behave, in the countries of both North and South, shows that interest rationality is not always uppermost. What, for example, of agents who behave according to several different rationalities, and who, instead of constantly calculating and seeking their own short-term advantage, pursue now a logic of honour or prestige, now one of subsistence or reproduction, now one of redistribution?[41] Or one might consider the whole field of gifts and counter-gifts – ritual presents made on the occasion of anniversaries, weddings or end-of-year festivities, but also bequests and all non-market activities,[42] whether in the setting of primary sociality (the family and personal relations) or in that of secondary sociality (the social system) where the injunction to be generous also holds sway.[43] Ahmet Insel, who has tried to evaluate the weight of gifts in contemporary French society, concludes that it 'is roughly three-quarters the size of GDP'.[44] If that is the case in the North, what can one say of societies of the South, where reciprocity systems operate much more extensively

---

41. See, in particular, the work of Christian Comeliau, e.g.: 'Rentabilité et sociéte', in Sophie Mappa, ed., *Ambitions et illusions de la coopération Nord–Sud*, Lomé IV, Forum de Delphes, Paris: L'Harmattan, 1990, pp. 146–55; and 'Pour un renouveau des études de développement', *Revue Tiers Monde*, XXXIV, (135), July–September 1993, pp. 687–701.

42. All these practices have been perfectly analysed by Jacques T. Godbout (in collaboration with Alain Caillé) in *L'Esprit du don*, Paris: La Découverte, 1992.

43. 'Companies would not function for a second if they did not mobilize their employees' support; the State, without an ethic of public service, is just an empty shell; and science progresses only when researchers more or less feel they are participating in a common enterprise.' Alain Caillé, 'Sortir de l'économie', in Serge Latouche, ed., *L'Économie dévoilée. Du budget familial aux contraintes planétaires*, Paris: Autrement (159), 1995, p. 185.

44. 'Inheritances, money gifts between households, ritual or spontaneous gifts within households, "helping hands", the giving of blood and body organs ... do not enter into this estimate.' Ahmet Insel, 'La part du don, essai d'évaluation', in MAUSS (Mouvement anti-utilitariste dans les sciences sociales), *Ce que donner veut dire. Don et intérêt*, Paris: La Découverte, 1993, pp. 221–34.

through clientelist networks, tontine schemes and matrimonial bride wealth, and where the 'accursed share' spent on ceremonies of every kind assumes quite major proportions? The scale of practices not dependent (or only partly dependent) on the market becomes considerably greater if it includes the whole 'informal sector' which – according to one of those who have studied it best – blows apart the categories traditionally used in economics.[45]

A general theory that recognizes such diverse rationality among economic agents is not *a priori* impossible, but it must be said that one does not exist at present. Instead, the dominant approach is inevitably reductionist – which means that a host of practices for which theory must find a place conflict with it. If economics is incapable of seeing what happens now, why should one think that it can foresee what will happen in the future? Why should one treat as science the whole fairy story of market, scarcity and rational calculation? The economist is like someone who goes out under a streetlamp to look for his missing key, on the grounds that he can see better there. It is true that 'one sees better' when exchange is organized by the market; the models one might put forward have the merit of consistency, and their explanatory value is not insignificant. The only problem is that the cases to which they apply are extremely rare, as soon as one goes beyond the highly general point that an abundant supply of a good leads to a fall in its price (and a shortage to a rise in its price).[46]

But these simplistic models of behaviour are not the only defect of mainstream economics. More fundamental still are all those 'mental blanks' in neoliberal theory – the things that are supposed not to exist because it does not have the means to conceptualize them. Since it is all about counting, why not count everything? If production is to be totalled up, why not include the destruction which is part and parcel of it, and which would challenge the mechanistic paradigm of economics and its blindness to the irreversibility of time? The creation of value does not take place *ex nihilo*,[47] for man is not a demiurge; so-

45. Jacques Charmes, 'De l'économie traditionelle à l'économie informelle', in *L'Économie dévoilée*, pp. 144–59.

46. Although the 'law' of supply and demand explains quite well the price variation of basic goods (at least for those traded on the London or Chicago exchanges), it is much less useful in accounting for the 'mood' or 'volatility' of securities exchanges whose reactions are often described as 'irrational'. And Marshall Salins pointed out long ago that only 'cultural reasons' explain why the price of ox tongue is lower than that of steak.

47. Except perhaps in the case of money, which – as we have seen – belongs more and more to the realm of the virtual.

called processing activities actually involve numerous costs that the
market price fails to reflect. Another simplification concealed by
monetary calculation is the inclusion of stocks in the category of flows.
Is it not the presence of a 'general equivalent' which allows energy
produced on the basis of renewable flows and limited stocks to be sold
at the same price?[48] Or again, is it enough to calculate a few externalities to gain the real measure of damage to the environment?

These points are not new: the effects of globalization did not have
to make themselves felt before the imperfections of economic theory
became apparent. But perhaps we can see the consequences better since
the fences erected by the State have gradually come down. In the end,
it is the 'scientific' character of economics itself which is in question –
for two reasons. First, if the distinguishing feature of science is that it
bases itself on minute analysis of a complex reality, then mainstream
economics (as we have tried to show) omits too much from its investi-
gation to satisfy this condition. Second, if the distinguishing feature of
science is that it formulates universally valid propositions,[49] then mainstream economics is not a science because its models have only limited
validity. (The various rationales pursued by economic agents, for
example, are far from combining everywhere in the same way.) These
reservations about the scientific character of economics are all the more
necessary in that they are so little recognized. They also form a starting
point from which to question the core belief of the system – that is,
the universal necessity of growth.

As we have seen, the history of 'development' is also – and perhaps
mainly – the history of a belief shared by most of the 'decision-makers'
of the epoch, even though it is Western in origin and can make no claim
to universality. This belief first made it possible to justify the incredible
'progress of opulence' in the countries of the North; then it underwrote
five decades of messianic enthusiasms during which everything was done
in both North and South (though without success) to spread a model
of material well-being from the so-called 'developed' countries to the
rest of the world; and finally, it persists in the form of a heavenly but
virtual Beyond of the 'as if', which legitimates the process of globalization and its dramatic effects experienced daily here below.

---

48.   To be more specific, the interconnection of electricity grids allows a uniform
price to be charged for energy of classical, hydraulic and nuclear origin. See also the
remarks above in the chapter on the environment and the Brundtland Report.

49.   This point of view was first advanced by Dudley Seers more than thirty years
ago. See pp. 106–8 above.

It is time to get out – to move from the realization of failure to an act of rejection, from illusion to reality (although nowadays everything encourages us to confuse the two), from reassuring dreams to serious questions, from high-minded utopias to scandalous truths. And the first such truth is that the 'development' celebrated in ultra-solemn declarations will never exist, because it presupposes infinite growth that is in reality impossible. This observation is also valid for the globalization process that seeks to solve the problem by denying it. What is the problem exactly? It is that in any competitive situation (even one open to all) the winners cannot fail to realize that their success is also creating losers, because the race is always based on the knockout principle. The task and the stakes are truly enormous, for the process unleashed is not viable in the long run if it stays on the same track. It will certainly be necessary to tackle the questions posed by the relationship between work and employment (that is, the forms of social integration), by the degrees of national or local self-reliance within the framework of globalization, by the relationship between the State and the market, by the ecological consequences of predatory use of natural 'resources', by the need to master social change conceived as a social and political (rather than a market) process, by the alarming growth of inequalities, and above all by the inadequacies of economic theory. These concerns are neither imaginary nor novel.[50] If existing work in this direction remains little known, it is because belief (even of an absurd kind) is a social phenomenon which forces itself on one and all, albeit in the euphemistic form of 'as if'. As reality cannot be looked in the face, the most comfortable course is to re-enchant it and to transfer it to the hyperreal world of fiction.

Yet the problems persist – indeed, everywhere the situation is worsening dramatically. Only the spell of fiction, gradually acquiring force from habit, makes it possible to avoid the truth – until the day when one is forced to admit that the emperor has no clothes. It is well known that paradigms die hard; for a long time they can shift and adapt to facts that contradict them, by producing more and more *ad hoc* hypotheses which, more often than not, serve to protect powerful interests. But when the many solutions offered to a problem falter and collapse, is it not legitimate to inquire whether it was wrongly posed in the first place? *Is it then not necessary to challenge the belief, even if it has*

---

50. Paradoxically, these questions ought to be at the heart of ... 'development studies'! But in fact, the latter is entirely concerned with 'development assistance', neglecting any critical function with regard to the hegemonic system.

the advantage of giving intellectual comfort to the faithful? It is true that the mind, perhaps more than nature, abhors a vacuum. But it is a vacuum that now has to be confronted.

If the task is so difficult, this is because we must bracket out not only the postmodern imaginary (the reality effect produced by the virtual), but above all the deep-seated collective imaginary, the source of value-enhancing and value-receiving practices, which still proclaims the necessity of 'development' despite the negative verdict of history. Does this mean that care for other people – which, in this case, joins concern for oneself and for future generations – should therefore disappear? Certainly not. The stakes are too high, and the situation is too grave. But tinkering around with old strategies will not be of any use. Only a new paradigm can alter, not the way things are, but our way of conceiving them. That is, it can make it possible for us to think what is today unthinkable. History shows us a series of turnarounds that have changed the face of the world. What value today have the certainties of Galileo's adversaries, of the Inquisitors hunting down witches, of the colonizers so full of their sacred trust of civilization? How will people tomorrow judge the 'age of development'? It is too early to say. But it is high time to pose the question – so that the imagination can be called into struggle against what appears self-evident.

CHAPTER 13

SOME THOUGHTS ON WHAT
IS TO BE DONE

Before outlining a few points for further reflection, it may be useful to recall briefly, and very succinctly, some of the main themes of the preceding chapters.

First, the 'development' problematic is inscribed in the very core of the Western imaginary. That growth or progress should be able to continue indefinitely – that is an idea which radically distinguishes Western culture from all others. This characteristic, as strange as it is modern, sets up between nations a division far greater than all those forged in the course of history to justify the ostensible superiority of the West (savages/civilized peoples; oral/written cultures; societies without a history/historical societies, etc.). For all manner of reasons having to do with military, economic and technological domination, one can find everywhere today this way of looking ahead to a future that constant growth of production will make self-evidently better. This hegemony of 'development', however, could establish itself only through a kind of semantic conjuring, through the construction and dissemination of a concept of 'underdevelopment'. By breaking with a tradition of dichotomy and creating a 'false opposite', the universalization of the Western mode of production was made to seem a possibility. The subsequent transformation of the term 'underdeveloped countries' into 'developing countries' simply reinforced the illusory promise of material prosperity for all.

The 'development' paradigm has now changed into a belief shared by every leader of the various nation-states (and therefore by all the international organizations), as well as by nearly all the economic technocrats and the immense majority of the population. In private, to be sure, everyone can sometimes catch themselves doubting – such is the lot of every believer – but it does not stop them praying with one voice when they take part in collective rites. For every belief gets used to temporary uncertainties, and even feeds off them; anyway, they do not challenge the social consensus. However much one may hesitate privately, it still seems that there is nothing else to be done, since everyone believes that everyone else believes. Shared belief thus gives rise to social constraint that is expressed in the form of obligatory practices reinforcing commitment to the belief. This defines the circle within which the definition of problems, and the ways of solving them, are inscribed. There is scarcely any difference between the believer who thinks an illness is due to a sin against God or one's ancestors – and so considers forgiveness the first step to a cure – and the economist who identifies unemployment with weak demand and looks to renewed growth (and consumption) as the solution. In both cases, there is a premiss which grounds the initial belief and determines the answer to the question posed. The believability structure necessarily confirms the belief as that which cannot be refuted; no one could prove that God does not exist.

It is in the nature of 'development' not only to make an overabundance of goods available to consumers, but also to produce inequality and exclusion. All the texts on 'development' are unanimous in concluding that the gap between North and South (but also between rich and poor in each) is continually widening. The blindness that strikes thinking on the subject makes it possible to act as if this gap were a 'given' whose only connection with the ensuing discourse were to provide it with legitimacy. In fact 'development' itself, far from bridging the ritually deplored gap, continues to widen it. If this mechanism of cumulative causation passes unnoticed, this is not only because it cannot be integrated into the belief, but also because the spectacular enrichment of the well-off fuels hopes of a possible redistribution among those left out in the cold. People cling to these hopes all the more tightly in that some advance signs seem to be visible: some food surpluses have reached areas of chronic undernourishment, or have enabled destitute authorities to pay their staff; a few tens of billions of dollars, distributed each year by the rich countries as 'development assistance', finance publicly useful infrastructure, plug budget deficits or encourage the purchase of military hardware; NGOs mobilize civil society in the well-off countries (without neglecting extra public funds) in order to send gifts to the most disadvantaged sections of the world population, to take financial responsibility for a clinic, to provide

backing for co-operative ventures, to support educational institutions
or credit provision; international conventions seek to stabilize income
from certain basic products or to open up a little the market of the
industrial countries; financial institutions grant loans on favourable conditions and – with the usual provisos – reschedule the debts of cash-
starved States. There seems every reason to believe, then, that solidarity
is possible and that common interests will win through in the end –
even if official 'development assistance' re-enters the economic circuit
of donor countries, even if it is more advantageous to sell off agricultural surpluses than to keep stockpiling them, even if price-stabilization
agreements are neither signed nor respected by the major buyers, and
even if a few billion are well worthwhile to keep the international
monetary and financial system from collapse. The essential thing is to
keep the belief going. Every religion requires sacrifices. The Ancient
Greeks, who were far from stupid, used to divide a sacrificial animal
into two parts: the bones and fat were left in honour of the god, while
the meat was consumed by humans.

Whatever is done, a kind of lassitude sets in. No doubt a few miracles
are still reported, as in every religion, mainly concentrated in South-
East Asia; far from spreading terror, the 'dragons', large and small, are a
source of enthusiasm.[1] No doubt the 'return of growth' is still announced from time to time, when interest rates fall over here or rise
over there, or when some figure regarded as more orthodox than his
predecessor comes to power. In essence, however, the scenario barely
changes: some 'develop', others are left out. And whereas the main
dividing line has so far run between North and South, it is now
establishing itself within each nation-state, and making ever less appropriate the conventional vocabulary (rich countries, poor countries,
North, South, industrial societies, Third World) with which the present
work has itself had to make do. Each now seems powerless as it watches
the others' (good or bad) fortune unfold, often irreversibly. To avoid
having to admit that 'development' can never become general, a pretence
is made of believing that it is simply far away; patience is then maintained by proposing various emergency measures. In countries that
consider themselves wealthy, these might involve the opening of soup
kitchens, the arrangement of a few metro stations for the homeless, the
provision of a basic minimum for unemployed people no longer entitled
to benefits, the encouragement of the well-off to hire more domestics,

---

1. Except among those who live there and have to bear the ecological costs of
'development'. See Jean-Claude Pomonti, 'L'Asie défigurée', *Le Monde*, 17 June 1995.

or the creation of more employment involving personal care. In the so-called countries of the South, charity work is a riskier business: the main priority is weaker sections of the population (women and children, to be precise), as is the custom in the event of a shipwreck; anything else requires precautions such as a well-armed and well-trained military escort (as in Somalia). The task is no longer the saving of souls – which might take some time – but the saving of lives – which is more in keeping with the value accorded to immediacy, urgency, 'real time'. This remark is evidently cynical. Isn't it better to do that, at least, rather than do nothing at all? It certainly is – even if, it might be added, one should not be duped by the selectiveness of 'theatres of operations', nor by the political ulterior motives that lie behind humanitarian inter-vention. The horror of Rwanda is unbearable, and a hands-off attitude unjustifiable. Nevertheless, the narrowing of a once-universalizable 'development' to humanitarian relief for groups suffering the stigma of exclusion is one of the gravest signs of the crisis of 'development'.

The question 'what is to be done?' cannot be avoided in this con-clusion. Of course, it would be possible to get round it by pleading that the problem is too complex, and that it is impossible to offer a valid solution *urbi et orbi*. The two arguments are not devoid of any founda-tion. But while there is probably no point in proving the first, we should simply say that to dwell so much on the Western specificity of the 'development' belief would have been rather futile if one were then to claim that one's own conclusions were universal. Respect for cultural diversity, then, prohibits generalizations. There are numerous ways of living a 'good life', and it is up to each society to invent its own. But this in no way justifies the injustices of the present day, when some continue to 'develop' while others have to make do with a 'happy poverty' – on the false grounds that this corresponds to their particular culture. Whether one likes it or not (and why shouldn't one?), a number of products linked to the Western way of life (the telephone, antibiotics, computers, electricity, the internal combustion engine, etc.) are used everywhere in the world. Their mere presence has transformed social relations. Such was the case with all technological innovations in every epoch of history, whether they were spontaneously accepted or forcibly introduced. Of course, technology is never culturally neutral, but access to the same technology does not inevitably lead to cultural homogeni-zation; one has only to compare the countries of the North to be convinced of this. The demonstration effect associated with 'develop-ment' is certainly real enough, but all possible interpretations and appropriations are left open. When the many 'failures of development' have not been programmed to make the donors rich, they too represent a triumph for cultural diversity – if not for the 'authenticity' evoked by nostalgic spirits.

Even if we refuse to speak for others, however, the question remains: what is to be done? There would seem to be three possible paths. They may not be in competition with each other (because different actors are involved), but they are not necessarily compatible, and may lead in different directions. Still, they all share an opposition to the way in which the present system functions.

The first path is the one taken by Christian Comeliau.[2] Having convincingly exposed the roots of 'development' in Western values, as well as the fact that generalization of the dominant model is 'at once obligatory and impossible',[3] he proposes a set of measures that we shall here outline merely in part. Growth, he argues, remains a legitimate aim because it is necessary for the improvement of living conditions in the so-called poor countries, although the actual structure must be consciously geared to the production of certain goods. Loans may be considered so long as they provide the capacity to pay them back, while integration of the countries of the South into the world system ought to depend on the benefits they can derive from it, instead of simply conforming to the principle of free trade. International agreements on basic products should allow prices to be stabilized in a way favourable to all parties, thanks to the existence of an effective common fund. Finally, the multinationals should agree to transfer their technology to the countries of the South when these countries ask them to do so, but this does not mean that the quest for more suitable technologies should be given up.

This is a seductive approach that rests upon a critique of the hegemony of the productivist market economy – an economy which appears as a panacea but whose only aim is its own indefinite expansion, thereby excluding those who are unable to participate in it. Comeliau has also thought seriously about the problem of values, and his conception of solidarity happily escapes the usual fuzziness by defining it as an objective situation which compels all members of a group to co-operate in solving the problem posed.[4] This ought to have specific consequences, especially with regard to international inequalities, peace, law and the environment. Seemingly 'responsible' and 'reasonable' proposals are then

2. Christian Comeliau, *Les relations Nord–Sud*, Paris: La Découverte, 1991.
3. Ibid., p. 49.
4. Ibid., p. 91.

put forward, to move in the right direction without demanding in advance a complete transformation of the system.

It is doubtless important to note that some immediate measures could be taken which would substantially raise popular living conditions. Disillusionment or discouragement threatens to make people forget. But realism demands that the question be asked: what is the real scope of a normative discourse? Or – to be more precise – which actors have the power to make it part of the realm of facts? How can it not be seen that, despite their constant declarations of good intentions, all the players are cheating? Reason is powerless as soon as the issue is political: those in power have no interest in change (whatever they say to the contrary), and those who want change do not have the means to impose it. Moreover, the time horizon of political figures, tied as it is to the next election or to fears of a *coup d'état*, is incompatible with the pursuit of long-term objectives. An attempt must be made, of course, to understand phenomena on a worldwide level, to grasp their interrelations, to identify the various elements that make up the system. But once that is done, is it also possible to propose worldwide solutions? Here we reach the limits of all international strategies: they invoke the general interest to convince actors who listen only to their particular interest. Of course, we are talking of strategies that are based on non-market economics. But that implies powers of arbitration covering the system as a whole, and things which are possible at a local or national level may not be possible at a world level. The stakes are of cardinal importance. That is why there is no need to hope before embarking on something, nor to succeed as a condition for perseverance.

The second answer to the question of what is to done draws upon the experience of social movements in the South which have stopped expecting everything to come from the good will of those in power, and no longer believe either in aid or in international co-operation. They therefore organize among themselves, inventing new forms of social linkage and new ways of securing their existence.[5] The diversity of their social and geographical location makes it difficult to summarize the positions of these movements, but all of them can be said to share the view that all the 'development' measures of the last few decades have resulted in material and cultural expropriation. The failure has

---

5. See Gilbert Rist, Majid Rahnema and Gustavo Esteva, *Le Nord perdu*, Lausanne: Editions d'En Bas, 1992 (which contains a bibliography of articles and books within this perspective). The reader may also refer to the remarks at the end of the chapter above on self-reliance.

been so complete that it would be futile to want to go on as before; that would lead only to an increase in poverty and inequality. Hence the main task is to restore the political, economic and social autonomy of the marginalized societies. No more hopes can be placed in international trade, and not much can be expected of the State either, except that it should refrain from stifling the initiatives of grass-roots groups. All that matters is that each society should regain the right to organize its existence as it sees fit, outside the system now in place, by limiting the role of economics, giving up the accumulation of material goods, encouraging creativity and ensuring that decisions are taken by those directly concerned. The idea, then, in spite of 'development', is to organize and invent new ways of life – between modernization, with its sufferings but also some advantages, and a tradition from which people may derive inspiration while knowing that it can never be revived.[6]

These are minority movements, of course, but they are not without importance. Let us take just three examples. The Swadhyaya movement in India brought together 300,000 members at a single meeting, and in villages where they are influential the style of life has radically changed. In Mexico, Gustavo Esteva reports that four hundred associations embracing half a million people are struggling 'to regenerate their local space'. And in West Africa, movements are spreading in numerous villages simply on the basis of sharing successful experiences.[7] Contrary to what might be thought, these do not revolve around activism or practical expedients verging on 'how to cope' – in fact, what they all have in common is a new way of looking at the self and the world or, in other words, an epistemological turn. As Emmanuel Ndione puts it, quoting an African proverb: 'You are poor because you look at what you do not have. See what you possess, see what you are, and you will discover you are astonishingly rich.'[8] The approach is not unlike that of the American Blacks who, having had enough of constant denigration, proudly declared: Black is beautiful. So today, large numbers of the excluded are claiming exclusion as the basis of their autonomy.

---

6. See Alfredo L. de Romaña, 'L'Économie autonome. Une alternative sociale en émergence', *Interculture* (Montreal), XXII (3 and 4), Summer–Autumn 1989.

7. See Majid Rahnema, 'Swadhyaya: The Unknown, the Peaceful, the Silent yet Singing Revolution of India', *IFDA Dossier*, 75–76, January–April 1990, pp. 19–34; Gustavo Esteva, 'Regenerating People's Space', *Alternatives*, XII, 1987, pp. 125–32; Emmanuel S. Ndione, *Réinventer le présent. Quelques jalons pour l'action*, Dakar: ENDA GRAF Sahel, 1994.

8. Ibid., p. 37.

In every case, because the interpretative grid changes, reality itself is transformed: not by magic, but through a break with the dominant system that is no longer seen as a model or paradigm to be adopted at any cost. The frustration caused by impossible imitation of a false and alienating ideal thereby comes to an end, and the energies it has formerly mobilized can be invested in a new approach: namely, the rediscovery of a law of one's own. The important thing is not what happens in people's heads but the practices that flow from it. Those who remain prisoners of 'development' – and measure everything by the yardstick of per capita income – will maintain that this does not do away with material poverty. But for those going through the experience, the opposite is true. Very quickly, self-confidence liberates people's initiative, restored social ties lead to the revival of solidarity, refusal to obey the old powers opens up new ways not only of opting out but also of acquiring new resources. This is why account must be taken of the numerous social movements which, in varying degrees and in the most varied places, share this new vision of the world.[9] Even if they are not recognized by the media, and even if their experiences do not figure in international declarations, this does not prevent them from existing and multiplying. Of course, these many ways of rejecting 'development' do not add up to a 'theory' that could be contrasted to others, or that one might think of exporting to other places. However many people are mobilized by them, these approaches remain 'local' (that is, adapted to their specific context), but the change they bring about is real. Should the conclusion be that the initiatives of those excluded by 'development' are to be preferred to an anyway impossible transformation of international structures?

A third answer to the question remains to be considered. If one refuses to situate oneself solely at the level of international relations and to speak in the place of others, if one also takes seriously the roots of 'development' in Western culture, then it is necessary to question the underlying concepts (especially in economics) and to propose others in their stead. This is a radical approach in the sense that it addresses the problem at the root, and offers a critique of the prevailing economic imaginary. The main difficulty then becomes how to shatter the religious structure which protects 'development'; how to thwart the self-

---

9. Similar social movements exist in Europe – most notably, those which have set up LETS or Local Exchange Trade Systems. Through the creation of 'fictitious currencies' (which it makes no sense to accumulate), they are trying to escape the market by reconstituting a collectively administered 'gift economy'.

immunizing mechanisms of the dominant thinking in economics. Is not the 'mythical charge' that positively overdetermines the concept of growth too powerful for there to be any hope of passing it by?

Yet even authors least inclined to question the Western premises of 'development' are forced to admit that 'the theorization of post-development is probably the essential task today'.[10] Thus, in parallel to the proliferation of dissident experiences in the South, there is clearly an area of theory in which research needs to be organized. But agreement is more difficult to reach when it comes to defining the framework for such research. For either it is considered (in common with most economists) that the seriousness of one's conclusions must be guaranteed by the concepts and models of 'normal science', in which case there is a risk of not discovering anything new; or else one starts by attaching greater importance to history and anthropology, for example, and exposes oneself to the accusation of scientific light-mindedness. Nevertheless, there are several reasons why the second alternative should be preferred. First, the 'anomalies' of 'normal science' are too numerous to pass as insignificant;[11] one cannot denounce 'the crisis of development studies' or deplore 'the failures of development' and, at the same time, continue to think within a paradigm that is at its last gasp. The real 'scientific light-mindedness' is not where it is said to lie but, rather, on the side of those who persist in using outworn concepts.[12] Their strong resistance (itself quite 'normal') changes nothing. As Feyerabend said, you can move science forward only by elaborating hypotheses which

10. André Guichaoua and Yves Goussault, *Sciences sociales et développement*, Paris: Armand Colin, 1993, p. 151. The authors are especially critical of the theses of Serge Latouche, Hassan Zaoual and François Partant (and would doubtless also be of Gustavo Esteva, Ashis Nandy and Majid Rahnema), on the grounds, among others, that they lack theoretical depth. A vigorous plea for 'post-development' may be found in Arturo Escobar, *Encountering Development: The Making and Unmaking of the Third World*, Princeton, NJ: Princeton University Press, 1995.

11. On the concepts of 'normal science' and 'anomaly', see Thomas S. Kuhn, *The Structure of Scientific Revolutions*.

12. A professor of macroeconomics and director of a banking and financial management institute (whose name will be omitted out of charity) recently declared: 'It is a problem teaching this subject [macroeconomics]: on the one hand, you have a workable but outdated theory, and on the other, you have a more satisfactory but partial theory which in many respects is still at the level of basic research. In undergraduate teaching, at least, we put forward the old theory and present fragments of the new ones. But it doesn't really matter, because few students will go on to use these tools on a regular basis.' The basic Keynesian model, he continued, is 'a very practical tool derived from the old theory and familiar to all economists. It can also be easily employed – which is an advantage in teaching.' Supplement to the *Journal de Genève*, 29 May 1995, p. 37.

correspond neither to theories nor to 'well-established facts'; and – more provocatively – 'we need a dream-world in order to discover the features of the real world we think we inhabit'.[13] Nothing forces us to be intimidated by the terrorism of those who make science out to be the truth. After all: 'only scientists believe that others believe in something as they believe in the sciences'.[14] In other words, 'science' is neither truer nor more absurd than some other belief; it is itself a social product which varies over time and cannot claim the privilege of infallibility.

There can be no question, in this conclusion, of working out the details of such a research programme; at the most we can sketch a few themes. These should be enough to show that what is needed is not just more action in favour of the least advantaged (which is not to say that that should cease), or new rules to govern the 'world order' (which does not mean that thought should not be given to them). The first priority is to gain some distance from the belief in 'development', to bring out the numerous ways in which it covers up its own contradictions. This 'belief-dissolving' task cannot be entrusted to the economists who live on the belief; it lies, rather, with history and comparative anthropology, which make it possible to relativize the various forms of rationality by illuminating their historical links with the exercise of power. The next task – and some economists have already got down to it – is to challenge certain 'evident ideas' that form part of the ordinary discourse of economics – for example, the concept of an 'economic circuit' (which belongs to the mechanistic paradigm of equilibrium and ignores phenomena of irreversible destruction bound up with production), or the concept of 'utility' that serves to legitimate many circular arguments (because it is always possible to show *a posteriori* that a given actor had an interest in doing what he did, even in showing himself to be altruistic). Thirdly, it is necessary to study exchange phenomena by constructing explanatory models other than the hegemonic one of the market, which rests upon a notion of price characterized by equivalent and instantaneous benefits, and therefore excludes the qualitatively and quantitatively important cases of reciprocal giving. Lastly, thought needs to be given to a general economics that is capable both of including 'non-economic' factors such as prestige or unproductive expenditure, and of distinguishing between various (historically and culturally determinate) modes of the definition, production and appropriation of

13. Paul Feyerabend, *Against Method*, London: Verso, 1978, p. 32.
14. Bruno Latour, 'Quand les anges deviennent de bien mauvais messagers', *Terrain*, 14, March 1990, p. 76.

wealth. This list is not exhaustive, nor does it constitute a programme. But it does allow us to identify a number of themes (not all of them new), on the basis of which a different conceptualization should be possible of the many aims that men and women pursue as they produce, destroy, exchange, consume and waste.

We have thus considered three answers to the question: what is to be done? The first seeks to manage without illusions a system that is known to be perverse: since one cannot sit with arms folded in the face of all the misery in the world, one should try to achieve certain general aims by inflecting as much as possible a number of tendencies that run counter to them – even though this means confronting the huge problem of moving from norm to application. The second consists in a wager on the positive aspects of exclusion: marginal groups should make a virtue out of necessity by profiting from the fact that they are not allowed to share in the booty of 'development'. It is a bold and risky path, because the conditions in which it is pursued cannot be controlled. But a number of reports concur that there are some places where it is not only possible but successful. Whereas 'development' offered hope, the rejection of 'development' produces new wealth. The third answer departs from the practices encountered in history and places the emphasis on theory – not through any taste for speculation, but to extricate thought from the circle of belief. If the presuppositions of 'development' are to be flushed out, there has to be an external critique unencumbered by either scientific appearances or common sense.

These three answers are not offered by the same actors, and their pertinence varies with the place and context. What they have in common is that they are all strategies of transgression. It is always sacrilegious to challenge a shared belief and to refuse to accept the compulsory behaviour it entails. This applies whether it is a question of combating the hegemony of the market in the name of a non-market path, or of turning away from the illusions of 'development' to imagine other forms of existence, or of struggling against the domination of outworn economic paradigms. In all three cases, the point is to prepare the ground for 'post-development' – which should not be confused with 'anti-development'. To want to do something different from what has been done so far does not mean doing the opposite. That would be too simple! History shows that 'development' is a recent invention. If the world could live without it for so long, surely it is right to think that life will continue when it has disappeared. Instead of the certainty of errors past and present, should we not prefer the uncertainty of the world that lies ahead?

PRESIDENT TRUMAN'S POINT FOUR MESSAGE

Fourth, we must embark on a bold new program for making the benefits of our scientific advances and industrial progress available for the improvement and growth of underdeveloped areas.

More than half the people of the world are living in conditions approaching misery. Their food is inadequate. They are victims of disease. Their economic life is primitive and stagnant. Their poverty is a handicap and a threat both to them and to more prosperous areas.

For the first time in history, humanity possesses the knowledge and skill to relieve the suffering of these people.

The United States is pre-eminent among nations in the development of industrial and scientific techniques. The material resources which we can afford to use for assistance of other peoples are limited. But our imponderable resources in technical knowledge are constantly growing and are inexhaustible.

I believe that we should make available to peace-loving peoples the benefits of our sum of technical knowledge in order to help them realize their aspirations for a better life.

And, in cooperation with other nations, we should foster capital investment in areas needing development.

Our aim should be to help the free peoples of the world, through their own efforts, to produce more food, more clothing, more material for housing, and more mechanical power to lighten their burdens.

We invite other countries to pool their technological resources in this undertaking. Their contributions will be warmly welcomed. This should be a cooperative enterprise in which all nations work together through the United Nations and its specialized agencies whenever practicable. It must be a worldwide effort for the achievement of peace, plenty, and freedom.

With the cooperation of business, private capital, agriculture, and labor in this country, this program can greatly increase the industrial activity in other nations and can raise substantially their standards of living.

Such new economic developments must be devised and controlled to the benefit of the peoples of the areas in which they are established. Guarantees to the investor must be balanced by guarantees in the interest of the people whose resources and whose labor go into these developments.

The old imperialism – exploitation for foreign profit – has no place in our plans. What we envisage is a program of development based on the concepts of democratic fair-dealing.

All countries, including our own, will greatly benefit from a constructive program for the better use of the world's human and natural resources. Experience shows that our commerce with other countries expands as they progress industrially and economically.

Greater production is the key to prosperity and peace. And the key to greater production is a wider and more vigorous application of modern scientific and technical knowledge.

Only by helping the least fortunate of its members to help themselves can the human family achieve the decent, satisfying life that is the right of all people.

Democracy alone can supply the vitalizing force to stir the peoples of the world into triumphant action, not only against their human oppressors, but also against their ancient enemies – hunger, misery, and despair.

On the basis of these four major courses of action we hope to help create the conditions that will lead eventually to personal freedom and happiness for all mankind.

Public Papers of the Presidents
20 January 1949

DECLARATION ON THE ESTABLISHMENT OF A NEW INTERNATIONAL ECONOMIC ORDER

We, the Members of the United Nations,

Having convened a special session of the General Assembly to study for the first time the problems of raw materials and development, devoted to the consideration of the most important economic problems facing the world community,

Bearing in mind the spirit, purposes and principles of the Charter of the United Nations to promote the economic advancement and social progress of all peoples,

Solemnly proclaim our united determination to work urgently for THE ESTABLISHMENT OF A NEW INTERNATIONAL ECONOMIC ORDER based on equity, sovereign equality, interdependence, common interest and co-operation among all States, irrespective of their economic and social systems which shall correct inequalities and redress existing injustices, make it possible to eliminate the widening gap between the developed and the developing countries and ensure steadily accelerating economic and social development and peace and justice for present and future generations, and, to that end, declare:

1. The greatest and most significant achievement during the last decades has been the independence from colonial and alien domination of a large number of peoples and nations which has enabled them to become members of the community of free peoples. Technological progress has also been made in all spheres of economic activities in the last three decades, thus providing a solid potential for improving the well-being of all peoples. However, the remaining vestiges of alien and colonial domination, foreign occupation, racial discrimination, *apartheid*

and neo-colonialism in all its forms continue to be among the greatest obstacles to the full emancipation and progress of the developing countries and all the peoples involved. The benefits of technological progress are not shared equitably by all members of the international community. The developing countries, which constitute 70 per cent of the world's population, account for only 30 per cent of the world's income. It has proved impossible to achieve an even and balanced development of the international community under the existing international economic order. The gap between the developed and the developing countries continues to widen in a system which was established at a time when most of the developing countries did not even exist as independent States and which perpetuates inequality.

2. The present international economic order is in direct conflict with current developments in international political and economic relations. Since 1970, the world economy has experienced a series of grave crises which have had severe repercussions, especially on the developing countries because of their generally greater vulnerability to external economic impulses. The developing world has become a powerful factor that makes its influence felt in all fields of international activity. These irreversible changes in the relationship of forces in the world necessitate the active, full and equal participation of the developing countries in the formulation and application of all decisions that concern the international community.

3. All these changes have thrust into prominence the reality of interdependence of all the members of the world community. Current events have brought into sharp focus the realization that the interests of the developed countries and those of the developing countries can no longer be isolated from each other, that there is a close interrelationship between the prosperity of the developed countries and the growth and development of the developing countries, and that the prosperity of the international community as a whole depends upon the prosperity of its constituent parts. International cooperation for development is the shared goal and common duty of all countries. Thus the political, economic and social well-being of present and future generations depends more than ever on co-operation between all the members of the international community on the basis of sovereign equality and the removal of the disequilibrium that exists between them.

4. The new international economic order should be founded on full respect for the following principles:

(a) Sovereign equality of States, self-determination of all peoples, inadmissibility of the acquisition of territories by force, territorial integrity and noninterference in the internal affairs of other States;

(b) The broadest co-operation of all the States members of the international community, based on equity, whereby the prevailing disparities in the world may be banished and prosperity secured for all;

(c) Full and effective participation on the basis of equality of all countries in the solving of world economic problems in the common interest of all countries, bearing in mind the necessity to ensure the accelerated development of all the developing countries, while devoting particular attention to the adoption of special measures in favour of the least developed, land-locked and island developing countries as well as those developing countries most seriously affected by economic crises and natural calamities, without losing sight of the interests of other developing countries;

(d) The right of every country to adopt the economic and social system that it deems the most appropriate for its own development and not to be subjected to discrimination of any kind as a result;

(e) Full permanent sovereignty of every State over its natural resources and all economic activities. In order to safeguard these resources, each State is entitled to exercise effective control over them and their exploitation with means suitable to its own situation, including the right to nationalisation or transfer of ownership to its nationals, this right being an expression of the full permanent sovereignty of the State. No State may be subjected to economic, political or any other type of coercion to prevent the free and full exercise of this inalienable right;

(f) The right of all States, territories and peoples under foreign occupation, alien and colonial domination or *apartheid* to restitution and full compensation for the exploitation and depletion of, and damages to, the natural resources and all other resources of those States, territories and peoples;

(g) Regulation and supervision of the activities of transnational corporations by taking measures in the interest of the national economies of the countries where such transnational corporations operate on the basis of the full sovereignty of those countries;

(h) The right of the developing countries and the peoples of territories under colonial and racial domination and foreign occupation to achieve their liberation and to regain effective control over their natural resources and economic activities;

(i) The extending of assistance to developing countries, peoples and territories which are under colonial and alien domination, foreign occupation, racial discrimination or *apartheid* or are subjected to economic, political or any other type of coercive measures to obtain from them the subordination of the exercise of their sovereign rights and to secure from them advantages of any kind, and to neocolonialism in all its forms, and which have established or are endeavouring to establish effective control over their natural resources and economic activities that have been or are still under foreign control;

(j) Just and equitable relationship between the prices of raw materials, primary commodities, manufactured and semi-manufactured goods exported by developing countries and the prices of raw materials, primary commodities, manufactures, capital goods and equipment imported by them with the aim of bringing about sustained improvement in their unsatisfactory terms of trade and the expansion of the world economy;

(k) Extension of active assistance to developing countries by the whole international community, free of any political or military conditions;

(1) Ensuring that one of the main aims of the reformed international monetary system shall be the promotion of the development of the developing countries and the adequate flow of real resources to them;

(m) Improving the competitiveness of natural materials facing competition from synthetic substitutes;

(n) Preferential and non-reciprocal treatment for developing countries, wherever feasible, in all fields of international economic cooperation whenever possible;

(o) Securing favourable conditions for the transfer of financial resources to developing countries;

(p) Giving to the developing countries access to the achievements of modern science and technology, and promoting the transfer of technology and the creation of indigenous technology for the benefit of the developing countries in forms and in accordance with procedures which are suited to their economies;

(q) The need for all States to put an end to the waste of natural resources, including food products;

(r) The need for developing countries to concentrate all their resources for the cause of development;

(s) The strengthening, through individual and collective actions, of mutual economic, trade, financial and technical co-operation among the developing countries, mainly on a preferential basis;

(t) Facilitating the role which producers' associations may play within the framework of international co-operation and, in pursuance of their aims, *inter alia* assisting in the promotion of sustained growth of the world economy and accelerating the development of developing countries.

5. The unanimous adoption of the International Development Strategy for the Second United Nations Development Decade[1] was an important step in the promotion of international economic co-operation on a just and equitable basis. The accelerated implementation of obligations and commitments assumed by the international community within the framework of the Strategy, particularly those concerning imperative development needs of developing countries, would contribute significantly to the fulfilment of the aims and objectives of the present Declaration.

6. The United Nations as a universal organization should be capable of dealing with problems of international economic co-operation in a comprehensive manner and ensuring equally the interests of all countries. It must have an even greater role in the establishment of a new international economic order. The Charter of Economic Rights and Duties of States, for the preparation of which the present Declaration will provide an additional source of inspiration, will constitute a significant contribution in this respect. All the States Members of the United Nations are therefore called upon to exert maximum efforts with a view to securing the implementation of the present Declaration, which is one of the principal guarantees for the creation of better conditions for all peoples to reach a life worthy of human dignity.

7. The present Declaration on the Establishment of a New International Economic Order shall be one of the most important bases of economic relations between all peoples and all nations.

2229th plenary meeting
1 May 1974

---

1. Resolution 2626 (XXV).

BIBLIOGRAPHY

Achard, Pierre, Chauvenet, Antoinette, Lage, Elisabeth, Lentin, Françoise, Nève, Patricia and Vignaux, Georges: *Discours biologique et ordre social*, Paris: Le Seuil, 1977.

Addo, Herb, ed.: *Transforming the World Economy? Nine Critical Essays on the New International Economic Order*, London: Hodder & Stoughton, 1984.

Amin, Samir: *Accumulation on a World Scale: A Critique of the Theory of Underdevelopment* [1970], Hassocks: Harvester Press, 1974.

Amin, Samir: *Unequal Development: An Essay on the Social Formations of Peripheral Capitalism* [1973], Hassocks: Harvester Press, 1976.

Amin, Samir: *Imperialism and Unequal Development* [1976], Hassocks: Harvester Press, 1977.

Assidon, Elsa: *Les théories économiques du développement*, Paris: La Découverte, 1992.

Aubry, Pierre: *La Colonisation et les colonies*, Paris: Octave Doin & Fils, 1909.

Aziz, Sartaj: *Rural Development: Learning from China*, London: Macmillan Press, 1978.

Badie, Bertrand: *La Fin des territoires. Essai sur le désordre international et sur l'utilité sociale du respect*, Paris: Fayard, 1995.

Badinter, Elisabeth and Robert: *Condorcet (1743–1794): Un intellectuel en politique*, Paris: Fayard, 1988.

Baeck, Louis: *Post-War Development Theories and Practice*, Paris: UNESCO and the International Social Science Council, 1993.

Baran, Paul A. and Sweezy, Paul M: *Monopoly Capital: An Essay on the American Economic and Social Order* [1966], Harmondsworth: Pelican, 1968.

Baudrillard, Jean: 'La genèse idéologique des besoins', in *Pour une critique de l'économie politique du signe*, Paris: Gallimard, 1972.

Baudrillard, Jean: *The Perfect Crime* [1995], London: Verso, 1996.

Beaud, Michel: 'Face à la croissance mortifère, quel développement durable?', *Revue Tiers Monde*, XXXV (137), January–March 1994, pp. 131–50.

Becker, Gary: *The Economic Approach to Human Behavior*, Chicago: University of Chicago Press, 1976.

Bernis, Gérard Destanne de: 'Développement durable et accumulation', *Revue Tiers Monde*, XXXV (137), January–March 1994, pp. 95–130.

Bourguignat, Henri: *La Tyrannie des marchés. Essai sur l'économie virtuelle*, Paris: Economica, 1995.

Bruckner, Pascal: *The Tears of the White Man: Compassion as Contempt* [1983], New York: The Free Press.

Buell, Raymond Leslie: 'Backward Peoples under the Mandate System', *Current History*, XX, June 1924, pp. 386–95.

Buffon, Georges Louis Leclerc, comte de: *Histoire universelle*, vol. X [1749], extracts in *De l'homme*, Paris: Maspero, 1971.

Butler, Rex: 'Acheter le temps', *Traverses*, 33–34, January 1985, pp. 142–151.

Canetti, Elias: *Crowds and Power* [1960], Harmondsworth: Penguin Books, 1973.

Cardoso, Fernando Henrique: *As idéias e seu lugar, ensaios sobre as teorias do desenvolvimento*, Petrópolis: Vozes, 1980 [quoted and translated here from the French edition, *Les idées à leur place*, Paris: PUF, 1984].

Cardoso, Fernando Henrique and Faletto, Enzo: *Dependency and Development in Latin America* [1969], Berkeley: University of California Press, 1973.

The Challenge to the South: The Report of the South Commission, Oxford: Oxford University Press, 1990.

Chaumont, Charles: *L'ONU*, Paris: PUF, 1962.

Chauveau, Jean-Pierre: 'Participation paysanne et populisme bureaucratique. Essai d'histoire et de sociologie de la culture du développement', in Jean-Pierre Jacob and Philippe Lavigne-Delville, eds, *Les Associations paysannes en Afrique. Organisation et dynamiques*, Marseilles: APAD/Karthala/IUED: Geneva/Paris, 1994.

Chazelas, Victor: *Territoires africains sous mandat de la France: Cameroun et Togo*, Paris: Société d'éditions géographiques, maritimes et coloniales, 1931.

Chesnais, François: *La Mondialisation du capital*, Paris: Syros, 1994.

Chesnaux, Jean: 'Science, machines et progrès chez Jules Verne', *La Pensée, Revue du rationalisme moderne*, 133, June 1967, pp. 62–85.

Colard, Daniel: *Vers l'établissement d'un nouvel ordre économique international*, Paris: La Documentation française, 1977.

Comeliau, Christian: 'Rentabilité et société', in Sophie Mappa, ed., *Ambitions et illusions de la coopération Nord–Sud*, Lomé IV, Forum de Delphes, Paris: L'Harmattan, 1990, pp. 146–55.

Comeliau, Christian: *Les Relations Nord–Sud*, Paris: La Découverte, 1991.

Comeliau, Christian: 'Pour un renouveau des études de développement', *Revue Tiers Monde*, XXXIV (135), July–September 1993, pp. 687–701.

Comeliau, Christian: 'Développement du "développement durable" ou blocages conceptuels?', *Revue Tiers Monde*, XXV (137), January–March 1994, pp. 61–76.

Comte, Auguste: *System of Positive Polity* [1854], vol. 1, London: Longmans, Green & Co., 1875.

Condorcet, Antoine-Nicolas de: *Sketch for a Historical Picture of the Progress of the Human Mind* [Year 3 of the Republic], London: Weidenfeld & Nicolson, 1955, p. 173.

Corm, Georges: *Le nouveau désordre économique mondial. Aux racines des échecs du développement*, Paris: La Découverte, 1993.

Cornia, Giovanni Andrea, Jolly, Richard and Stewart, Frances: *Adjustment with a Human Face*, vol. 1, *Protecting the Vulnerable and Promoting Growth*, Oxford: Clarendon, 1987.

Cox, Robert W.: 'Ideologies and the New International Economic Order', *International Organization*, 33 (2), Spring 1979, pp. 257–302.

Duchet, Michèle: *Anthropologie et histoire au siècle des Lumières* [1972], Paris: Flammarion, 1977.

Ducrot, Oswald: *Dire et ne pas dire. Principes de sémantique linguistique*, Paris: Herrmann, 1991.

Duignan, Peter and Gann, L.H., eds, *Colonialism in Africa 1870–1960*, London: Cambridge University Press, 1975.

Durkheim, Émile: *The Rules of Sociological Method* [1895], New York: The Free Press, 1964.

Durkheim, Émile: *The Elementary Forms of Religious Life* [1912], New York: The Free Press, 1995.

Emmanuel, Arghiri: *Unequal Exchange: A Study of the Imperialism of Trade* [1969], London: New Left Books, 1972.

Escobar, Arturo: *Encountering Development: The Making and Unmaking of the Third World*, Princeton, NJ: Princeton University Press, 1995.

Esteva, Gustavo: 'Regenerating People's Space', *Alternatives*, XII, 1987, pp. 125–52.

État de désarroi. Les répercussions sociales de la mondialisation, Geneva: UNRISD, 1993.

Etat des savoirs sur le développement: Trois décennies de sciences sociales en langue française (under the direction of Catherine Choquet, Olivier Dollfus, Etienne Le Roy and Michel Vernières), Paris: Karthala, 1993.

Etemad, Bouda: *Le débat colonial. Tendances récentes de l'histoire de la colonisation*, University of Geneva, Faculty of Social and Economic Sciences, 1987.

Evans-Pritchard, Edward: *Witchcraft, Oracles, and Magic among the Azande* [1937], Oxford: Clarendon Press, 1976.

Fals-Borda, Orlando: *Ciencia propia y colonialismo intelectual*, Bogotá: Editorial Oveja Negra, 1971.

Feyerabend, Paul: *Against Method*, London: Verso, 1978.

Fontenelle, Bernard Le Bovier de: *Poésies pastorales avec un Traité sur la nature de l'églogue et une Digression sur les Anciens Poètes & Modernes*, The Hague: Louis van Dole and Estienne Foulque, 1688.

Fontenelle, Bernard Le Bovier de: 'De l'origine des fables', in *Oeuvres complètes*, ed. G.B. Depping, Geneva: Slatkine Reprints, 1968, vol. 2.

Fornel, Michel de: 'Les paradoxes du vrai-faux', *Traverses (Le fantôme de la vérité)*, 8, Winter 1993, pp. 28–39.

Frank, André Gunder: 'Sociology of Development and Underdevelopment of Sociology', in *Latin America: Underdevelopment or Revolution*, New York: Monthly Review Press, 1969.

Frank, André Gunder: 'North South and East West: Keynesian Paradoxes in the Brandt Report', *Third World Quarterly*, II (4), October 1980, pp. 669–80.

Fröbel, Volker, Heinrichs, Jürgen and Kreye, Otto: *Die neue internationale Arbeit-steilung. Strukturelle Arbeitslosigkeit in den Industrieländern und die Industrialisierung der Entwicklungsländer*, Reinbek: Rowohlt, 1977.

Galtung, Johan: *Poor Countries vs. Rich: Poor People vs. Rich: Whom Will NIEO Benefit?*, University of Oslo, 1977.

Galtung, Johan and Nishimura, Fumiko: *Von China lernen?*, Opladen: Westdeutscher Verlag, 1978.

Galtung, Johan, O'Brien, Peter and Preiswerk, Roy, eds: *Self-Reliance, A Strategy for Development*, Geneva: IUED/London: Bogle-L'Ouverture Publications, 1980.

George, Susan: *How the Other Half Dies: The Real Reasons for World Hunger*, London: Penguin, 1981.

George, Susan and Sabelli, Fabrizio: *Faith and Credit: The World Bank's Secular Empire*, Harmondsworth: Penguin, 1994.

Georgescu-Roegen, Nicholas: *The Entropy Law and the Economic Process*, Cambridge, MA: Harvard University Press, 1971.

Gerbet, Pierre: *Les Organisations internationales*, Paris: PUF, 1960.

Ghai, D.P., Khan, A.R., Lee E.L.H. and Alfthan, T., eds: *The Basic-Needs Approach to Development: Some Issues Regarding Concepts and Methodology*, Geneva: International Labour Office, 1977.

Ghebali, Victor-Yves: *L'Organisation internationale du travail*, Geneva: IUHEI, 1987.

Girardet, Raoul: *L'idée coloniale en France, 1871–1962*, Paris: La Table ronde, 1972.

Godbout, Jacques T. (in collaboration with Alain Caillé): *L'Esprit du don*, Paris: La Découverte, 1992.

Grinevald, Jacques: 'Science et développement. Esquisse d'une approche socio-épistémologique', in *La pluralité des mondes*, Geneva: Théories et pratiques du développement, Cahiers de l'IED, 1975, pp. 31–98.

Guenin, G: *L'épopée coloniale de la France racontée par nos contemporains*, Paris: Larose, 1932.

Guichaoua, André and Goussault, Yves: *Sciences sociales et développement*, Paris: Armand Colin, 1993.

Haas, Peter M., Levy, Marc A. and Parson, Edward A: 'Appraising the Earth Summit: How Should We Judge UNCED's Success?', *Environment*, 34 (8), October 1992.

Halle, Louis J.: 'On Teaching International Relations', *The Virginia Quarterly Review*, 40 (1), Winter 1964, pp. 11–25.

Harborth, Hans-Jürgen: *Dauerhafte Entwicklung (Sustainable Development), Zur Enstehung eines neuen ökologischen Konzepts*, Berlin: Wissenschaftszentrum Berlin für Sozialforschung (FS II 89–403), 1989.

Hardy, Georges: *Nos grands problèmes coloniaux*, Paris: A. Colin, 1929.

Hettne, Björn: *Development Theory and the Third World*, Helsingborg: Swedish Agency for Research Cooperation with Developing Countries [SAREC], 1982.

Hettne, Björn and Tamm, Gordon: 'The Development Strategy of Gandhian Economics', *Journal of the Indian Anthropological Society*, 6 (1), April 1976, pp. 51–66.

Hirschmann, Albert: 'The Rise and Decline of Development Economics', in

Essays in Trespassing: Economics to Politics and Beyond, Cambridge: Cambridge University Press, 1981, pp. 1–25.

Holly, Daniel: 'Les Nations unies et le nouvel ordre économique mondial', *Études internationales* (Quebec), VII (3), September 1977, pp. 500–15.

Hopkins, Michael: *A Basic-Needs Approach to Development Planning*, World Employment Programme, Working Paper 3, Geneva: ILO, 1977.

Human Development Report, 1990 et seq., Oxford University Press, 1991 *et seq.*

Ibn Khaldun, *The Muqaddimah: An Introduction to History*, 2 vols, trans. Franz Rosenthal, London: Routledge & Kegan Paul, 1958.

Insel, Ahmed: 'La part du don, esquisse d'évaluation', in Mouvement anti-utilitariste dans les sciences sociales, *Ce que donner veut dire. Don et intérêt*, Paris: La Découverte, 1993.

Jalée, Pierre: *The Pillage of the Third World* [1967], New York: Monthly Review Press, 1967.

Kantowsky, Detlef: 'Gandhi – Coming Back from West to East?', *IFDA Dossier*, 39, January–February 1984, pp. 3–14.

Kuhn, Thomas S.: *The Structure of Scientific Revolutions*, Chicago: University of Chicago Press, 1962/1970.

Lacoste, Yves: *Contre les anti tiers-mondistes et certains tiers-mondistes*, Paris: La Découverte, 1985.

Latouche, Serge : *Critique de l'impérialisme*, Paris: Anthropos, 1979.

Latouche, Serge: *Faut-il refuser le développement?*, Paris: PUF, 1986.

Latouche, Serge: *La Planète des naufragiés. Essai sur l'après-développement et peuples autochtones*, Paris: La Découverte, 1991.

Latouche, Serge: 'La fiction et la feinte: développement et peuples autochtones', *Ethnies* (review of *Survival International*), 13, Spring 1991.

Latouche, Serge, ed.: *L'Économie dévoilée. Du budget familial aux contraintes planétaires*, Paris: Autrement, 159, 1995.

Latour, Bruno: 'Quand les anges deviennent de bien mauvais messagers', *Terrain*, 14, March 1990, pp. 76–91.

Latour, Bruno: *We Have Never Been Modern* [1991], New York: Harvester Wheatsheaf, 1993.

League of Nations: *The Mandates Systems: Origin, Principles, Application*, Geneva, 1945.

Lederer, Katrin (in collaboration with Johan Galtung and David Antal): *Human Needs: A Contribution to the Current Debate*, published by the Berlin Science Center, Cambridge, MA and Königstein: Oelgeschlager, Gunn & Hain, Anton Hain, 1980.

Leibniz, Gottfried Wilhelm: *La naissance du calcul différentiel*, introduction and notes by M. Parmentier, Paris: Vrin, 1959.

Lemercier de la Rivière, Pierre-François: *L'Ordre naturel et essentiel des sociétés politiques*, London: Jean Nourse/Paris: Desaint, 1767.

Lepage, Henri: *Demain le libéralisme*, Paris: Le Livre de Poche, 1980.

Leroy-Beaulieu, Paul: *De la colonisation chez les peuples modernes* [1874], Paris: Félix Alcan, 6th edn, 1908, 2 vols.

Lévi-Strauss, Claude: *Le racisme devant la science*, Paris: UNESCO, 1952.

The Limits to Growth: Report to the Club of Rome, London: Pan Books, 1972.

Lipietz, Alain: *Mirages et miracles. Problèmes de l'industrialisation dans le tiers monde*, Paris: La Découverte, 1985.

Lizot, Jacques: 'Économie primitive et subsistance', in *Libre*, Paris: Petite Bibliothèque Payot, 1976, pp. 69–114.

Lugard, Frederick: *The Dual Mandate in British Tropical Africa*, Edinburgh/London: W. Blackwood & Sons, 1922.

McNamara, Robert S.: *The McNamara Years at the World Bank: Major Policy Addresses of Robert S. McNamara 1968–1981*, Baltimore, MD: Johns Hopkins University Press, 1981.

McNamara, Robert S.: *In Retrospect: The Tragedy and the Lessons of Vietnam*, New York: Times Books of Random House, 1995.

Malinowski, Bronislaw: *A Scientific Theory of Culture*, Chapel Hill: University of North Carolina Press, 1944.

Marglin, F.A. and Marglin, S.A, eds: *Dominating Knowledge: Development, Culture and Resistance*, Oxford: Clarendon Press, 1990.

Marseille, Jacques: *Empire colonial et capitalisme français. Histoire d'un divorce*, Paris: Le Seuil, 1984.

Marx, Karl: *A Contribution to the Critique of Political Economy*, London: Lawrence & Wishart, 1971.

Marx, Karl: 'Manifesto of the Communist Party' [1848], in *The Revolutions of 1848*, London: New Left Review/Penguin, 1973.

Marx, Karl: 'Economic and Philosophical Manuscripts' (1844), in *Early Writings*, Harmondsworth: Pelican/New Left Review, 1975.

Marx, Karl: *Capital Volume 1*, Harmondsworth: Pelican/New Left Review, 1976.

Marx, Karl and Engels, Friedrich: *On Colonialism*, Moscow: Foreign Languages Publishing House, n.d.

Masini, Jean: 'Introduction', *Revue Tiers Monde*, XXXV (137), January–March 1994, pp. 9–29.

MAUSS [Mouvement anti-utilitariste dans les sciences sociales], *Ce que donner veut dire. Don et intérêt*, Paris: La Découverte, 1993.

Meienberger, Norbert: *Entwicklungshilfe unter dem Völkerbund. Ein Beitrag zur Geschichte der internationalen Zusammenarbeit in der Zwischenkriegzeit unter besonderer Berücksichtigung der technischen Hilfe in China*, Winterthur: P.G. Keller, 1965.

Meier, Gerald M.: 'From Colonial Economics to Development Economics', in Gerald M. Meier, ed., *From Classical Economics to Development Economics*, New York: Saint Martin's Press, 1994.

Morgan, Lewis H.: *Archaic Society*, London: Macmillan & Co., 1877.

Morin, Edgar: *Pour sortir du vingtième siècle*, Paris: Fernand Nathan, 1981.

Moss, Alfred George and Winton, Harry N.M., eds: *A New International Economic Order: Selected Documents, 1945–1975*, New York: UNITAR Document Service, 3 vols (n.d.).

Myrdal, Gunnar: *Asian Drama: An Inquiry into the Poverty of Nations*, 3 vols, Harmondsworth: Penguin Books, 1968.

Nandy, Ashis: 'Shamans, Savages and the Wilderness: On the Audibility of Dissent and the Future of Civilisations', *Alternatives*, XIV, 1989, pp. 263–77.

Nassar, Nassif: *La pensée réaliste d'Ibn Khaldun*, Paris: PUF, 1967.

Ndione, Emmanuel: *Le don et le recours. Ressorts de l'économie urbaine*, Dakar:

ENDA, 1992.

Ndione, Emmanuel: *Réinventer le présent. Quelques jalons pour l'action*, Dakar: ENDA GRAF Sahel, 1994.

Nisbet, Robert A.: *Social Change and History: Aspects of the Western Theory of Development*, New York: Oxford University Press, 1969.

Nnoli, Okwudiba: *Self-Reliance and Foreign Policy in Tanzania: The Dynamics of the Diplomacy of a New State, 1961 to 1971*, New York/London/Lagos: NOK Publishers, 1978.

North–South: A Programme for Survival – Report of the Independent Commission on International Development Issues, London: Pan Books, 1980.

Nyerere, Julius: *Freedom and Socialism*, Dar Es Salaam: Oxford University Press, 1968.

Nyerere, Julius: *The Arusha Declaration: Ten Years After*, Dar Es Salaam: Government Printer, 1977.

Partant, François: *La fin du développement. Naissance d'une alternative?*, Paris: Maspero, 1982.

Pearson, Lester B.: *Partners in Development*, New York: Praeger, 1969.

Perrault, Charles: *Parallèles des Anciens et des Modernes* [1688], Geneva: Slatkine Reprints, 1971, vol. 1.

Perrot, Marie-Dominique: 'Passager clandestin et indispensable du discours: le présupposé', in Gilbert Rist and Fabrizio Sabelli, eds, *Il était une fois le développement*, Lausanne: Éditions d'En Bas, 1986, pp. 71–91.

Perrot, Marie-Dominique, ed.: *Dérives humanitaires. États d'urgence et droit d'ingérence*, Geneva: IUED/Paris: PUF, 1994.

Perrot, Marie-Dominique, Rist, Gilbert and Sabelli, Fabrizio: *La Mythologie programmée. L'économie des croyances dans la société moderne*, Paris: PUF, 1992.

Perroux, François: *L'Économie au XXᵉ siècle* [1961], Paris: PUF, 1964.

Perroux, François: *L'Économie des jeunes nations: Industrialisation et groupements de nations*, Paris: PUF, 1962.

Perroux, François: 'Dialectiques et socialisation', in Maximilien Rubel, ed., *Karl Marx: Oeuvres*, vol. 1, 1965.

Piault, Marc-Henri: 'La colonisation: pour une nouvelle appréciation', *Cahiers ORSTOM*, série sciences humaines, XXI (1), 1985, pp. 5–12.

Piciotto, Robert: *Putting Institutional Economics to Work: From Participation to Governance*, Washington, DC: World Bank Discussion Papers (304), 1995.

Pietilä, Hilkka: 'Environment and Sustainable Development', *IFDA Dossier*, 77, May–June 1990, pp. 61–70.

Poerksen, Uwe: *Plastic Words: The Tyranny of a Modular Language* [1989], University Park, PA: Pennsylvania University Press, 1995.

Polanyi, Karl: *The Great Transformation: The Political and Economic Origins of Our Time* [1944], Boston, MA: Beacon Press, 1957.

Polanyi, Karl: *Primitive, Archaic and Modern Economies*, ed. George Dalton, New York: Anchor Books, 1968.

Praxmarer, Peter: *Development: On the Sociogenesis, Political Usage and Theoretical Possibilities of a Concept*, Institut universitaire de hautes études internationales, University of Geneva, 1984, mimeo.

Preiswerk, Roy: 'Is the New International Economic Order Really New?', *The*

Caribbean Yearbook of International Relations, Trinidad and Tobago, 1977, pp. 147–59.

Public Papers of the Presidents of the United States, Harry S. Truman, Year 1949, 5, United States Government Printing Office, Washington, DC, 1964.

Rachline, François: *De zéro à epsilon. L'économie de la capture*, Paris: Hachette, 1994.

Radkowski, Georges-Hubert de: *Les jeux du désir. De la technique à l'économie*, Paris: PUF, 1980.

Rahnema, Majid: 'Swadhyaya, The Unknown, the Peaceful, the Silent Yet Singing Revolution of India', *IFDA Dossier*, 75–76, January–April 1990, pp. 19–34.

Reshaping the International Order: A Report to the Club of Rome, Jan Tinbergen, co-ordinator, Antony J. Dolman, editor, Jan van Ettinger, director, New York: E.P. Dutton & Co., 1976.

Resolution of the Central Committee of the CPC on the Guiding Principles for Building a Socialist Society with an Advanced Culture and Technology, 28 September 1986, Beijing: Foreign Languages Press, 1986.

Rist, Gilbert: *Towards a 'New' United Nations Development Strategy? Some Major United Nations Resolutions in Perspective*, Nyon: International Foundation for Development Alternatives (IFDA), 1977, mimeo.

Rist, Gilbert: 'The Not-so-New International Order', *Development* (SID), XX (3–4), 1978, pp. 48–52.

Rist, Gilbert, ed.: *La Culture, otage du développement?*, Paris: L'Harmattan, 1994.

Rist, Gilbert, Rahnema, Majid and Esteva, Gustavo: *Le Nord perdu. Repères pour l'après-développement*, Lausanne: Éditions d'En Bas, 1992.

Romaña, Alfredo L. de: 'L'Économie autonome. Une alternative sociale en émergence', *Interculture* (Montreal), XXII (3 and 4), Summer–Autumn 1989.

Rosset, Clément: *L'Anti-nature. Éléments pour une philosophie tragique* [1973], Paris: PUF, 1986.

Rostow, Walt W.: *The Stages of Economic Growth: A Non-Communist Manifesto*, Cambridge: Cambridge University Press, 1960.

Rousseau, Jean-Jacques: 'Preface to *Narcissus, or The Lover of Himself* [1782], in *The Collected Writings of Rousseau*, vol. 2, Hanover, NH: University Press of New England, 1992.

Rousseau, Jean-Jacques: 'Discourse on the Origin and Foundations of Inequality among Men' [1755], in *Collected Works*, vol. 3, ed. Roger D. Masters and Christopher Kelly, Hanover, NH: University Press of New England, 1992.

Rufin, Jean-Christophe: *L'Empire et les nouveaux barbares*, Paris: J.-C. Lattès, 1991.

Sabelli, Fabrizio: *Recherche anthropologique et développement*, Neuchâtel/Paris: Institut d'ethnologie, Maison des sciences de l'homme, 1993.

Sachs, Wolfgang: 'L'Archéologie du concept de "développement"', *Interculture* (Montreal), XXIII (4), Autumn 1990, Cahier 109.

Sachs, Wolfgang, ed.: *The Development Dictionary: A Guide to Knowledge as Power*, London: Zed Books, 1992.

Sachs, Wolfgang, ed.: *Global Ecology: A New Arena of Political Conflict*, London: Zed Books, 1993.

Sahlins, Marshall: *Stone Age Economics*, Chicago: Aldine–Atherton, 1972.

Sarraut, Albert: *La Mise en valeur des colonies françaises*, Paris: Payot, 1923.

Say, Jean-Baptiste: *Cours complet d'économie politique* [1828], Brussels: Société typographique belge, 1843.

Schmidheiny, Stephan: *Changing Course: A Global Business Perspective on Development and the Environment*, Cambridge, MA: MIT Press, 1992.

Seers, Dudley: 'The Limitations of the Special Case', *Bulletin of the Oxford Institute of Economics and Statistics*, 25 (2), May 1963, pp. 77–98; reprinted in Gerald Meier, *Leading Issues in Economic Development*, New York: Oxford University Press, 3rd edn, 1976, pp. 53–8.

Seers, Dudley: 'North-South: Muddling Morality and Mutuality', *Third World Quarterly*, II (4), October 1980, pp. 681–93.

Serres, Michel: 'Le savoir, la guerre et le sacrifice', *Critique*, vol. 33 (367), December 1977, pp. 1067–77.

Smith, Adam: *The Wealth of Nations* [1776], London: Methuen, 1961, 2 vols.

Stavenhagen, Rodolfo, ed.: *Agrarian Problems and Peasant Movements in Latin America*, Garden City, NY: Doubleday & Co., 1970.

Stavenhagen, Rodolfo: *Las clases sociales en las sociedades agrarias*, 7th edn, Mexico City: Siglo XXI, 1975.

Steppacher, Rolf: 'L'ingérence écologique et la globalisation de l'économie de marché', in *Écologie contre nature. Développement et politiques d'ingérence*, (3), Geneva: IUED/Paris: PUF, pp. 99–114.

Stokke, Olav: 'Sustainable Development: A Multi-Faceted Challenge', *The European Journal of Development Research*, 3 (1), June 1991, pp. 8–31.

Ten Basic Human Needs and Their Satisfaction, Sarvodaya Community Education Series, 26, Moratuwa, Sri Lanka, 1978.

Thuillier, Pierre: 'La correspondance Darwin–Marx: une rectification', *La Recherche* 77, April 1977.

Tracts surréalistes et déclarations collectives 1922–1939, vol. I, Paris: Terrain vague, 1980.

Trainer, Ted: 'A Rejection of the Brundtland Report', *IFDA Dossier*, May–June 1990, pp. 71–84.

Turgot, Anne Robert Jacques: 'A Philosophical Review of the Successive Advances of the Human Mind' [1750], in *Turgot on Progress, Sociology and Economics*, trans. and ed. Ronald J. Meek, Cambridge: Cambridge University Press, 1973.

UNDP, *Human Development Report 1991*, Oxford: Oxford University Press, 1991, p. 1.

Valette, Jacques: 'Note sur l'idée coloniale vers 1871', *Revue d'histoire moderne et contemporaine*, vol. 14, April–June 1967.

Virilio, Paul: *La Vitesse de libération*, Paris: Galilée, 1995.

Vylder, Stefan de: *Sustainable Human Development and Macroeconomics: Strategic Links and Implications*, a UNDP discussion paper, 1995, mimeo.

What Now: The 1975 Dag Hammarskjöld Report, prepared on the occasion of the Seventh Special Session of the United Nations General Assembly, 1975, published as a special issue of the Hammarskjöld Foundation journal, *Development Dialogue*, 1975.

Weiller, Jean and Carrier, Bruno: *L'Économie non conformiste en France du XXe siècle*, Paris: PUF, 1994.

World Commission on Environment and Development, *Our Common Future*, with an introduction by Gro Harlem Brundtland, London: Fontana Books, 1988.

Zorn, Jean-François: *Emancipation et colonisation*, unpublished paper presented to the seminar 'L'émancipation comme problème', Paris, 18–20 September 1989.

INDEX

absolute, 162, 163; causes of, 79,
169; fight against, 127, 136; 'happy',
137, 241; reduction of, 186
pragmatism, 223
Prebisch, Raúl, 109, 113
privatization, 13, 208, 222
producers' associations, 148, 161
production: dissociated from
consumption, 186; geared to
demand, 17; growth of, 16, 168, 184
productivism, 196, 216
productivity, 98, 142, 171; growth of,
78; low, 96; of the poor, 163
profit, gearing to, 13
progress, 22; as result of human vices,
38; having same substance as history,
40; ideology of, 37; infinite, notion
of, 35–40
public development assistance, 92, 163,
172, 191, 198, 207, 221, 240; targets
for, 92 see also aid
public service cuts, 173
public spending, 207

Quesnay, François, 206
Quinzaine coloniale, 53

Ramphal, Shridath, 199
Rappard, William, 59
rationality: diverse, 234; of interest, 233
Ratsiraka, Didier, 138
raw materials, 146, 158; prices of, 202
(falling, 219); supplies of, 152
Raynal, Abbé, 49
Reagan, Ronald, 170, 220
reference man of FAO, 166, 167
religion, 168, 216, 218, 245; as product
of social causes, 20; definition of, 20;
requirement for sacrifice, 240
religiosity, migration of, 21
relocation of production, 122, 153
resources: destruction of, 187;
exhaustion of, 141; exploitation of,
186, 189, 236; human, 213; non-
renewable, 14, 45, 187; transfer of,
201; use of, diachronic view of,
187
restructuring, 153, 220, 231
return of the same, 34
revelation, in history, 32
revolution, 87, 112, 113, 175
Revue des Deux Mondes, 53
Rhodesia, 126, 141; Southern, 126
Ricardo, David, 206

Rio Conference, 179, 192, 193, 194,
195
Rio Declaration, 189
Romania, 69
Rostow, Walt W., 6, 93–103, 107, 111,
118, 138, 198, 217; The Stages of
Economic Growth, 93–103
Rousseau, Jean-Jacques, 37, 38, 41, 49
Ruanda-Urundi, 64
Rubel, Maximilien, 104
Russian Revolution, 81
Rwanda, 197, 209, 241

Sabelli, Fabrizio, 6
Sabri-Abdalla, Ismaïl, 199
Sachs, Ignacy, 155
Salah, Ahmed Ben, 155
salinization, 151
Sandinistas, 174
Sarraut, Albert, 57
sarvodaya, 124
Saudi Arabia, 82
savage, as contemporary ancestor, 41
Say, Jean-Baptiste, 40, 49
Scandinavia, 159, 219
Schumpeter, Joseph Alois, 73
science, 58; anomalies of, 246; as social
product, 247; break with history, 29;
decline excluded, 36; predictivity of,
211; proximity with myth, 43;
Western, 40
secularization, 21
Seers, Dudley, 106–8; 'The Limitations
of the Special Case', 106
self-confidence, liberatory aspect of, 245
self-defence, right to, 83
self-determination, right to, 79, 83
self-interest, 17, 18, 91
self-reliance, 123–39, 143, 148, 157, 159,
161, 169, 198, 199; adverse effects
of, 135–6; collective, 86; principles
of, 134–6; theory of, 125
Sen, Amartya, 205
Senghaas, Dieter, 109
Shah of Iran, 174, 211
shantytowns, 231
shipping rates, review of, 84
slavery, 39, 48, 49, 52, 60, 74; abolition
of, 51; opposition to, 51
small is beautiful ideology, 169
Smith, Adam, 18, 49, 206, 215; An
Inquiry into the Nature and Causes of
the Wealth of Nations, 39
smuggling, 172

80; independent alternatives for, 121;
scholarships for, 88
Third World Forum, 165, 205
Third Worldism, 110, 175; challenge to,
175; demise of, 174, 176; triumph
of, 140–70
Tienanmen Square massacre, 197
time, ambivalent relationship to, 45
Tinbergen, Jan, 159
Tito, Josip Broz, 88
Togo, 89, 197
Torres, Camilo, 120
Touré, Ahmed Sékou, 123, 197
trade, international, 13, 72, 119, 125,
148, 200, 244; as engine of growth,
150, 185; freedom of, 85; growth of,
78, 84, 149, 186, 216, 231;
liberalization of, 4
trade barriers, 91
tradition, 21, 121
traditional society, 94, 95, 96, 102
Trans-Jordan, 59
transnational companies, 14, 141, 147,
187, 198, 224; interference of, 148;
regulation of, 149
transport: individual, limiting of, 196;
public, 157, 164
Traoré, Moussa, 197
Treaty of Versailles, 59
Tricontinental, 88
Truman, Harry S., 6, 75, 77, 89, 198;
Point Four see Point Four
Tunisia, 82
Tupamaros, 120
Turgot, Anne Robert Jacques, 58

ujamaa strategy, 125–34, 156
underdevelopment, 100, 118, 238; as
apparently causeless, 76; as natural
state, 95, 120; as new world view,
72–5; causes of, 142, 162;
development of, 148; history of
concept, 6; seen as lack, 79
unemployment, 22, 141, 142, 160, 195,
220, 231, 239, 240
unequal exchange, 115, 117, 119
Union coloniale française, 50, 53, 56
Union of Soviet Socialist Republics
(USSR), 28, 69, 87, 98, 99, 124,
176; colonialism of, 86; demise of,
178, 197, 211, 219, 220
United Kingdom (UK), 4, 47, 50, 56,
59, 75, 102, 120, 125, 126, 158 see
also British Empire

United Nations, 69, 70, 71, 72, 80, 81,
82, 92, 127, 141, 145, 146, 151, 156,
158, 159, 164, 179, 188, 210, 220,
251, 255; agenda for action, 89;
Charter, 82, 145 (Article 55a, 88);
Development Decades, 90;
modification of system, 156; rhetoric
of, 146
UN Children's Fund (UNICEF), 173,
174, 209, 220
UN Conference on Environment and
Development (UNCED), 188–92;
unofficial, 188
UN Conference on Trade and
Development (UNCTAD), 85, 113,
143, 146, 198
UN Development Programme
(UNDP), 9, 11, 78, 89, 90, 91, 192,
197, 198, 209, 220, 222, 232; and
human development, 204–10;
resident representatives system, 65,
66
UN Economic and Social Council
(ECOSOC), 88, 89, 90, 190
United Nations Economic Commission
for Latin America (CEPAL), 109,
113, 115, 116
UN Environmental Programme
(UNEP), 155, 189, 192
UN Educational, Scientific and Cultural
Organization (UNESCO), 57, 158,
169, 220; US and UK walk-out,
158
UN Expanded Programme of Technical
Assistance, 78, 85, 88, 89
UN General Assembly, 23, 83, 89, 90,
143, 148, 154, 178, 198
UN Permanent Advisory Commission
on International Commodity Trade,
84
UN Security Council, 81
UN Sustainable Development
Commission, 190
United States of America (USA), 65, 66,
68, 69, 71, 72, 77, 78, 80, 86, 88,
109, 119, 158, 164, 170, 173, 189,
195, 207; floating of dollar, 141;
hegemony of, 75–6; military
alliances of, 87; neo-Marxism in
111–13; opposition to, 110
Universal Declaration of Human
Rights, 69, 73
universalism, 62
universality, of Augustine's schema, 33

LEADING ZED TITLES IN DEVELOPMENT STUDIES

John Martinussen, *Society, State and Market: A Guide to Competing Theories of Development*

Majid Rahnema with Victoria Bawtree (compiled and introduced), *The Post-Development Reader*

Nalini Visvanathan et al. (editors), *The Women, Gender and Development Reader*

Michel Chossudovsky, *The Globalization of Poverty: Impacts of IMF and World Bank Reforms*

Wolfgang Sachs (editor), *The Development Dictionary: A Guide to Knowledge as Power*

Frans J. Schuurman (editor), *Beyond the Impasse: New Directions in Development Theory*

Denis Goulet, *Development Ethics: A Guide to Theory and Practice*

Hans-Peter Martin and Harald Schumann, *The Global Trap: Globalization and the Assault on Prosperity and Democracy*

Raff Carmen, *Autonomous Development: Humanizing the Landscape: An Excursion into Radical Thinking and Practice*

Samir Amin, *Capitalism in the Age of Globalization: The Management of Contemporary Society*

Serge Latouche, *In the Wake of the Affluent Society: An Exploration of Post-Development*

Nassau A. Adams, *Worlds Apart: The North–South Divide and the International System*

Rosi Braidotti, Ewa Charkiewicz, Sabine Hausler and Saskia Wieringa, *Women, the Environment and Sustainable Development: Towards a Theoretical Synthesis*

Manfred Max-Neef, *Humanscale Development: Conception, Application and Further Reflections*